Implications of Current Research on Social Innovation in the Basque Country

Edited by

Ander Gurrutxaga Abad and Antonio Rivera

Current Research Series No. 4

Center for Basque Studies
University of Nevada, Reno

Published in conjunction with the University of the Basque Country
UPV/EHU

Current Research
Selections of the ongoing work done by the faculty of the University of
the Basque Country (UPV/EHU), www.ehu.es/

Current Research Series, No. 4
Center for Basque Studies
University of Nevada, Reno
Reno, Nevada 89557
http://basque.unr.edu

Library of Congress Cataloging-in-Publication Data

Implications of current research on social innovation in the Basque
Country / edited by Ander Gurrutxaga Abad and Antonio Rivera.
    p. cm. -- (Current research series ; no. 2)
Includes bibliographical references and index.
Summary: "Collection of articles on social innovation in the Basque
Country"--Provided by publisher.
ISBN 978-1-935709-05-3 (pbk.)
1. Pais Vasco (Spain)--Social conditions. 2. Basques--Social conditions.
3. Economic development--Social aspects. I. Gurruchaga, Ander. II.
Rivera, Antonio. III. University of Nevada, Reno. Center for Basque
Studies.
HN590.P275I45 2011
303.440946'6--dc22
                                2011001951

Contents

Introduction

ANDER GURRUTXAGA ABAD and ANTONIO RIVERA

Translated by Jennifer R. Ottman

Some interpretive keys can help us comprehensively understand the dynamics of social innovation. Most important among these is the way it is diffused and spread, without which any one of its elements is practically meaningless. In order to encourage innovation, there need to be appropriate contexts and terrain. Similarly, the value of the interactions it promotes and the connectivity it generates stands out more than, for example, the stocks of knowledge that can be found in particular geographical locations. Knowledge is mobile, fluid, and unstable, and as a result, it can never be a static piece of property. Social innovation is a cultural exercise where success is a matter above all of shared culture, of the dynamism of networks of knowledge transfer, learning from one another, and specific factors that facilitate the exchange of information among different parties.

The human networks that interconnect and globalize the world are primarily networks of knowledge and information transfer with the ability to sustain interactive processes of learning and innovation. Once knowledge and information are extensively shared, the dynamics of innovation experienced in all the connected spaces are accelerated. In this way, the formation of a culture of innovation takes shape as the clearest exponent of tendencies that drive change.

Human networks and the culture of innovation they contain are not born out of nothing, but rather are built on preexisting foundations that enable them to function and reproduce. They unfold in a process that takes time and manifests different traits in different geographical areas.

The presence of suitable initial conditions does not entail the immediate creation of a culture of innovation; rather, it needs a period of maturation in which synergies among different elements can forge shared codes of interests and trust. It is the fruit of interactive and communicative relationships among actors, agencies, and resources with the capacity to build networks of knowledge transfer and social spaces of innovation and active learning. Therefore, undoubtedly its dynamics are processes with a strong sociocultural component. But what are the fundamental pillars of social networks that make interaction, communication, and collective learning possible? This question necessarily leads us to consider the social and cultural factors that make it possible for repeated situations of relationship-building, association, and trust to flourish in certain geographical areas.

Social innovation locates the basis for innovation in the ability to take advantage of a society's social intelligence in the attempt to resolve problems and build futures, linking the relationship among human beings to the capacities they acquire when it comes time to confront, for example, "conflict," "diversity," "climate change," "culture," "the city and its new spaces," and so on. The result is that innovating means producing systems of tolerance that accept some basic aspects of the existing situation in order to modify it, whether these are tangible (products, technologies, and so forth) or intangible assets (values, ideas, and institutions). If the process is successful, the transformed aspects acquire new uses and meanings. In this view, the thing invented is the tangible and hence modified embodiment of existing (intangible) knowledge. Innovation can also be the product of chance and luck.

Innovating does not mean following a path predetermined by any institution, but rather that the dynamics innovation creates and on which it builds acquire a variety of traits and trajectories in the places where they spread. The problem appears when we observe that some societies lack dynamics of innovation. These processes exist alongside societies and countries that are incapable of finding either paths or answers for improving their citizens' quality of life.

Interactive processes of learning are possible thanks to shared sociocultural and institutional contexts that generate a climate of trust and related objectives. It is problematic, as a consequence, to draw a clear line between innovation on the one hand and the attainment of concrete, tangible objectives on the other, especially in the areas of social and cultural innovation.

Should we not consider the small transformations that pass unnoticed in institutions such as the family and daily life as substantial parts of social and cultural innovation? Is there no innovation in mundane or artistic spheres without concrete objectives? Innovation should be associated with the search for solutions to daily problems, with the discovery of new facts in diverse societies, and with reinterpretation through use, praxis, and experimentation, more than with the attainment of pragmatically or rationally defined objectives. With time, objectives and initial ideas are diluted and modified in such a way that use, practice, and the utility of what already exists are what generate the emergence of new ideas and distinct objectives. Innovation is not always "for a purpose"; instead, innovation takes place through improvisation or "because it turns out that way."

Processes of comprehensive innovation, those that "cast their net" over society as a whole, modifying its pillars and structures, in some cases pass through a sequence of stages in which an initial phase is followed by phases of consolidation, transformation, and collapse. In other cases, however, we not infrequently find societies that remain stuck in one of these phases, and we can likewise observe faster or slower transitions from one phase to another, depending on each society's particular characteristics. Therefore, this constant movement has the result that the trajectory of diffusion resembles an "S" more than a straight line. Innovation is possible thanks to the transfer of knowledge accumulated as a result of previous innovations, with the implication that experience with practices of social innovation reproduces social innovation and prepares societies to accept more innovation. There is no reason that this process should follow a single rhythm of progressive change or constant improvement, but whatever the case, its end result is to increase a society's complexity and foster a greater need for innovation.

Once the consolidation phase is reached, there frequently emerges a certain fatigue that affects the process of reproduction and creates "bottlenecks" that can lead to the stagnation of the dynamics previously operating. Other innovations can refresh them, incorporating novel practices and dynamics and suitable structures for confronting the pertinent transformations, creating principles that channel the fatigue arising from these processes. Complexity grows along with these processes in such a way that it becomes trapped in a whirlwind of questions without answers or in the eternal struggle against contingency, chance, and unforeseen or unwanted problems.

Social innovation is understood not as a rationally based solution capable of solving economic, business, social, environmental, or cultural problems, but rather as an asset with which to confront such problems and one that necessarily leads to episodes that problematize the solutions designed and attempted. Innovation does not always result in benefits, but can instead lead both to prosperity and to collapse or failure due to poor management of the resources available. Likewise, innovation is not necessarily universally beneficial, but instead, in many cases, leads to the perpetuation of unequal geographical development.

In the case of the Basque Country, which we analyze in this book, the region's social structure is undergoing a process of transition between the gradual disappearance of industrial society and the emergence of a knowledge society. In other words, industrial society is not the force that rules daily life, but neither has a knowledge society yet been fully constructed. There is no completed model to serve as a reference for societies like that of the Basque Country. Its construction depends on exogenous variables and on endogenous factors.

1

The History of Innovation in the Basque Country

Antonio Rivera

Translated by Robert Forstag

In their recent study, Alfonso de Otazu and José Ramón Díaz de Durana (2008) analyze and document why many individuals from the Basque Country have distinguished themselves both at the helm of companies and in spearheading innovative initiatives of all kinds: economic, cultural, organizational, religious, and even political. Concentrating on the crisis of the Middle Ages as well as on modern times, these authors identify factors such as being forced to take to the world's oceans and seas to seek one's fortune, the establishment of entities like guilds and brotherhoods, companies that pooled community efforts in order to achieve commercial success, the organization of the migratory process to the Americas, the advantages that came from their self-conceptualization as noblemen, the consequences that operated both in favor and against their longstanding legal traditions, and their unique relationship with different religious orders. These and other explanations are rooted in historical logic—how individuals who identified themselves as Basque successfully resolved over the course of many centuries the difficulties and challenges they faced by resorting to imaginative and effective strategies. This is how the human spirit manifests itself in history: how one sees oneself and is, in turn, seen is nothing more than a reflection of repeated patterns of collective behavior and of the uniqueness of a specific group—in this case, the Basque people—that are forged as a result of being confronted with the challenge of resolving problems arising from their struggle to survive and quest to thrive in a hostile world.

On the basis of this singular historical background—a formidable burden to be sure—and on the basis of the fundamental assumption that a people does not have some sort of inherent essence, but "only" its history, I will address the same question strictly within the context of modern history. There can be no doubt that this same enterprising and innovative capacity demonstrated by Basques in previous centuries once again came into play in the 1980s and 1990s. A small people in terms of geographic extension and total population, but endowed with a strong sense of uniqueness and difference with respect to "those on the outside" (although with concomitant difficulties in seeing itself as a unified entity), the Basques have faced the challenges of contemporary living by applying its intelligence to such dramatic effect that, by the end of the twentieth century, the Basque Country was one of the most advanced regions on the Iberian Peninsula and all of Europe. In the absence of abundant natural resources (with some notable exceptions, as we will see), its development has instead been primarily based on the capacity of its people to create and assimilate new procedures and structures in order to successfully meet a series of historical challenges.

The beginnings of this modern history were not especially propitious in either the Basque Country specifically or in Spain generally. Two wars against revolutionary and Napoleonic France were followed by two civil wars (the Carlist Wars), the second of which did not conclude until 1876. ·The results of the second Carlist War led to a significant realignment of the status quo of the residents of the Basque provinces—specifically in terms of the change from being "in Spain" to "being Spanish." The eternal dilemma of how to effectively mix water and oil—in this case, reconciling the Basque antiegalitarian legal tradition with a new and uniform national constitution—was resolved, after various fits and starts, with the definitive abolition of regional law in 1876 (ameliorated, of course, by the continuity of highly effective autonomous tax collection procedures—the fiscal pacts). This instrument, which was managed by the provincial elites, gave them a decisive competitive advantage. At the same time, the abolition of regional law—a fact of regulatory and political importance that had an impact on a number of different levels—occurred at the same time as another historical process was coming to an end on a community level: As in other areas, liberal individualism and capitalism became the order of the day, giving rise to a new logic regarding commerce and continual progress.

Industrialization

It was within this historical frame of reference that the rurally (but not exclusively agriculturally) based Basque Country, traditional in character and precarious in terms of its natural resources, became transformed into an industrialized, urbanized, rich, and even modern society (although a society that always maintained one foot planted firmly in the secure foundations of its past traditions). Among the longstanding Basque occupations were mineral exploitation and iron working. Iron was now more important than ever, but in a qualitatively different context. In short, the privatization of mines allowed for its unrestricted exploitation. The owners of these mines gradually established a highly beneficial relationship with other industrialists—mainly those in Britain. Immersed in the nearly century-long process of industrialization, British foundries had access to the quantities of coke needed to supply energy and enable mineral conversion, but did not possess sufficient quantities of iron. Basque miners began to supply them high-quality iron in abundance: Its composition was ideal for the new conversion technology being carried out by means of Bessemer converters, invented in 1856. They shipped raw materials to the British Isles. During the last quarter of the nineteenth century, the Basque Country quintupled its extractive capacity. During each year of this period, there were 2,500 to 3,000 journeys between the port of Bilbao and the British ports of Northumberland, Durham, and Middlesbrough. To a lesser, although still significant, extent, there was similar trade between the Basque Country and Wales, Holland, France, and Belgium.

Such activity generated capital that was unheard of in that era: The sale of iron extracted in the final quarter of the nineteenth century resulted in profits exceeding 1 billion pesetas. Although under partial foreign ownership, the mining companies were Bizkaian, and it was Bizkaians who retained the majority of the profits. Yet those who reaped the benefits of this bonanza were few in number, even though the general economy of Bizkaia (Vizcaya) benefited to a considerable extent from investment in the infrastructure necessary to conduct exploitation activities (e.g., railroads, cable cars, wagons, and port development) as well as from production expenses of all kinds (salaries, administration, and partnerships) Thus, a select number of local families—the Ybarras, Martínez Rivases, and Chávarris, and then later the Echevarrietas, Aznars, Gandarias, Lezama Leguizamones, Sotas, and others—were in a position of being able to mobilize this capital in order to diversify their business activities and thereby obtain greater added value. These families became involved in the steel industry by profiting from their previous commercial activities and benefiting from the considerable knowledge they had acquired. Important steel companies were founded from the late 1870s through the 1880s: San Francisco, the Altos Hornos de Bilbao (AHB), and the Sociedad Vizcaya, which belonged, respectively, to the Rivas, Ybarra, and Chávarri mining families. Raw material continued to be shipped to England, but the ships began to return with coal (which also arrived in Bilbao by railroad from other locations in Spain, such as the basins of Asturia and León). Part of the production process now began to take place in Spain itself: first ingots and later more elaborate products. Thus, the capital invested in mining began to yield greater added value and lay the foundations for the subsequent diversified industrialization of Bizkaia.

Early on, Victor Chávarri realized just how promising such development was. He wrote that, "Making ingots exclusively will never allow us to generate money in proportion to the capital invested" (1883, n.p.). By the end of the 1880s, some capital was diverted to equipment for the purposes of producing warships for the Spanish fleet or metallurgical material for large infrastructure projects. Therefore, the Spanish state and Spanish markets became, respectively, the main buyer and the primary venue of iron and steel manufacturers, two developments that had important repercussions. In the meantime, other capital was invested in the manufacture of finished and semi-finished metallurgical products (e.g., wire, pipes, sheet metal, brass articles, beams, and tin plate). All of this was done to generate a higher percentage of money "in proportion to the capital invested." This laid the foundation for a fundamental shift in Basque industrialization: from mining to iron and steel metallurgy. And this phenomenon, in turn, led directly to the development of each of the necessary production sectors, until a highly diversified and vertically structured industry eventually took shape. Shipping companies were founded in order to ensure continued participation in maritime trade. Large shipyards were created for the purpose of manufacturing and repairing ships. Traditional banks (in Bilbao and other areas of Bizkaia) were strengthened, and new banks were founded in order to meet the increased need for capital and loans. Railroad networks were expanded to more efficiently transport materials (and eventually people). Concessions for various minerals and metals were purchased throughout Spain in order to ensure adequate supply to factories. And insurance companies were created.

At the beginning of the twentieth century, the Basque Country joined the "new industrial revolution," and as a result new sectors—such as chemical, explosive, and hydroelectric industries—emerged. In addition, new markets for investment were sought, and new businesses were developed in fields such as wine production, passenger transport, water supply, and other services needed for the burgeoning cities. In 1901, the creation of a metallurgical society, Altos Hornos de Vizcaya (AHV), the largest company in Spain, signaled the verticalization and maturation of Basque industrialization. This entity was created as the result of the merger of the firms Vizcaya, AHB, and Iberia.

In little more than a quarter of a century, the small population of the Basque Country—or rather the Bizkaian heartland clustered around the mouth of the Nervión River—had carried out a very wide-ranging and radical transformation of its industrial processes. This development saw the metamorphosis of a rural and agrarian region into an urban and industrial society. In addition, various sectors of Spanish production came to be almost completely dominated by Basques: the iron and steel industry; banking and financing (to a large extent); the hydroelectric industry; shipping transport; and the construction of ships and railroads (to a considerable degree). Other industries would soon arise, such as the paper industry (particularly important in Gipuzkoa [Guipúzcoa]) and even the wine industry (involving large investments in the region of La Rioja).

Bizkaians had successfully met the challenge of attaining the level of other industrialized regions, and had done so as a result of a determined effort to concentrate resources on a number of levels: an industrial concentration in the mining and iron/steel sectors over the course of many years; a spatial concentration on the small region of the Lower Nervión; a concentration of capital among a few select families; a concentration of manual labor (that was to a large extent provided by immigrants); and a concentration on executing a transformative process within a relatively short amount of time. At the beginning of the twentieth century, Gipuzkoans definitively joined the industrial process as well. But in their case, they did so by means of a diffusion and diversification of efforts: In Gipuzkoa, all of the province's various regions were industrialized as much as possible. Primary materials in each of the regions were utilized for this purpose: rivers and water energy for textiles, paper manufacturing, and metallurgy; marlstone and lignite for cement production; and fishing for the preparation of conserves. Agreements with Bizkaians were made for the manufacture of equipment (i.e., mobile railroad equipment). These same agreements and the products of steel (and lead and other) mines led to the production of finished metallurgical products. Previous manufacturing traditions were employed for the manufacture of arms and jute. Sector diversification occurred here early on as a result of the absence of a single primary material in abundant quantities. In other words, diversification in Gipuzkoa was not a result of gradual development. Capitalization within the province resulted in the creation of small and, in some instances, medium-sized businesses, and of entrepreneurs that functioned at these same levels and who had close ties to the places where they lived. The process, which took a considerable amount of time, allowed the coexistence of traditional and modern production methods, intensive and extensive labor, and both artisan and technical modes of work. Manual labor was recruited within each separate region of the province, with "mixed workers" (those who divided their work hours between labor in factories and their own homes) frequently being employed. During World War I, particular sectors and companies within Gipuzkoa were of critical importance within Spain as a whole. These included railroad vehicles and related equipment in Beasain; the paper industry in Tolosa and Errenteria (Rentería); cement manufacturing; arms manufacturing in Eibar; finished iron and steel works; and even the manufacture of berets for both soldiers and civilians. In Araba (Álava) and Navarre, with the exception of a number of medium-sized factories in their respective capitals, there was no corresponding degree of industrial innovation, which had important social repercussions. These two territories continued to be firmly anchored in the traditions of the past, and in all respects their culture and economy were closely tied to their physical territories. Their provincial capitals, Vitoria-Gasteiz and Iruñea-Pamplona, functioned as service providers and also witnessed increasing administrative growth. Whatever modest signs of modernity were to be found in Araba and Navarre were strictly limited to their two capitals.

Modernization

The differing responses in each of the Basque territories to the challenge of industrial modernization resulted in correspondingly different societal evolution. In the most general terms, the rapid transformation of Basque society resulted in the replacement of traditional elites by a new elite class, and at the same time changed the internal balance of power within the society: The reserved merchants of Bilbao and the traditional rural *jauntxos* (rural overlords) saw their status usurped by a new and more dynamic class who had acquired wealth in the iron business. Bilbao and the manufacturing and mining centers of the Bilbao Estuary gained a dominant position vis-à-vis the "other" more traditional Basque Country.

Their basic political duality, with liberal republicans on one side and rural and urban Catholic traditionalists on the other, was displaced by a new tripartite division that, broadly speaking, represented the three emerging social classes. The most important mine owners and manufacturers aligned themselves with the various governmental factions of the Spanish monarchy. Some displaced *jauntxos* and some of the urban middle class, who longed for a reversion to the status quo, created Basque nationalism. And the industrial proletariat identified with Marxist socialism. Within a very short time encompassing the end of the nineteenth and beginning of the twentieth centuries, these groupings emerged as the new social and political agents within society—the protagonists of the "Basque triangle."

In contrast, the temporal and spatial progress characteristic of industrialization in Gipuzkoa made it possible for traditional elites to retain power there: republicans, liberals, and conservatives in the capital and in certain towns and districts (Eibar, Irun, and Bergara, for example), and Catholic traditionalists in the rest of the province. All these Gipuzkoan elites, whatever their ideological differences, continued to have one foot in the modern world and another in the old traditions. They created and owned shares in capitalist enterprises while they zealously defended traditional cultural and social forms (i.e., communitarianism, the Basque language, a distinctive Basque identity, classist and territorial antiegalitarianism, and Catholicism). As a consequence, Basque nationalists and socialists—the new political groupings that had emerged in Bizkaia—did not evolve in Gipuzkoa until some time later, and when they finally did, it was on the frontier between these two Basque provinces (the Bergara district and Eibar).

This evolutionary difference was most dramatic in Araba and Navarre, where the continuity of traditional socioeconomic forms meant that the traditional elites retained their time-honored status. These elites were overwhelmingly traditional in their politics, with some republican or liberal-conservative exceptions in the capitals and in certain regions (such as the Erribera or Ribera region of Navarre).

During this fin de siècle period, the city gained ground on the country in the Basque Country. The change was mainly quantitative in nature: Araba, Bizkaia, and Gipuzkoa nearly doubled their population during the fifty-three-year period between 1877 and 1930 (from 450,699 to 891,710), but the geographic distribution was markedly uneven, with population growth mainly concentrated in industrial and urban districts (Bilbao, the Left Bank of the Nervión, and Donostia-San Sebastián). Much of this gain was due to immigration. In 1920, 70 percent of Basques lived in towns of more than three thousand inhabitants (a figure reduced to 57 percent when the criterion was a population of five thousand and to 36 percent when the criterion was ten thousand). Bilbao surpassed the population mark of 100,000 (with a population of 112,819 in 1920). Donostia-San Sebastián experienced accelerated growth during the first decades of the century, and by 1920 had a population of 61,774. Even Vitoria-Gasteiz and Iruñea-Pamplona had become consolidated as "inland cities (with populations of 34,785 and 32,635, respectively).

The urbanization of the Basque Country ran parallel to the process of demographic transition: specifically, the transformation of traditionally high birth and death rates to a situation in which these rates where markedly reduced as a result of both public policies (that resulted in a reduction of infectious diseases and improved hygiene), including later health, hospital, and housing policies, as well as private behavior (i.e., hygiene practices, cultural changes, economic rationalization, and birth control). The emerging urban culture came to be seen as a "social product" par excellence—a space specifically created for people. The rational design of city expansion (devised in the nineteenth century but definitively implemented at the beginning of the twentieth) was questioned on various grounds as a result of the simultaneous conversion of these new urban territories into arenas of both social conflict and social control (with their *sequalae* of vertical and horizontal segregation), as well as on the grounds of their providing an opportunity to increase real estate revenue and profits.

The new, expanded city, in contrast to the traditional city centers, became the vital hub for the emerging ruling class, who not only took up residence in the new quarters, but also conducted all of the activities emblematic of their new values there, whether economic or mercantile (bank headquarters and the Stock Exchange), political (newly constructed institutional buildings and party headquarters), or social (private social circles and casinos, exclusive clubs, and cafes). The main city streets also migrated to the new neighborhoods (the Gran Vía in Bilbao, the Dato in Vitoria-Gasteiz, and the Boulevard in Donostia-San Sebastián) as did communications, transport, and entertainment centers (the editorial offices of newspapers, railroad stations, and theaters). This spatial hierarchy served as an ongoing reminder of the new class structure of society, indicating not only the space reserved within this society for each of its separate components, but also the accompanying social hierarchy (by means of what Weber termed the "routinized charisma" acquired by the newly rich).

At the same time, each city was acquiring a profile that was conducive to specialization, both within Basque society and beyond. The painter Adolfo Guiard summed up this process as follows: "Bilbao was striving to become a huge factory, San Sebastián a huge hotel, and Vitoria a huge sacristy" (Orueta 1952, 174). One might add that the mission of Iruñea-Pamplona was to continue to serve as the capital of the old world (or kingdom) of Navarre.

In sum, these developments involved a voluntary specialization of functions that had an impact on the urban settings in question. Thus, Donostia-San Sebastián eschewed the construction of a large port on the Urumea River and instead concentrated on the development of La Concha Bay, mindful of the fact that, ever since the middle of the nineteenth century, this area of the city had become a summer tourist destination, which now constituted one of its primary sources of revenue. In contrast, the almost complete lack of promenades and parks in Bilbao led its inhabitants to appreciate what could be gained from a stroll through the industrious, varied, bustling, and not particularly attractive area around the estuary, and to particularly value the hustle and bustle of its busy piers. In Vitoria-Gasteiz and Iruñea-Pamplona, the clash between modernists and traditionalists was resolved in favor of a kind of middle ground that in fact reflected the values of community, religion, and continuity in preference to industry, modernity, and risk.

The attitude, wealth, and efficiency of Bilbao's (and, to some extent, Gipuzkoa's) elite stood in stark contrast to the conservative stance of the inland provinces. In the Bizkaian capital, especially, a ruling class emerged that was acutely conscious of the fact that the short-term future of their region depended on making good and timely personal decisions. In addition, in Bizkaia a small but cohesive group was responsible for not only developing the new manufacturing economy, but for creating cultural and educational infrastructures that served to legitimize the new elite. This small group included, among others, the entrepreneurs and politicians

Víctor Chávarri Salazar, Horacio Echevarrieta, and Ramón de la Sota (as well as Rafael Picavea in Gipuzkoa and the Ajuria family in Araba); and intellectuals, artists, and publicists, such as the Urquijo family in Bizkaia, the Herrán family in Araba, Miguel de Unamuno, Ramón Basterra, Pablo de Alzola, Francisco Goitia, José de Orueta, Gregorio Balparda, and Julio de Lazúrtegui.

Their achievements can be seen in the creation of important institutions such as the Engineering School (1899) in Bilbao, the University of Deusto (1886; with its School of Business Administration opening in 1916); the founding of newspapers such as *El Liberal* and *La Gaceta del Norte* (1901), and *El Pueblo Vasco* in Donostia-San Sebastián (1903); the establishment of economic lobbies such as the Liga Vizcaína de Productores (Bizkaian Producers' League) in 1894, and political lobbies such as the liberal-conservative "La Piña" group in 1897; the founding of political parties and unions with modernist ideologies such as the Basque Nationalist Party (1895) and the Metallurgy Workers of the UGT (Unión General de Trabajadores, General Workers' Union) of Bizkaia (1914); the establishment of cultural magazines such as *Hermes* (1917); and the founding of very large companies such as AHV and Astilleros Euskalduna (1900), among many other examples. In short, a number of areas in Basque society had been highly modernized even before the democratic experience of the Second Republic during the 1930s. The region of Bilbao and the Bilbao Estuary, as well as Donostia-San Sebastián had been modernized, but these were enclaves within inland areas that were far more traditionalist in orientation and more closely tied to agrarian and rural economies and societies, with a strong communitarian spirit that showed no signs of abating, and under the strong influence of the highly influential Catholic Church.

The Community

The social challenges represented by these changes have been met in the Basque Country by the creation of a number of mechanisms that fostered the transformation of its structures while taking care not to completely undermine its past traditions. A concerted effort was made to ameliorate the divisive impact of these change and modernization processes by means of measures that retained the profound sense of community within the Basque Country. Preserving this sense of community—which was originally local or provincial in nature but in time encompassed the entire

Basque Country—was not only as an expression of the region's profound sense of territorial identity, but to an even larger extent, a means of cleaving to age-old traditions that provided a sense of security and continuity—an essential element in coping with the risks of any societal transformation.

The Basque guilds, brotherhoods, and societies of the past translated in the modern context into very dense socialization networks, both in terms of organizations promoting their own interests (economic lobbies, unions, political entities, and religious associations) as well as in informal and everyday activities (those following traditional religious injunctions, participation in traditional festivities, or *cuadrillas*—specific and extended groups of friends). Throughout history, both modernists and traditionalists have seen the community as one of the bulwarks of Basque society. This has resulted in Basques developing a strong resistance to the disintegrative (or individualizing) tendencies of modernity. Yet this should not blind us to the often profoundly oppressive nature of community ties when these function during times of dissension to determine who belongs to "our group" and who is defined as "an outsider," a classic dilemma in the sociology and politics of place.

On the other hand, the Basque Country has often responded to economic change and its accompanying social transformation in very modern ways. There are many examples of this. The Vitoria-Gasteiz Seminary of the 1930s, a group headed by Father José Miguel Barandiarán, conducted excellent and advanced sociological surveys in various locales in order to determine the state of the Catholic religion (and of the Church) as well as of its opponents, for the purpose of promoting the continued preeminence of the Church. Basque nationalism itself, although it originally emerged as a reaction to certain disintegrative tendencies at the end of the nineteenth century, adopted some organizational and expressive forms that were unprecedentedly modern in nature—forms that were more closely in tune with the newly emerging mass society than with nineteenth century politics: mobilization, the stimulation of collective passions, the reinforcement of traditional iconography, the construction of a historical narrative, and the combination of both horizontal and vertical internal and external structures.

Basque society at the end of the nineteenth century represented both the continuity of past traditions and the beginning of new traditions. Although this society was rigidly divided along class lines (a rigidity that became even more pronounced with the progressive and differential development of each region), it maintained or incorporated wide-ranging institutions, policies, and large scale social welfare networks. The Triano Miners Hospital, founded by physicians such as Enrique Areilza and José Madinabeitia (among others, in addition to the hygienists of a previous generation), the Las Nieves Psychiatric Asylum (founded in 1907 in Vitoria-Gasteiz), a highly developed system of charity, as well as municipal taxes earmarked for charity are all examples of the constant preventive and ameliorative efforts that were undertaken by both the private and public sectors.

Several decades later, the same process was repeated: In Vitoria-Gasteiz, which experienced a high degree of immigration following the opening of new factories in the 1950s and 1960s, a group within the Catholic Church (led by Carlos Abaitua, José María Setién, Juán María Uriarte, and Ricardo Alberdi) drafted provisions in collaboration with local property owners, politicians, and boosters, together with representatives of both labor and business, in order to build workers' districts in the city (Adurza and Errekaleor). These districts were seen as an integrated (and even self-managing) social unit, and were constructed with a view to preventing the kinds of conflicts and controversies that had emerged in the recent past. This kind of planning resulted in the almost complete absence of shantytowns in what was arguably the fastest-growing European city during that historical period.

Another example of this social concern was the 1956 "Mondragón cooperative experiment." Building on previous experiments of production cooperatives, such as the Alfa factory created by Socialists in Eibar in 1920, and consumer cooperatives affiliated with either Socialism or Christian Socialism, it was the brainchild of the pragmatic and visionary priest José María Arizmendiarrieta. The first thing that Arizmendiarrieta tried to do was to reconstitute a community in Arrasate-Mondragón that had been profoundly divided into victors and vanquished after the Spanish Civil War. With this purpose in mind, he devised a project that attempted to introduce modernization and economic development in and even beyond the area by means of a cooperative organization that was at the same time compatible with the reorganization and reintegration of the local community, incorporating a traditional Christian Socialist political program and even newly constructed symbols of Basque identity. These ideas were closely linked to the dominant and entrenched political tradition in the area—Basque nationalism. Modernity and tradition were thus once again united in an unusual social experiment. As one final example of this, the persistence of local traditions, especially during times of change when cultural expressions or modifications were not always internally consistent, was a way of preserving the image of the locality as "one big family"—as a community that had a future in spite of the threats posed by a progress that was both inevitable and desirable.

We can thus see the continual union of two apparently mutually exclusive processes in the Basque Country. The forced juxtaposition of these two processes led to socioeconomic development that was largely free of the negative effects of social disintegration. The result of this was a general continuity of a certain sense of community (which, to be sure, was not equally strong throughout all of the Basque Country). Politics came to be a critically important feature of this sense of community, which in fact arose as a social defense mechanism responding to particular historical circumstances. Similarly, this coexistence of the two apparently antithetical forces of innovative modernity and comforting tradition combined for the purpose of yielding socially beneficial practical results, has its parallel in "instrumental modernity." This is defined by the longstanding local tendency to resort to advanced formulas of analysis and action for the ultimate purpose of maintaining social tradition in particular circumstances of economic change.

General Transformation

In the late nineteenth and early twentieth centuries, the diverse industrialization of a number of Basque regions placed them in the vanguard of Spanish economic development. Although this growth was halted temporarily by the Spanish Civil War (1936–37 in the Basque Country; until 1939 in the rest of Spain), the economy soon recovered by placing itself in the service of the conflict, especially when the whole Basque territory fell into the hands of the rebels led by General Francisco Franco. The large industrial facilities of Bizkaia and of the rest of the Basque Country (whose owners were generally sympathetic to the future dictator) mobilized on behalf of the war effort, manufacturing war materiel. Then, after the conclusion of hostilities and within the framework of an autarchic economy, these same facilities played a central role in the manufacture of the equipment necessary for the reconstruction of the country.

In addition, certain industrial sectors in Gipuzkoa took advantage of the continuation of mandatory "import substitution" and specialized in a tradition that had its roots in the Eibar arms industry. The machine tool industry in Gipuzkoa (and later of the Basque Country as a whole) began to "copy with appropriate modification," and with an uncanny sense of innovation, the patents and practical solutions that were being employed in other places. The result of this process was the extraordinary recovery of production levels following a period during which the economy was closed and strongly regulated, and which coincided with a new phase in international economic expansion during the late 1950s and 1960s. And once more the Basque economy went through a process it had experienced a half century earlier: the industrialization of new regions, the intensification of industrialization in those regions where the process had already been introduced, the arrival of large groups of rural immigrants from the interior of the Basque Country, from bordering regions, and also from distant regions (in the case of Extremadura, Galicia, or Andalucía).

In addition, this new process saw the even greater concentration of the population in cities and the progressive expression of a social modernity that went hand in hand with the economic transformation: an increase in social conflicts and political dissidence, the growing influence of foreign cultures, changes in customs, and the social emergence of new cohesive groups such as women and youth. By then, nearly all of the Basque Country had become industrialized and urban. People left various rural areas, such as the Araba plains or certain zones of Navarre, for their respective provincial capitals. Vitoria-Gasteiz and Iruñea-Pamplona became industrialized, as had earlier happened in both Bilbao—with its strong manufacturing sector—and the principal towns in Gipuzkoa. These cities had the additional advantage of possessing newer and more diverse industries that, at the same time, were more dependent on the large multinational companies that were located in their manufacturing sectors: Mercedes Benz and Michelin in Ehari-Ali-Gobeo and Gamarra, Vitoria-Gasteiz; and Volkswagen in Landaben, Iruñea-Pamplona. In Bizkaia, industry expanded in the Kadagua and Ibaizabal valleys and toward the Aiara (Ayala) Valley in Araba. In Gipuzkoa, industry developed along the whole Deba River and throughout Donostia-San Sebastian. In the meantime, the steel industry was developed in Bera (Vera), Lesaka (Lesaca), and Altsasu (Alsasua) in Navarre.

The 1960s saw a marked degree of economic and social development, with the four Basque-Navarrese provinces, along with Madrid and Barcelona, at the head of the list of Spanish regions in terms of revenue and GDP. The two coastal provinces intensified and developed their previously existing industries to the maximum extent possible—until they no longer had room in their own territories for further development and had to transfer factories to Vitoria-Gasteiz, the greatest beneficiary of those boom years. The capital of Araba, which had maintained the fiscal pact (along with Navarre, but unlike Bizkaia and Gipuzkoa) during the Franco years, was able to exploit its advantages as a result of astute decisions on the part of local authorities that made cheap and well-organized land available for the installation of new industrial plants. At the same time, its social policies, which were rooted in communitarian and welfare traditions, achieved high levels of economic development without having to pay the price of excluding large sectors of its population. Finally, the constant commitment to contracting qualified manual labor contributed added value to all of the Basque industries.

Fin de Siècle Crisis and Responses

In the mid-1970s, a new historical era began in the Basque Country (and Spain as a whole). The death of the dictator led to the institution of a democratic system after a short, complex, and uncertain transition process. Since 1980, the new democratic reality has served as the framework for self-government underpinned by new administrative institutions. Finally, the progressive industrial development of the 1960s ended in the mid-1970s as a result of the impact of the international oil crisis on production processes that had grown obsolete and that had come to be artificially sustained. By 1985, the previously vigorous Basque industrial sector (that had contributed 56 percent of the total raw added value to the region) was suffering unemployment rates that reached 25 percent. The hyper-industrialization that had justified its previous levels of development left the economy highly vulnerable to the effects of a crisis that specifically affected the industrial sector. A decrease in demand, along with the obsolescence of some sectors and the alternative of a more profitable collaboration with strategies at the state level, led to the forced rationalization of traditional Basque industries such as steel manufacturing, shipbuilding, the production of electrical appliances, and to a lesser extent, the machine tool industry.

Given these circumstances, hyper-industrialization gave way to the development of the service sector. This continued to grow in a way befitting a clearly postindustrial society that benefited during the 1980s from expansion of a public sector as a result of the new regional self-government institutions that also served to decrease deficits in social infrastructure (in the areas of health, education, and communications). By the 1990s, public services had definitively surpassed metal products and machines in terms of its contribution to the raw added value of the Basque economy.

This profound crisis—which was a part of the subsequent crisis of the mid-1990s—led to the emergence of a radically transformed country. Some of the iconic companies of longstanding Basque "secular" industrial capitalism simply disappeared after having languished for years. AHV became defunct in 1996, Papelera Española in 1994, while Astilleros Euskalduna had already ceased operations in 1984. This crisis left Basque society in a profound state of social depression—a depression that became more intense as a result of both ETA's deadly terrorist activities and, especially, rising unemployment rates. The Basque Country emerged from this crisis via two different routes. In principle, and despite the fact that it was experiencing an industrial crisis, the strongest component of Basque productive capacity continued to endure and eventually rebounded as soon as the crisis was past. An awareness that the obsolescence of some sectors had intensified the crisis was conducive to a growing appreciation of the importance of innovation.

This process found expression in a number of different ways. First, there was the long-delayed creation of two public universities: the Universidad del País Vasco/Euskal Herriko Unibertsitatea (UPV/EHU) in 1980 and the Universidad Pública de Navarra/Nafarroako Unibertsitate in 1987. This was followed by the creation of Mondragon Unibertsitatea in 1997. In addition, networks of technology parks were created in Zamudio (1985), Miñano (1995), and Miramón (1997), together with a network of other technology centers in 1986. All of these developments were instrumental in emerging from the crisis. Various sectors that each contributed high added value, whether technological or operating in highly competitive environments on an international level, replaced the old steel industry after modernizing their operations: commercial services (Eroski), banking services (BBVA), energy (Iberdrola, Petronor), pharmaceutical companies, machine tool manufacturing, transportation and automotive industries, and information systems, among others. Even the old steel industry found a place in the new economy with the founding of the company Aceralia. Also contributing to the emergence from the crisis was the transformation of the Basque Country into a society with a strong and permanent industrial emphasis that at the same time was open to other options.

Two developments were emblematic of this transformation. First, the Swedish multinational company Ikea moved into facilities previously occupied by AHV (among other places, in the Barakaldo shopping center). This change of tenants symbolized larger changes in social cultures, labor, class structure, and production and consumer trends. Another symbolic change occurred in 1997 when the Guggenheim Museum of Bilbao (as well as other public infrastructure assets such as the Bilbao Metro and the Euskalduna Conference Center and Concert Hall) relocated in old shipyards. This represented at once the culmination and the catalyst of a general process involving the recuperation of the Bilbao Estuary specifically and of Bilbao more generally. The previous image of the city as a gray and declining industrial capital had been rehabilitated, and it became the modern, international, and attractive city dominated by the service sector that it is today. The public corporation "Bilbao Ría 2000," involving an equal participation of Basque and state administrative entities, played a crucial role in this process. This corporation has served as an important tool for the redefinition and creation of a new metropolitan Bilbao (projected to extend as far as Barakaldo).

In history, some dramatic episode often finds a place in the collective memory as a means of identifying a new and promising turn of events. In the case of the Basque Country, such an event may well have taken place in the summer of 1983, when Bilbao and other towns on the Nervión River suffered a severe flood. This episode took place in the midst of both a profound economic crisis as well as an equally grave social and political crisis that had led to a high degree of institutional instability. One can hardly compare the circumstances in the Basque Country at the beginning of the twentieth century with this later crisis: a stock market crash, an abrupt halt to industrialization, a marked degree of social conflict, a progressive change in political and cultural forms, and the gradual emergence of characteristics typical of mass society. Yet it is interesting that, in both cases, both the Nervión region and the Basque Country as a whole resorted to formulas that allowed them to catch up to the most progressive regions of the European continent.

In both circumstances, certain individuals' perception of the importance of personal and collective decisions regarding a number of key matters was crucial: the importance of training and professional qualifications for large sectors of the population available to take part in production processes; the introduction of mechanisms by entrepreneurs that would ensure greater profitability; the progressive modernization of society and institutionalized expression of its interests; and an awareness of the fact that change should occur—insofar as possible—without incurring the risk of either social schism or the disintegration of the core community. In each instance, the success of the process of innovative adaptation was associated with the names of different individuals, entities, and companies. Yet in both instances, an innovative spirit was the common denominator.

References

Chávarri, Victor. 1883. *Memoria descriptiva de las instalaciones para la fábrica de hierro y acero en las marismas de Sestao por la Sociedad de metalurgia y construcciones Vizcaya.* Bilbao: Archivo Foral de Vizcaya, AHV0013/09.

Orueta, José de. 1952. *Memorias de un bilbaíno.* San Sebastian: Nerea.

Otazu, Alfonso de and José Ramón Díaz de Durana. 2008. *El espíritu emprendedor de los vascos.* Madrid: Silex.

2

The Human Face of Basque Social Innovation: Demography, Family, and Human Capital, 1860–2000

Manuel González Portilla and José Urrutikoetxea
Lizarraga

Translated by Robert Forstag

An Initial Reflection

Growth and innovation are challenges that have confronted every society, each of which has striven to find the ideal balance between its population and its resources. The accumulation and distribution of resources, a social hierarchy, regulations, and both individual and collective behavior are key variables for understanding the history of human populations. To speak about innovation within the context of the last century of Basque history without discussing those individuals who were its greatest exponents would hardly make sense.

The Demographic and Family Context

The development of historical demography within Basque historiography has a long history, and a wide range of studies have been published during the past half century. Among other important works within this sub-genre are the contributions of the members of the Historical Demography and Urban Planning Group of the Department of Contemporary History at the Universidad del País Vasco/Euskal Herriko Unibertsitatea (UPV/ EHU), under the leadership of Manuel González Portilla.

This group initially focused on a rather general introductory approach. They were mainly interested in understanding population evolution, general tendencies, cycles, and critical points of development. When they began to analyze the fundamentally important variables (marriages, baptisms/births, and deaths), they soon detected distinctive Basque demographic patterns. This caused them to move away from constructing the image that had been typical of traditional historiography. Continuing their research along these lines, a particular focus on migratory movements began to occupy a central space in their research. Later, and imperceptibly, studies began to focus on the family as the most meaningful context of their findings, for it was within the family that they began to detect individual and collective projects, leadership roles and strategies, social imperatives, and values. Far from being a neutral entity, the family proved to be an active protagonist of the first order in the process of defining, reproducing, and renovating the social models that constituted the context of their development. In addition to the diversity of models and the complexity of components, a third point of focus began to emerge: that of the dynamism of family and demographic behavior that inevitably accompanies the process of social innovation experienced within the wider society.

The Distinctive Perception of Contemporaries: The Connective Thread of Discourses

Throughout the last 140 years—and as has occurred in other societies that have undergone intense transformations—Basque society has experienced a marked degree of tension between experienced reality and reality as formulated in discourses that attempted to turn back the clock. Between the cracks of an increasingly urban reality, it was possible to discern a longing for an idealized past:*"Han bizi naiz ni pakean."* ("Back there, I am at peace.") If "to innovate" means "to introduce what is new" or "to stimulate change and improvement," then it is evident that not all who have played a role in this history have internalized the concept in exactly the same way.

Decades would pass until some measure of critical recognition was expressed of the achievements that had been made as a result of the modernization process. The current rhetorical dispute regarding who can preach the new faith in research development and innovation (RDI) is a relatively recent phenomenon. When, back in 1882, the men who drafted the Primary Education Reform Project in Bilbao—men who were the direct heirs of the Free Education Institute—dreamed of bringing about a true "social revolution" as a result of their undertaking (Ruiz de Loizaga 2010), they were not reflecting the typical thinking of the intelligentsia of their era.

For almost a century, people in the Basque Country have lived, worked, thought, and amused themselves within urban settings while they have longed for and venerated a supposedly agrarian past that, in the majority of instances, they have not actually experienced themselves. For a long time, the legitimate right to claim the ongoing maintenance of the legacy of past traditions has been predominantly characterized by a primitive fear of change and of a rejection of the present, all in the interest of feeding a longing for a past that, to a large extent, never existed. History has thus run the risk of becoming stuck in the (largely reconstructed) past, with the geography of the Basque Country tending to be reduced to its rural dimension and with truly leading figures and important events drawing little interest. This way of thinking has led to innovation being viewed as a threat. The list of those who have either knowingly or unwittingly contributed to the strengthening of such a tendency is as respectable as it is extensive.

Reducing the rich panorama of Basque socio-familial models to a bare minimum was perhaps the first step in the process of engendering a uniform image of Basque history. First Frédéric Le Play (1878) and then later the Basque nationalist Engracio de Aranzadi ("Kizkitza") went from stating a number of unobjectionable facts to making sweeping assertions regarding the supposed eternal essence that constituted "Basqueness," establishing a sort of Manichean dualism that proposed an opposition between (good) rural life and (evil) modern urbanization.

A fair number of writers embraced this dualist scheme that divided the Basque reality into good and evil. These men inveighed against the wickedness of industrialization, represented most powerfully by railroads. For example, Pierre Loti (2008, 14) wrote that railroad trains were "rather ugly, dingy, noisy, stupidly insistent things, passing fast, faster, making the earth tremble and disturbing the exquisite calm of nature with their whistles and clunking noises: Railroads! . . . The railroad is more leveling than time itself, bringing hither and yon the trinkets produced by industry and spreading modern ideas, making the world, here and everywhere, a more banal place, a place more and more comfortable for idiots!" Arturo Campión (1935, 318) went even farther in his discourse, crossing the line of mere xenophobia: "I now understood everything. It wasn't the Moors who were coming but their brethren. Madrid was spewing out its wretched refuse upon Gipuzkoa from the 'pleasure trains.'"

More than anyone else, it was José Miguel de Barandiarán and Manuel de Lecuona who developed a discourse that was most strongly opposed to modernization. Their trenchant denunciation was aimed not only at the process of change itself but on the factors of urban life that promoted change. Thus, industrialization, immigration, urbanization, and "imported articles" became the focal points of this "other environment or social form, opposed not only to the Catholic religion but to all religion, which was now rearing its head in our villages . . . as part of the new urban society" (Barandiarán 1924, 171).[1]

While the Process Ran Its Course

But the real everyday life of ordinary human beings goes on, and is often oblivious to the rhetoric of intellectuals who seek to influence the course of events. Thus, while the study of different discourses is fundamentally important, not only to properly understanding social processes, but to how such processes are understood by various contemporary thinkers, it is the analysis of the processes themselves that is crucial to comprehending what is really going on within a society. Taking this important distinction into consideration, there is one undeniable fact: The Basque Country was constructed during the "long century" of growth and change. This construction took place in the face of the various discourses that gained momentum in Basque society, whether such discourses were embraced, engaged dialectically, or rejected. What is undeniable, given the evidence, is that what took place acquires meaning from an examination of the efforts of those prominent individuals who promoted the society's growth.

Who were the individuals that constructed this new Basque Country? How did they live? What efforts did they make to assure that they met the needs of the society in which they lived? How were these efforts expressed

---

1. Manuel de Lecuona (1924, 47) was even more specific about the social processes that he saw as responsible for these changes that, he wrote, resulted "from contact with strangers who were not of our kind in workshops, factories, public work projects, sports, etc."

within the context of families? What was it that catalyzed these efforts? In what circumstances did the encounter between Basques and non-Basques take place? Do the daily activities of the lives of these men and women offer any answers in this regard? What we are in fact faced with is a long history of individuals and families: men, women, and workers—artisans, farmers, factory workers, and the middle class. The story is most definitely very rich and textured.

The Two Faces of a History of Modernization and Social Innovation

To speak of modernization is to make reference to a complex and profound process of social innovation that affects the many different facets of the social prism.

The Unequivocal Confirmation of Unprecedented Growth

The particular context in which modernization and innovation occurred within Basque society was one of unprecedented demographic and economic growth and a modernizing urbanism that radically transformed its character. The most obvious indication of the change that was taking place was the growth of the population. The figures presented in table 2.1 speak for themselves.

Table 2.1. Population evolution in the Basque Country, 1877–2001

Years	Araba	Index	Bizkaia	Index	Gipuzkoa	Index	Basque Country	Index
1877	93,517	100.0	189,954	10000	167,207	100.0	450,678	100.0
1900	96,385	103.1	311,361	163.9	195,850	117.1	603,590	133.9
1930	104,176	111.4	485,205	255.4	302,329	180.8	891,710	197.9
1950	118,012	126.2	568,688	299.4	374,040	223.7	1,061,240	235.5
1975	238,233	254.7	1,151,680	606.3	682,517	408.2	2,072,430	459.8
2001	286,387	306.2	1,122,637	591.0	673,563	402.8	2,082,587	462.1

Even though, strictly speaking, the starting point could be fixed a number of years earlier, it is undeniable that a tremendous qualitative leap was made within the course of one hundred years.

Figure 2.1 Evolution of population indexes in the Basque Country, 1877–2001

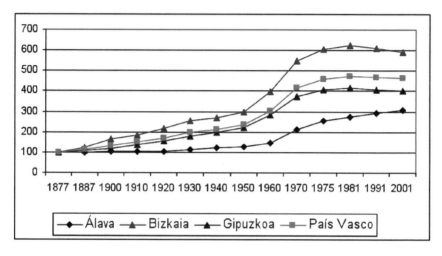

As can be seen in figure 2.1, this growth began in 1876 and ended with the world economic crisis in the 1970s. Although the definitive transfer of the Spanish customs offices to the coast in 1841 represents the very first step on the long road to modernization, the definitive march along this path actually began in 1876, when the *fueros* (laws granting special privileges to the Basque provinces) were abolished and the mining and steel industries were initially established. The repercussions of the energy crisis of the 1970s brought this long period of modernization and growth to a close—a period that Basque historiography has characterized as "the industrial century." Afterward, during a period of thirty years, Basque society witnessed the end of one economic model and had to construct a different one based on innovation and the knowledge-based economy.

The most striking thing about this entire process is the very magnitude of the growth that occurred. The data presented in both table 2.1 and in figure 2.1 are in this respect eloquent in a way that no narrative description could hope to match. Throughout the "industrial century," the Basque Country experienced the most spectacular demographic leap in its entire history. Having grown accustomed over a long period of time to "expelling" all but its first-born children to fend for themselves elsewhere, the Basque Country suddenly began to retain many of its children and even attracted a significant number of foreign workers. As a result, by 1975, the three Basque provinces had five times more inhabitants than they had in

1876. This represents a startling rate of population growth. Table 2.1 and figure 2.1 give a number of clues as to how this growth occurred.

What we see first and foremost is the living history of a people that met the diverse challenges they were faced with by employing a high degree of nuance and subtlety. Across the broad spectrum of Basque society, one can see how each of the three provinces came to define its own unique way of coping with these challenges.

Bizkaia displayed a precocious maturity in the rapidity of its modernization (Pareja Alonso 2000). By 1930, the end of the first phase of industrialization, this province had become definitively industrialized, as shown by a cumulative annual demographic growth of 1.79 for the period between 1877 and 1930. This initial momentum was sustained during the second period of industrialization (1950–75), with a rate of 2.86.

Although industrialization in Gipuzkoa also began at an early date, it proceeded at a rather slower pace, while going through nearly the same phases as the process in Bizkaia, but to a markedly less degree. During the period from 1877 to 1930, its cumulative rate of growth was 1.12. During the period 1930–50, its growth was higher than the mean level for the Basque Country as a whole. Later, as was the case in the other territories, the second industrialization period had a notable multiplying effect, with a cumulative annual growth rate of 2.43.

Araba was a notable exception to the general growth pattern. This province remained mired in the traditional way of life for decades and would not experience significant demographic growth until the second period of industrialization. Thus, during the period between 1877 and 1930, Araba's cumulative annual growth was a meager 0.20. However, between 1950 and 1975, it shot up to 2.85, thus attaining parity with the other two territories during the final phase of industrialization.

As a result of this complex historical dynamic, the Basque Country witnessed an unprecedented degree of growth and change, albeit in the context of uneven development among the three provinces. The demographic data show, on the one hand, the face of growth, change, and social innovation. Bizkaia grew 506 percent, Gipuzkoa 308 percent, and Araba 155 percent. Yet, as we have seen, there was differential progress among the three territories on the road to modernization. And they together must now face the new challenges posed by the twenty-first century.

Given its small size, the Basque Country is characterized by a remarkable richness and complexity, in terms of both its geography and the life of its people. This is but one example of a highly nuanced complexity that becomes evident as one studies a number of different salient variables. One finds there, paradoxically, both unity and diversity, and this paradox remains evident today, in the early years of the twenty-first century.

In any case, differentiation at the provincial level does not exhaust the possibilities of an intensive focus on a micro level—in other words, on the everyday life of individuals. Each of the three provinces itself displays a high degree of diversity within its borders. The analysis that follows, in providing an overview of each of the three territories, will reflect their internal diversity while attempting to be sensitive to historical changes that occurred during a period that encompasses more than one hundred years.

The first demographic phase lasted until the 1940s and coincided with the first wave of industrialization, the Spanish Civil War (1936–39), and the postwar period. Its origins lie in the more distant past and go back to the beginnings of the Spanish national market (i.e., the transfer of the customs offices to the coast in 1841) and industrialization. In the opinion of an observer cited by Pascual Madoz (1852), "An enduring peace and customs revenues led to the rebirth of industry in Gipuzkoa." As soon as the Carlist War (1872–76) concluded, political changes (the abolition of the *fueros*), the consolidation of a centralized national state, and economic and fiscal changes within the context of regional industrial development (the fiscal agreements) all took firm root in the region. These circumstances together created the context for the regional growth that would soon be experienced.

The responses to these developments also varied among the three provinces. At first, Bizkaia joined the new economy, resorting to the exploitation and exportation of iron. After the opening of the Santa Ana de Bolueta iron and steel factory in 1841, the Bilbao Estuary region quickly became a center of renovation. Mining, the iron and steel industries, the naval industry, port infrastructure, railroads, trade, banking, and various services allowed the region to more than double its population. It soon extended its development from the left to the right bank of the river. Technical innovations of various kinds (the Bessemer blast furnaces, the Siemens-Martin process) and capital investments were helped by an abundant supply of cheap manual labor that was more capable than is commonly supposed. Technicians from other European countries also took part in this process (González Portilla 1981, 1995, 2009).

In Gipuzkoa, modernization was principally a feature of the urban areas in two of the province's regions. Donostia-San Sebastián and its surrounding region (Donostialdea)—saw the development of the textile, paper, and metallurgical industries. Also economically important to Donostia-San Sebastián was tourism and the multiplying effect of railroad transport. At the other end of the geographical spectrum, the Deba Valley saw the development of a textile industry, yet this was overshadowed by the manufacture of arms, iron foundries, and the manufacture of locks. In all of these activities, the Deba Valley maintained close links with the Bilbao Estuary region. Longstanding traditions, a utilization of hydraulic energy, and openness to innovation collectively formed the basis for the region's rapid growth.

The growing demand for manual labor was initially met by workers from nearby rural areas. The "new urban social way of life" (Barandiarán 1924, 171) thus began to penetrate the traditional rural way of life. It later gradually expanded its radius of influence beyond the regional and provincial level.

The arrival of railroads—as well as the breadth of their extension—provided critical logistical support to these initial efforts. In general terms, innovation was placed at the service of economic, social, and cultural change. As we well know, the opponents of change did not see things this way. For them, the railroad was the symbol of the devastation that was being wrought by the change that was taking place.

As for Araba, its 0.20 rate of demographic growth during the period 1877–1930 is the most striking index of its slow progress. Its markedly high rate of literacy (the highest in all of Spain) was not sufficient in and of itself to constitute the basis of an equally high level of modernization. In spite of its high literacy rate, Araba continued to cleave to its traditional way of life, which was rooted in agriculture (and, in the case of its capital city, Vitoria-Gasteiz, in trade). But this state of affairs would not endure much longer.

Historical processes are a lot more tenacious than discourses. Thus, beginning in 1950, the second demographic phase, growth rates indicate that the new wave of industrialization ended up penetrating the entire Basque Country. This occurred once the most severe effects of the postwar period and of economic autarchy had been overcome. The iron and steel, metallurgical, naval, chemical, consumer, and automotive industries, along with the manufacture of tools and machines, sewing machines, and electrical appliances, as well as shipbuilding, banking, insurance, and other activities, all contributed to the highest levels of growth that had ever been experienced in the Basque Country. Both Bizkaia and Gipuzkoa far more than doubled their population, and Araba soon followed suit.

It is also true that each province grew at its own pace and in its own manner, and unevenly within the provinces themselves. Bizkaia and Araba employed a centralized model to promote growth, while Gipuzkoa was characterized by a marked degree of decentralization. The modernized Bizkaia, with its epicenter in the Bilbao Estuary, gradually expanded its growth to eventually encompass the southern end of the estuary basin (Etxebarri and Basauri), Durangaldea (the Duranguesado, the region around Durango), as well as the so-called other Bizkaia that was more rural and maritime in orientation (Delgado Cendagortagalarza 2008). Gipuzkoa, on the other hand, continued to stick to its decentralized model. The upper valleys of the Oria and Urola rivers (Beasain, Zumarraga, and Legazpi), as well as the middle valley of the Urola (Azpeitia and Azkoitia), joined the two previously mentioned regional axes (Donostialdea and the Deba Valley) and extended their networks to their immediate rural surroundings. Initially, family-based industries in Gipuzkoa recruited their manual labor from nearby rural districts. However, as demand for labor began to intensify, they resorted to more distant regions, and the demand was generally met from the same regions as those that supplied workers for Bizkaian industry.

Throughout this second demographic phase, Araba fully participated in the industrialization process. It grew at the same pace as the other two provinces, with growth concentrated in the urban area of Vitoria-Gasteiz and, to a lesser extent, in the middle valley of the Nervión river (Laudio [Llodio], Amurrio). This growth was based on a highly varied industrial development and supported by a labor force that very nearly depopulated the nearby countryside (with workers eventually having to be recruited outside the province). These were all important signs of the change that was taking place.

The "third phase" (1975–2000) is the well-known story of stagnation. This is clearly evident in the annual growth rate of 0.02 for the Basque Country as a whole during this period. Only Araba experienced a significantly positive growth rate during this period (0.96). Yet, although this period was indeed one of stagnation, it was also one of new challenges and responses that, far from showing a resignation to time-worn patterns, presented evidence of a search for new paths to progress. Foreign markets imposed conditions that required a response, the local economy attempted to respond to the challenges of the new situation, and the population of the Basque Country modified its strategies and behavior accordingly.

The City: The Framework and Engine of Modernization

It is abundantly clear exactly where "the new social way of life was taking shape: Bilbao, Gernika [Guernica], Durango, Irun, Iruñea-Pamplona, Altsasu [Alsasua] . . . These are the most important focal points from which new ideas fan outward to Basque villages" (Barandiarán 1924, 171). In effect, any attempt to link demographic growth with the new "social way of life" necessarily involved primarily urban frames of reference. The correlation among rates of urbanization, provincial growth models, and rates of growth is conclusive.

Table 2.2 Evolution of the urban population (>5.000 inhabitants) compared to total population, 1860–2001

Year	Araba	Bizkaia	Gipuzkoa	Basque Country
1860	20.10	17.20	28.70	22.30
1877	26.80	21.40	32.50	26.60
1900	31.80	52.80	44.00	46.60
1930	39.00	70.40	68.00	65.90
1975	82.63	91.82	90.61	90.37
2001	85.04	89.73	89.04	89.11

As is shown in table 2.2, in 1860, approximately 20 percent of the Basque population resided in towns of more than five thousand inhabitants. By 1930, this percentage had tripled for the provinces of Gipuzkoa and Bizkaia. Between 1950 and 1975, a period that represented the height of Basque urbanization, no less than nine of every ten inhabitants of all three provinces live in what can at least be nominally called urban settings. An urban environment inherently implies very specific activities that are far removed from those of the traditional Basque way of life. Artisans, workers, and the liberal professions form the bedrock of such an urbanized society. The city is, in the most general terms, the primary sponsor of innovation: It imposes a division of labor, encourages more efficient production methods, promotes the exchange of goods and services, serves as a catalyst for new projects, provides a venue for encounters among individuals and groups and for an exchange of ideas among them, and is a place of heightened individual freedom and a loosening of community bonds. The city is constantly reinventing itself.

Different Scenarios of Social Modernization

There are four fundamental analytical scenarios that we have attempted to employ as frames of reference for the purpose of explaining the primary causes of the modernizing process: demographic transition, family, migration/intermarriage, and human capital.

An examination of the demographic transformation provides a comprehensive understanding of the close connection among demographic trends, industrialization, and urbanization. Between 1876 and 1975 the Basque Country ended a complete cycle of a double demographic transition: that of mortality rates and that of birth and fertility rates. The factors that led to these developments are varied and are indicative of the close relationship among innovations in the areas of health, hygiene, urban planning, the social and occupational sphere, and educational innovation.

While traditional demographic models continued to be employed in most of the Basque Country,[2] the first modernizing impulse (1876–1900) was primarily centered in the mining region of the Bilbao Estuary. This model involved intensive demographic and urban growth, and its implementation had a high human cost as a result of obvious deficiencies in urban planning (Pérez-Fuentes 1993). High birth rates of around 40 percent were accompanied by high mortality rates that exceeded 38 percent, above the averages for Bizkaia as a whole (see table 2.3). Contagious diseases decimated the infant and juvenile populations. Within this context, growth can only have occurred as a result of immigration.

The second modernizing phase (1900–30), in contrast, was characterized by a higher quality of life. During this thirty-year period, mean life expectancy increased significantly. In the cities of the Bilbao Estuary, mean life expectancy increased from twenty to thirty years to fifty to fifty-five years, a jump unprecedented in the industrialized world (Livi-Bacci 1997). Innovation had made its presence felt in the form of improved health care and education. These factors, along with a (relatively slow) decrease in the birth rate (from 35–40 percent to 25 percent) helped encourage the growth that was taking place during this time. This dynamic applied in the industrialized regions of Bizkaia and Gipuzkoa.

---

2. We are referring here to the Atlantic region (where life expectancy was lower) and to the interior (where life expectancy was higher).

Table 2.3 Crude birth (CBR) and death (CDR) rates
in the Basque Country, 1885–2004

Period	CBR	CDR
1885–1894	35.53	27.49
1905–1914	32.37	19.78
1925–1934	25.67	15.43
1945–1954	20.02	9.88
1965–1974	21.58	7.44
1985–1994	8.23	7.55
1995–2004	8.01	8.67

Source: Movimiento Natural de la Población, EUSTAT.

The transition with respect to mortality culminated during the period between 1945 and 1975. As a result of the improvements that had manifested themselves in the previous period, the mortality rate was reduced to 10 percent. This change, together with a stable birth rate of 25 percent (as a result of a baby boom), along with significant levels of immigration, explains the spectacular growth of the Basque Country's population (including Araba). Life expectancy in 1976 was 69.6 years for men and 76.9 years for women. By 2000–1, it had risen to 76.4 years for men and 83.7 years for women. Thus, during the final quarter of the twentieth century, both sexes gained 3.26 months of life expectancy each year. The sum total of innovations and changes of all kinds has led to a distinctively modern demographic profile. The possibility of qualitative growth became a reality.

From 1950 until the end of the twentieth century, Basque demographics underwent its second transition: that of birth/fertility. By the beginning of the twenty-first century, the birth rate had reached an all-time historic low of 8.01 percent. But it was the dramatic decrease in the fertility rate (the total fertility rate; TFI) and the postponement of first pregnancy that provided the best evidence of the effects of the second demographic transition—while also raising questions regarding the capacity of the Basque population to avoid a long-term decrease of its population. In fact, the TFI decreased from 2.67 children/woman in 1976–76 to 1.03 in 2001–2. At the same time, the age of first pregnancy rose from 28.6 to 32.2. This constituted clear evidence of the second demographic transition (Arregi and Dávila 2005).

Changes in the economy, urban planning, and the labor market (which saw a marked rise in the proportion of female workers) along with improvements in hygiene and health, the transformation of family structure and behavior, the universalization of educational models, a change in cultural referents and in values, and an increasing encouragement of individual development were all fundamental components of the Basque demographic profile at the beginning of the twenty-first century.

The population pyramids for 1975 and 2001 clearly reflect the emerging profile of this final period. The pyramid for 1975 (figure 2.2) obviously reflects a very long-term trend of demographic growth that was only interrupted during the hiatus of the Civil War.

Figure 2.2. Basque Country population pyramid, 1975

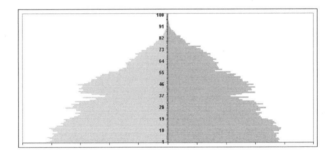

But that is where this long history of growth finally ends. From that moment forward, and as a result of various factors (most prominently the economic crisis and the end of the second demographic transition) the Basque population witnessed a gradual deformation of its age pyramid, as is shown in figure 2.3.

Figure 2.3. Basque Country population pyramid, 2001

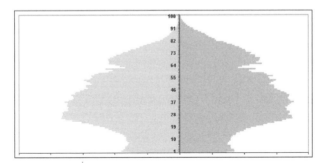

This is a development that has had an impact on Basque society at both age extremes. There has been an increase in the oldest age group as a result of both an increase in life expectancy and a general aging of the population. Concomitantly, at the base of the pyramid, there has been a dramatic reduction of population as a result of dramatically decreased birth and fertility rates.

A fertility rate that is among the lowest in the world, a dramatic increase in life expectancy, an imbalance in the age pyramid, an economic crisis, the extreme nuclearization of the family, and other factors depict a scenario that represents tremendous challenges. It is hoped that this scenario will lead to innovative thinking and a reinvention of the social model.

Throughout the distinct phases of the historical period under examination here, and insofar as it represents a fundamental locus of organization, reproduction, and adaptation to social realities, the family has been charged with the responsibility of reconciling the needs of the population with available resources, and with the framework and values established by the distribution of said resources, social hierarchies, inclusion, and exclusion.

The family finds itself in a position of needing to adapt to the new realities and, through a process of dialogue with them, of trying to define a proper place for each of its members and to improve their situation. And, while doing so, it also needs to support the new socioeconomic model. Breaking with old stereotypes and not-so-old realities, the family needs to reinvent itself as the key instrument of social innovation. Far from reflecting a supposedly universal traditional family, current family maps reveal a number of salient circumstances.

During the past 150 years, the Basque family has seen its dimensions shrink by 43.4 percent. As one might expect, this decrease has occurred at uneven rates in both geographical and temporal terms.

Once the difficulties of the initial period at the end of the nineteenth century were overcome, and with certain exceptions thereafter, the dimensions of the family were stable until 1930. This stability did not represent a return to supposed family structures of the past. It was simply a matter of adapting to circumstances. Once these circumstances changed, the entire second half of the twentieth century saw a rapid decrease in the size of the Basque family—a decrease that was truly spectacular during the period between 1975 and 2000. Yet lurking in the background of this phenomenon of decreased family size is another and more profound story regarding a change in behavior. To the extent that a society changes, the family itself becomes transformed, adapts, and changes its shape.

This transformation of the family took place within the context of the presence of two primary family models: the complex families of the rural Atlantic region and the Araba plains, on the one hand, and the nuclear families typical of the traditional industrial region, the coast, and the grape-producing regions on the other (González Portilla et al. 2003). In hindsight, everything seems to have pointed to the gradual but definitive triumph of the latter model. However, as recently as 1960, complex families still had a notable presence in urban settings. But things have changed since then. Despite external appearances, the relatively large number of extended families do not—and do not wish to—reproduce past patterns. On the contrary, they reinvent familial complexity as a way of coping with the double challenge of minimum salaries and of assuring stable living (García Abad 1999). Welcoming relatives and boarders into their homes are a means to this end. The woman—the "housewife"—thus takes on a crucially important role, and becomes the central figure in this balancing act that characterizes not only such families but the wider society of which they form a part.

Beginning in 1970, the outlook of families began to change. Complex families shrunk until they came to constitute only 10 percent of total families. The nuclear family thus became the reigning model. The new housing policy had something to do with this turn of events, but the data for 2001 point to a different factor. During the last two decades of the twentieth century, new realities surfaced that not only resulted in the replacement of the old complex models, but that even made inroads into nuclear family structures. Single-person families have quadrupled (from 5 to 20 percent), and single-parent families have also flourished (by 2001, they constituted 10 percent of all families). This phenomenon did not take account of changes in family configurations resulting from divorce, separation, or of combined families.

It is clear that the last one hundred forty years have witnessed a continued effort of readaptation and reinvention on the part of the family. Reconstituted family structures have been most characterized by the triumph of individuality. Underlying this process is an accumulation of profound changes. Industry, the growth of cities, innovations of all kinds, increasing individualism, and secularism have all contributed to this important innovation. Immigration is yet another critical factor.

Data regarding immigration are conclusive. By 1975, the end of the long period of growth, half of the Basque population was of outside origin, either directly or indirectly (García Abad 2005; Pareja Alonso 2000). This was one of the characteristics of its modernity.

Modernizing is a synonym of openness to foreign markets and of a willingness to employ foreign labor: One is not possible without the other. The Bilbao Estuary region set the tone in such matters, but allowing for geographical variations, all three provinces have followed the same pattern in this regard. Between 1877 and 1975, and in conjunction with the Basque Country's two periods of greatest economic growth, there were two periods in which immigration reached unprecedented heights.

Deficient urban development and health care, crowding, pollution, and high mortality rates were all consequences of the Bilbao Estuary's first stage of rapid industrialization (1877–1900), which was mainly driven by immigration. The first third of the twentieth century saw the consolidation of industrialization and social modernization, not only in Bizkaia but also in some of the regions of Gipuzkoa. By 1930, the majority of the population of both territories lived in cities: 70.4 percent in Bizkaia and 68 percent in Gipuzkoa. At that time, the involvement of Araba in this modernizing process was very limited.

The second period of high immigration occurred fifty years later (1950–75). With the first demographic transition well underway, the second period of industrialization affected all of the Basque Country. While the combination of a relatively high birthrate and a low mortality rate led to a marked natural increase, the increasing momentum of the second period of industrialization resulted in a demand for both outside workers and those native-born people as a result of the natural population increase. Thus, both the native-born and immigrants, in different proportions in the three provinces, together constituted the foundations of the new society.

The crisis of 1975–85 resulted in a sharp decrease in immigration, and particular socioeconomic patterns could be discerned with respect to both immigration and emigration. A certain proportion of qualified young people began to look for work outside of the Basque Country while small numbers of non-Basque workers continued to arrive to occupy niches in the labor market that had been vacated by the native population. Imbalance in the age structure of the population, the lack of interest in certain (both productive and service-oriented) jobs, and the problems of maintaining a welfare state all pointed to a short-term future filled with questions and challenges.

But while the scope of immigration provides a key to understanding the formation of our current society, information as to the origin of these immigrants, regarding the areas where they settled and concerning the ways immigration occurred, all help to understand the underlying causes of the population exchange that was occurring.

In regard to where the immigrants came from, it is possible to distinguish three different sources. Internal immigration has its own separate history of development. Within the Basque Country, there is a long history of movement among cities, towns, and provinces within the region. Yet such internal movements did not constitute the most important migration. Internal immigration mainly resulted from the initial experience of industrialization and was most intensive in those areas where industrialized development was most dense. Bizkaia experienced this immigration in the early days of its industrialization, and Gipuzkoa underwent this process to a greater extent during its initial period of industrialization. Araba, on the other hand, did not go through this process until the second period of industrialization. Wherever internal immigration occurred, its costs were relatively benign: a less dramatic uprooting of people, shared living arrangements (whether close to the factory or in parental homes), and the diversification of income.

But internal immigration was not the main source of immigration. It was instead more distant regions that contributed the highest proportion of the new infusion of manual labor: the northern Spanish *meseta* and the Cantabrian Coast (Castile-León, La Rioja, and Cantabria), during the first phase, and then Galicia, Extremadura, and Andalusia in the second phase, contributed the most significant proportion of human capital to the Basque modernization process. And it was this source of immigration that involved a more severe process of uprooting and higher human costs in general.

There were two ways that this external immigration occurred. Solitary immigrants were mainly seen during the first period of industrialization in Bizkaia and in the mining region. But such immigrants constituted a minority. The more common model throughout the entire period was based on those workers who came with their families. The establishment of industrialization, improved working conditions, and the meeting of expectations resulted in immigration being permanent, with any initial thoughts that immigrants may have had of returning to their original homes being indefinitely postponed in favor of permanent settlement in the Basque Country. The immigration of the youngest and most able workers with their families constitutes the largest source of supply of human capital. The demand for labor grew, and the increasing expectations of potential workers resulted in the expansion of the geographical regions from which immigrants were drawn, with movement intensifying. This process reinforced migration networks as well as the complexity of migration routes.

First generation immigrants and their second- and third-generation descendents became, along with the native-born, the foundation of the new project. Yet these new immigrants were not illegal (González Portilla et al. 2009). The relatively early, rapid, and intense nature of the "literacy transition" ("reading and writing") became a key factor in this history of innovation and growth as is shown in figure 2.4 (Domínguez Martín 2002).

Figure 2.4, Evolution of literacy rates, 1850–1930

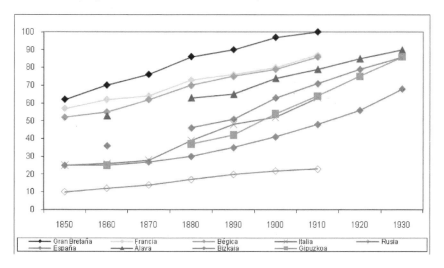

The literacy rates attained by the Basque population over the course of the past century are among the highest in all of Spain (Núñez 1992; Nuñez et al. 1997). By 1900, the three provinces had all surpassed the first literary "threshold," each exceeding 40 percent literacy (which supposedly guaranteed the maintenance of economic growth). The presence of a literate population constituted an important source of support for the modernization process that had been initiated.

Yet this source of support grew stronger in the coming years. By 1930, the end of the first period of industrialization, the population of the Basque Country, both male and female, had attained universal literacy (a literacy rate higher than 70 percent of the population; a level defined by experts as "the second threshold").

For many years, there continued to be important gender differences with respect to attaining secondary education (and, it goes without saying, university education as well). However, the early basic education received by girls helped prepare them to later assume their economic roles as "housewives," in which they acted as catalysts for modernization processes in the areas of hygiene, health, and education. Thanks to the efforts of this first generation of women, their daughters would later have more comprehensive access to secondary education, and their granddaughters would be able to gain admission to (and eventually attain a dominant presence in) universities. In the words of those who drafted the 1882 Primary Education Reform Project in Bilbao, the end of the twentieth century witnessed the achievement of what they characterized as their "social revolution."

Social Complexity and the Implementation of a New Process

The keys to understanding the past are not necessarily helpful in facing the future, but they do help us understand where we are heading. What seems a fundamentally sound course of action is to avoid a nostalgia that lacks any basis in reality, read the prevailing discourses with a critical eye, and, above all else, pay close attention to the reality of social processes.

The historical data that we have reviewed here reveal a parallel in historical circumstances separated by various decades, yet it points to the need to undertake a profound social renovation. With all of its problems, the first scenario (1876–1975) was one of challenges, but was also an era marked by projects, choices, realities, and changes. This period began with the first phase of industrialization in 1876. This was primarily characterized by an innovation that occurred in response to the urgent need to adapt to a new political, economic, and fiscal context.

Exports, capital accumulation, and the recourse to new technologies allowed for the possibility confronting the challenges involved in Western capitalist industrialization. Yet a solid base of human resources is also essential to meeting such challenges. Demographic transitions, improvements in health and hygiene, and immigration all helped provide this much-needed human capital. The road has not been easy and has taken its toll in human suffering. This is evident in so many different ways: the high mortality rates that prevailed during the initial phase of industrialization; the hard living and working conditions; housing problems; difficulties resulting from people living together in certain conditions; and the relegation of workers, women, and immigrants to the status of second-class citizens, cultural costs, and other problems. But there is little doubt that, as a result of the innovations that were undertaken—and taking full account of the terrible costs involved—the process in the end allowed the Basque Country to jump on the bandwagon of an urban-based modernization.

For all their importance, these are not the only innovations worth noting. Underlying all of these innovations has been the crucial supporting role of the educational system and the family. With a noteworthy and fairly early effort to promote literacy, the implementation of educational reform transformed the presence of a strong labor force into well-qualified human capital. In addition, in the background of this vast universe of challenges, projects, achievements, costs, and protagonists was the institution that made the monumental change that occurred possible: the family. The family made this change possible thanks to its constant efforts to reinvent itself in accordance with changing circumstances. And as the family reinvented itself, so too did women reinvent themselves. Underlying this reinvention process was the great revolution that was taking place within society: in its thinking, values, and behaviors. This revolution took place oblivious of most of the intellectual discourses (especially the most politically correct discourses) regarding what was happening.

In the second scenario, in the first decade of the twenty-first century, we are confronted with new challenges that require us to change course. New economic models, new rules of the game, and new frameworks are being considered to meet these challenges. Yet, far from resorting to past formulas, we are trying to learn from them within the context of a modern world in which subjects are more a part of modernity—a modernity that emphasizes human solidarity rather than "conquest" and production. What is needed is a profound transformation of old standards and ways of life that are no longer sustainable—a transformation that can take place only by means of new emphases and new ideas.

On the basis of such new emphases and ideas, we must take a fresh and more humanizing look at immigrants, women, and the new marginal class. To this end, it will be necessary to continually reconceptualize family models and the rules by which they operate—rules aimed at promoting optimal interpersonal relations. As part of this effort, we must assure universal access on the part of all sectors of society to comprehensive education, and to the means of education and training. All of these requirements point to the need for a "reconversion process" that can effectively navigate within the new framework of limited material goods that are unequally distributed (Larrea 2010).

References

Arregi, Begoña and Andrés Dávila, eds. 2005. *Reproduciendo la vida, manteniendo la familia: Reflexiones sobre la fecundidad y el cuidado familiar desde la experiencia en Euskadi.* Bilbao: Servicio de Ediciones y Publicaciones de la UPV/EHU.

Barandiarán, José Miguel. 1924. "Nacimiento y expansión de los fenómenos sociales." *Anuario de Eusko Folklore* 4: 151–229.

Campión, Arturo. 1935. "Contrastes. Cuadro de costumbres buenas y malas." In *Pedro Mari. Narraciones Baskas III.* San Sebastián: Beñat Idaztiak.

Delgado Cendagortagalarza, Ander. 2008. *La otra Bizkaia: Política en un medio rural durante la Restauración (1890–1923).* Bilbao: Servicio de publicaciones de la UPV/EHU.

Domínguez Martín, Rafael. 2002. *La riqueza de las regions: Las desigualdades económicas de España, 1700–2000.* Madrid: Alianza Editorial.

García Abad, Rocío. 1999. "Mercado de trabajo y estrategias familiares durante la primera industrialización vizcaína: el hospedaje." *Vasconia* 28: 93–115.

———. 2005. *Historias de emigración: Factores de expulsión y selección del capital humano en la emigración a la Ría de Bilbao (1877–1935).* Bilbao: Servicio Editorial de la UPV/EHU.

González Portilla, Manuel, dir. 1995. *Bilbao en la formación del País Vasco contemporáneo. (Economía, población y ciudad).* Bilbao: Fundación BBVA.

———. 2009. *La consolidación de la metrópoli de la Ría de Bilbao.* 2 vols. Bilbao: Fundación BBVA.

———. 1981. *La formación de la sociedad capitalista en el País Vasco (1876–1913).* San Sebastián: L. Haranburu Editor.

González Portilla, Manuel, et al. 2003. *Vivir en familia, organizar la socie-dad. Familia y modelos familiares: las provincias vascas a las puertas de la modernidad (1860)*. Bilbao: Servicio Editorial de la UPV/EHU.

Larrea, Pedro. 2010. "2009: La historia continúa." *El Correo* (January 4, 2010), 22.

Lecuona, Manuel de. 1924. "La religiosidad del pueblo." *Anuario de Eusko Folklore* 4: 1–47.

Le Play, Frédéric. 1878. "Le paysan basque du Labourd." In *Les ouvr-ières européens, étude sur les travaux, la vie domestique et la condition morale des populations ouvrières de l'Europe*. Tours: Ed. Alfred Mame et fils.

Livi-Bacci, Massimo. 1997. *A Concise History of World Population*. Trans-lated by Carl Ipsen. Malden, MA: Blackwell, 1997.

Loti, Pierre. 2008. *El País Vasco*. Donostia: Roger.

Madoz, Pascual. 1852. *Diccionario Geográfico-Estadístico-Histórico de España y sus posesiones de Ultramar*. Madrid: Imp. de P. Madoz y L. Sagasti, t. IX.

Núñez, Clara Eugenia. 1992. *La fuente de la riqueza: Educación y desarrollo económico en la España Contemporánea*. Madrid: Alianza Editorial.

Núñez, Clara Eugenia et al., eds. 1997. *La maldición divina: Ignoran-cia y atraso económico en perspectiva histórica*. Madrid: Alianza Editorial.

Pareja Alonso, Arantza. 2000. "The Demography of the Industrialized Province of Biscay in Northern Spain: Spatial Differences and Long-Term Changes." *The History of the Family* 5, no. 4: 431–448.

Pérez-Fuentes, Pilar. 1993. *Vivir y morir en las minas: estrategias famil-iares y relaciones de género en la primera industrialización vizcaína (1877–1913)*. Bilbao: Servicio editorial de la UPV/EHU.

Ruiz de Loizaga, María. 2010. "Primeras Letras: 'Revolución Social' y Modernización. El Bilbao de la Restauración: 1876–1920." Doctoral Thesis, UPV/EHU, Leioa.

3

Pathways to Social Innovation
in the Basque Country

ANDER GURRUTXAGA

Translated by Laura Bunt-MacRury

Most experts in innovative social learning agree that it is built through interactions rooted in the local level and in specific territories, although its aim is global.[1] Local spaces generate different forms of knowledge, creating differences in their ability to innovate. Some sites accumulate resources by creating environments that facilitate the emergence of innovative knowledge that can be transferred to other institutions, which leads to a propagation of ideas that synergize with other actors and areas. Thus, they generate a response to any contemporary challenges and issues that may arise. The resulting spaces should be conceptualized as "learning regions" due to their very same capacity to shape socioeconomic structures in adapting and adjusting to the requisites of innovation.

As stated in most research, development, and innovation (RDI) policies, training and education programs, public infrastructure, marketing strategies, and fiscal policies are ostensibly efficient factors to achieve this objective if they are linked and designed in unison between local and regional institutional networks. Innovative processes tend to con-

---

1. See Albuty and Mulgan (2003); Baumol, Litan, and Schramm (2007); Beck (1992); Beinhocker (2007); Berger and Huntington (2002); Berkun (2007); Rutten and Boekema (2007); Boekema (2003); Boutellier, Gassmann, and von Zedtwitz (2008); Bowler and Rhys Morus (2005); and Kapstein (1994).

centrate in urban metropolitan areas because they provide conditions conducive to the emergence of new sites and practices due to the advantages of spatial proximity and the concentration of agents and resources. These include the accumulation of technical support, qualified human resources, technological infrastructure, universities, support research, and venture capital.

How are the effects of innovation and learning that promote productivity, competitive businesses, and social environments generated? Is it enough to gather the actors, resources, and infrastructure involved in these effects in the same room? I argue that innovative processes go beyond technological and/or economic interpretations alone to the extent that they capture the complexity of the processes that occur in spaces, areas, and levels that synergize into multiple and not necessarily economic processes. Therefore, attention should be given to a variety of innovative sources and possible environments whether they are economic, business, social, cultural, or artistic. To innovate is to create and/or reproduce a cultural system based on tolerance by accepting a revision to some of its basic existing characteristics, whether tangible (processes, products, technology, or marketing) or intangible (values, ideas, emotions, or institutions) so that successful processes can acquire new uses and meanings.

Innovative societies merge well-trained human capital to extend quality education to the vast majority of citizens, to public policy development, and to institutional environments that support risk-taking. They reward novel and good ideas, and they put forth various business incentives. For example, certain mechanisms used to build opportunity structures from which to strengthen the relationship between the RDI and university systems have resulted in greater social well-being and quality of life.

Starting from a Fordist frame, the following chapter considers this issue in the Basque Country by trying to understand to what extent it displays the socioeconomic dynamics and cultural organization that constitute the paradigm of innovative societies. I am interested in understanding what happens when this paradigm—formerly dependent as in the case of the Basque Country on the production of iron, steel, and shipbuilding—gives way to the leisure and the service industries, in turn fragmenting industrial working-class culture (thereby creating alternative and individualized responses associated with the ethos of leisure and consumption).

Innovative Action

Not all societies innovate under the same circumstances, but rather follow different paths. Exchange and interaction under reciprocal conditions provide the foundation that nourishes cultural innovation and ultimately socioeconomic development. As Richard Florida (2004) has argued, competitive and dynamic cities create environments open to creativity and diversity. Such synergies are key to prosperity in the age of knowledge and occur easily in environments where talented people choose to work and live, for example in the case of Silicon Valley. The competitive advantage of cities is in their ability to create, attract, and retain a workforce that plays a significant role in knowledge production and innovation. However, while such talent is retained in city-regions, this is not the case of just any city-region. One theory posits that people are attracted to communities and populations where other creative people are concentrated—and although they may have similar jobs, they retain diverse identities. In this sense, knowledge-based economies are not founded on social cohesion but, rather, certain forms of social cohesion are the foundation of knowledge economies. Maintaining cohesion and social integration are, then, not burdens on states but instead two key mechanisms for boosting socioeconomic development.

Successful innovation depends on the establishment of many specific contexts. Some interesting lessons from innovative societies can be deduced through empirical analysis. For example, socio-structural contexts are dependent on specific territorial resources to develop innovative situations. Thus, it is common to find variables with high levels of cooperation between actors at the local, regional, and national levels that have the capacity to produce:

- mechanisms of social consensus in groups that promote change
- the adoption of an ethic that achieves a balance and openness toward social innovations
- good local economic and cultural systems of governance
- the creation of effective social policies with the involvement and participation of skilled citizens in the surrounding population
- a high educational level of citizens
- low levels of social exclusion
- a high concentration of and employment rate in the information and communication technologies (ICTs), communications, and knowledge industry business sectors

- a good transportation system with effective internal connections linking different regions
- high caliber cultural and educational institutions
- the production of new knowledge in scientific research, numerous patents, and scientific articles
- the concentration of research centers
- young demographic rates
- good logistics and international networking
- decentralization and local autonomy within neighborhoods and communities in decision-making processes
- good planning and urban design in cities hosting such knowledge industries and laboratories

The most significant elements in the experiences cited are: the ability of innovative systems in each country, the quality of universities, and the effectiveness of communication mechanisms, both of these entities with respect to business and human resources operating in the innovation and knowledge economy. The consolidation of these processes requires paying special attention to the importance of people's education and living conditions, the entrepreneurial culture, and financial resources invested in systemic development. Individual contexts differ because, for instance, not every country's industrial structure is the same. Moreover, business opportunities, social structure, and cultural tradition are not universal. Inversely, less opportunities for innovation stem from a lack of: innovation policies, quality university education, a flexible and tolerant institutional system, an adequate social structure attentive to the environment, and a culture that enables and protects creativity.

What this means is that there are different courses of action. This is significant, for example, when one considers that the societies that have best resolved the tensions caused by educational process, and managed to innovate and create frameworks for creativity in early childhood education, are those that have best solved the problems of growth and that have been most successful in formalizing transformation processes toward a knowledge-based society. Equally, there is a greater association between investment in RDI and success in innovation. Moreover, societies that better redistribute tax revenue are placed higher on the Gini coefficient or the index concerning democratic openness. The Gini coefficient, and success in economic and social modernization processes, refers to the proper functioning of institutions as one of the most feasible explanations when citing the value of successful innovation processes. In all these processes, a palpable theme is explicit: It is not necessary to occupy the highest echelons in global rankings of GDP distribution or per capita income to make things right. What is needed are well-governed societies capable of redistributing income, low levels of corruption, good health systems, and compulsory public education, as well as progressive investment in RDI.

A knowledge-based society, which supports economic development and its legitimization through innovation, develops the ability to participate in activities that require knowledge, especially in how it is created, applied, shared, and transferred. Some of these activities are related to explicit kinds of knowledge, research, development, training (whether formal or informal), or searching for information relevant to the area of activity concerned. Others, however, seek to facilitate the emergence of ethereal information, or rather tacit knowledge.

The Definition of Social Innovation

In the 1990s, widespread technological, social, and economic transformations affected the structure of global society, especially the emergence and spread of ICTs. Changes in scientific activity due to ICT are essential to scientific practice. Above all, scientific communities, universities, and research centers become part of national RDI strategies, which tend to be transnational and supranational, at least in the case of the United States, the European Union (EU), and some Southeast Asian countries. The transformation of science can be described in short by the fact that scientific knowledge, which during the modern scientific era was an end in itself, is now a means to an end. Science has now become technoscience, whose aim is not to know the world but to change it. Most technoscience is driven by private initiative and RDI businesses, whose objective is to enable innovations that improve their competitiveness and productivity. The companies that invest in RDI (given their ability to innovate) create wealth and gain power to reinvest in basic and applied research.

This is the result of a particular story. The OECD (Organisation for Economic Co-operation and Development) and Eurostat (the European Statistics Office) published the first edition of the *Oslo Manual* in 1992. It argues that if local, regional, and national innovation systems are aligned, they demonstrate that technological innovation—acknowledged (following Joseph Schumpeter) as the main source of economic growth—is not the only relevant form of innovation. The second edition (1997) stresses the importance of innovation in the service sector, and the latest edition (2005) distinguishes four types of innovation: product (goods and services), processes, organization, and marketing. In sum, the most significant economic and social innovation processes are more varied than originally imagined by Schumpeter and his followers, and, more generally, than envisaged by most economic or technological analysis.

Simultaneously, other organizations and institutions draw attention to other forms of innovation, such as social innovation. The Young Foundation in the United Kingdom asserts that social innovations are, "activities and services that are motivated by the goal of meeting a social need and that are predominantly developed and diffused through organizations whose primary purposes are social" (2006, 8). It also defines innovation in general as "new ideas that work" (11). This meaning has been adopted by the British government, for whom innovation is, "The successful exploitation of new ideas" (Department for Innovation, Universities & Skills 2008, 12–13). They argue that this approach to social innovation—new ideas, institutions, and ways of working—more effectively reaches targeted social needs. Often, social innovation requires not only new ideas, but also the new application of old ones. Innovations can be disseminated through a profession, a specialized sector, or social actions in the field of education or health. Not all relate to the products or services of individual organizations. Social innovations stem from many sources (academic research, political campaigns, socially responsible businesses, or new technologies, for example) and can be applied in many fields. However, the British definition is hampered by having only successful innovations in mind, whereas many such attempts fail, as the *Oslo Manual* notes and as any innovator can verify.

Elsewhere, for theorists at the Centre de recherche sur les innovations sociales (CRISES, Research Centre on Social Innovations) in Canada, innovation is the intervention of social actors responding to an aspiration, a wish, a solution, or the creation of an opportunity with the aim of changing social relations, transforming a field of action, and putting forward new cultural orientations. Social innovations can achieve long-term social efficiency that exceeds the original objectives for which they were originally constructed. Innovation might, then, represent a commitment to challenging social stability by generating long-term change. For the CRISES, such innovations can have a social impact, creating social change and fostering the emergence of new development models, all depending on the diffusion of the innovation itself. Such innovations can be generated in three distinct areas: a particular region, in certain life conditions, and in the workplace.

For the Boston Indicators Project (BIP), the process of developing and transforming a city or region through innovative (and perhaps some not so innovative) measures is based on the ability of the city and social environment to combine the skills of different actors and participants involved in resolving problems affecting society as a whole. An economic, social, political, and cultural pact mobilizes local councils, political parties, public institutions, associations, foundations, businesses, and sociocultural organizations within a process oriented toward social action. The process succeeds if all actors move in the same direction, toward the same goals, and there is a balance of power in areas of participation. The ability to change or enact social transformation depends on the skills, ideas, values, habits, cultures, and policies that can be put together. For the BIP, social innovation is based on this cooperation and two influential concepts that mutually reinforce one another. In other words, innovation is utilized to face the uncertainty of new problems, yet it is this joint response to problems that allows for a longer-term discussion about what is happening and how best to combine human practice and action in order to improve a social environment.

James A. Phills, Kriss Deiglmeier, and Dale T. Miller point out that, "social innovation is the best construct for understanding—and producing—lasting social change" (2008, 6). With this objective in mind they define innovation as, "A novel solution to a social problem that is more effective, efficient, sustainable, or just than existing solutions and for which the value created accrues primarily to society as a whole rather than private individuals" (36).

In short, social innovation involves a series of learning processes on the part of individuals who are learning to solve problems and creating solutions in interaction with others in the process who apply, share, seek, and create knowledge. Thus, taken as a whole, *interactive learning spaces* can be formed in many places: in business, in the interaction between business and workers, between businesses and consumers, between consumers and producers, in research teams, in the public sphere, in the development and implementation of social policies, in the exchange of ideas between social and academic groups, within civil society, or in everyday exchanges between different generations. The construction of learning spaces depends on having people trained to identify relevant knowledge regarding a particular problem, as well as the knowledge and organization needed. However, this is not enough in itself because opportunities must also arise to address problems collectively. The nutrients that enrich collective learning are inscribed in geographical space—as a cultural and human code—that encompasses everyone. This means that interactive learning processes are made possible by sociocultural and institutional conditions that generate a climate of trust and shared objectives.

The consequence of this is a shift from scientific values to tasks more befitting social and economic engineering, as well as old-fashioned technocracy. Basically, those who incorporate the social innovation paradigm into the world of economic and social practices seek to create an ethical basis for liquid capitalism, business, and economic practice with the goal of fostering good practices in public and social policies. The result is a type of social innovation with four characteristics: (1) It is a paradigm associated with the economy, society, the economic activity of companies, the social activity of government, social services planning, and activities specific to health care and the elderly; (2) It is pragmatic in pursuing specific functions based on the general idea of what should be good or sustainable practices; (3) It has an ethical connotation in which its postulates are intended to consolidate and legitimize a certain way of doing things that are associated with values such as creativity, respect, care, trust, and loyalty; and (4) It has a methodological dimension in which the success of social innovation depends on its ability to manage the procedures surrounding good practices, as well as procedures that encourage internalizing such values.

Pathways to Innovation in the Basque Country

As regards this process of socio-industrial restructuring, the case of the shipbuilding and iron and steel industries in the Basque Country is paradigmatic in that it offers us a glimpse of how change, social innovation, and uncertainty are all interconnected. I will therefore analyze this case in order to originate a hypothesis and to chronicle the structural transformation of a society (the Basque Country), a region, an economic growth model (based on shipbuilding and iron and steel), a cultural structure, and the living conditions shaped by the predominance of a working-class industrial culture. I will examine the characteristics and consequences of innovative processes when they transcend the "essence" of technology in order to become social and cultural processes that alter the traditional lifestyles of an impacted community. Ultimately in this case, processes emerge that lead to the creation of an innovative model that transcends Fordist logic to remake this landscape—via an *industrial logic* in the era of knowledge—into one of malls dedicated to leisure and consumption.

Innovation processes encourage responses to the crisis of the Fordist industrial model, but the restructuring of the shipbuilding and iron and steel industries has not followed the same routes used by the industrial tradition that originally welcomed this developmental model. On the contrary, we are currently witnessing an end to more than 150 years of industrial history that this "narrative" had sustained. I use this case to show how some innovative processes that come about as the result of structural change involve factors that are sometimes unforeseen in the journey from the Fordist model to more flexible forms of work. In this case, paradoxically, the industrial tradition was a factor in both encouraging innovation and resistance to change.

The Basque Country is symbolic of the industrialization model that was developed in Spain in the second half of the nineteenth century. The Basque industrial framework was led by two large companies—Altos Hornos de Vizcaya in the iron and steel sector, and the shipbuilding yards of the Astilleros company—that in turn, generated a network of subsidiary companies to service them. And this led to the emergence of a traditional working class, working-class industrial culture, and an urban structure characteristic of this type of industrial development.

In this case, then, the historical logic of social innovation is associated with the defense of the industrial tradition and the lifestyle created by industrial working-class culture. Likewise, the urban structure was driven by an industrial logic that can also be used to describe Altos Hornos and its auxiliary businesses. The region's economic development was conditioned by the social logic of modernization in that the industrial setting was the vessel that drove innovation. Yet the Basque Country had to reconsider its way of life when, in the 1980s, the economic growth model based on the iron and steel industry and shipbuilding fell apart. Innovation, which until that time was associated with the everyday use of an industrial and working-class tradition that underpinned the iron and steel industry, no longer lent a sense of industrial security to the region. Thousands of jobs directly or indirectly related to industry were lost, and workers who had previously so identified with a particular industry, communitarian working-class culture, and a rhythm of life now faced a jobless future.

The disappearance of the traditional industrial structure and the restructuring of the labor force led to a reframing of the terms and meaning of innovation. Yet, before this could occur, and while the city's manufacturing livelihood still depended upon the original economic growth model, socio-industrial development had relied on five foundations: (1) population growth; (2) an industrial structure based on the subsectors of iron and steel and shipbuilding together with auxiliary businesses; (3) an urban structure with a developed center and a periphery that grew as the population increased; (4) a lifestyle shaped by the meaning derived from industrial work and a culture based on the idea of work as vocation, community commitment, and group solidarity; and (5) a political and institutional logic subjected to industrial whim and the hegemony of large companies over public institutions.

The iron and steel industry is an example of the prevailing industrial model in Spain during the period of protectionism, which kept it away from the challenges posed by competition in open markets. One way or another it survived and even expanded during an era of Spanish development in the 1960s, thanks to the protection granted by the nationalization of production and captive markets. Yet it did not develop any capacity for competition or technological innovation that it would have been forced to do by having to compete in the pace of the open market. As a result, company profits were not reinvested in technological innovation or in the formation of products and services, and the industry gradually declined.

One visible impact of this was that thousands of workers were forced into early retirement. Moreover, young people who had believed that their first natural step into the workplace would, like their fathers and grandfathers, be the "factory," had their expectations destroyed and became unemployment statistics without having entered the labor market. In addition, other industries were affected by the demise of the steel industry. Most shipbuilding companies ceased production, and those that survived were downsized so much as to have barely any industrial presence whatsoever. Others still began a downward spiral that led to their disappearance shortly after. Those that strove to survive found that they had to adapt to new times, resulting in significant cuts in labor and production. The results varied, but the general trend was unavoidable: The industrial and social crisis was followed by a restructuring of the region's productive framework. In the 1990s, then, this model of economic development came to an end after more than one hundred years.

The region thus lost its industrial presence, and in its place emerged the service sector. The policy of attracting business investment was successful in two areas: in leisure companies and service industries that emerged as a result of the growing service economy, creating jobs in flexible organizations; and in construction and public works that were increasingly important as a result of urban regeneration activity. Alongside these developments, a previously unheard of issue emerged in the 1990s: the novel experience of addressing "innovation"—or, better-stated, how to convert industrialized urban areas. Clearly, at the time both "hard" statistics and everyday life pointed to the harsh consequences of the crisis of socioeconomic model to that date: unemployment, urban decay, a cultural crisis, and a socio-industrial life cycle broken by the effects of industrial decline and downsizing.

Given the situation, the innovation model adopted would depend on two processes working: First, there would have to be an urban regeneration of the region with strategic use of the material and economic value of the land vacated by traditional industry. To address this issue, two institutions were created—Bilbao Metropoli-30 and Bilbao Ría 2000—with different purposes and functions, and a series of plans (funded by a series of public bodies from the provincial to the EU level) were implemented to coordinate the transformation. Second, corporate activity was also key, especially that of the leisure and service industries that were installed in the strip malls on the outskirts of Bilbao. Indeed, by the late 1990s this sector had become the major source of jobs in the area. Thus, institutional politics—the political work of representative institutions and the public economy from above—articulated and regulated regional innovation, as if the various agents suddenly understood that the time had arrived for the elected institutions.

These processes responded, in general, to a series of realities: By this time the Fordist industrial model had ceased to exist or, at best, was simply residual. Processes of change began when social and institutional actors defined the problem and began to address it by seeking solutions to the questions that were hitherto intractable or had not been raised. At that juncture, they began to look elsewhere and raise new questions.

The measures taken followed a definition of the problems, and among those that stood out were: plans to promote the use of former industrial land, a policy of attracting companies and soil decontamination, urban regeneration schemes, the creation of a cultural structure, promoting positive action for the elderly (for example, in housing and travel), and employment campaigns. Innovative institutions were dependent on the politics of large public institutions, which gave rise to agencies and agents aimed at reinforcing top-down transformation processes, with little citizen involvement, and designs based on expert knowledge and a technocratic means of redefining the meaning of place and space in a city that the industrial crisis left battered.

Further, this expert knowledge was integrated into international networks, with the Basque Country's problems publicized in changing communities in other Spanish regions, as well as in Europe and North America. These communities were supposed to be experiences from which to learn how other cities and regions in similar circumstances reacted and found solutions to the problems, and in these interdependent processes, the fundamental value was knowledge transfer. One key innovative solution was the creation of industrial parks, which provided a means of both attracting and creating work for the young people. Therefore, we see now that the dominant economic model has little to do with that of classic industrial society.

It is now based on knowledge-intensive production, with ever advancing machines, as well as goods and services rich in information. Knowledge-based training contrasts with the training system of classic industrial society. Industrial activity requires learning through *habitus*, whereas work in the knowledge society brings ideas and innovation. Individuals are integrated cognitively—they manage and work with information-based skills required by discursive reflection and rationality. The production that ensues does not produce goods but singularities and prototypes. This means that if one wants to add value to innovation, one must traverse the specific sites that define the knowledge economy.

Business can follow different paths: They can maintain the traditional business structure, although on a reduced scale, in the belief that smaller firms are more flexible and better able to resist the impact of a major downturn than their larger counterparts. Alternatively, they can seek to attract new businesses, especially in the service sector. For example, in the aforementioned strip malls, the commercial activity of small and medium-sized enterprises (SMEs) in the leisure and service industries helps to revitalize urban areas, and are one of their principal attractions. Finally, they can create business with high added value in knowledge and research. While in this option there are not as many companies, and they do not create the same numbers of jobs, their design activity demands an indirect workforce and, above all, leads to the establishment of networks composed of knowledge and high tech companies.

Finally, all these plans had to take into account a new configuration of communitarian and solidarity networks that historically defined the Basque Country's social capital. The dependence of this social capital on history and tradition was significant because modernity itself had been expressed through industrial working-class culture that was born in and tied to this region.

Innovation Cultures in the Basque Country

Innovation in the cultural structure stems from the aforementioned crisis of the industrial model, and it articulates new ways of creating social capital. It is based on the maxim of "keeping up to date," which, in social and cultural terms, means embracing a culture devoid of strong signs of identity and that is characterized by individuals in consumerist structures. This is the culture that deinstitutionalized the working-class industrial tradition and established a new form of institutionalization through its introduction of consumerist structures facilitated by leisure practices. In the Basque case, its effects were significant because new generations were retrained within the frame of the new cultural paradigm. In contrast, older generations were stuck in a tradition—that of factories, heavy industry, and shipyards—that no longer existed and could not be altered. Not surprisingly, then, communitarian ties were either transformed into more individualist activity or suffered from a lack of community organizations that might have maintained such common bonds.

Social capital is linked to group and community in two ways in the Basque Country. One, found among young people, relies on leisure structures and is associated with consumer industries and investment of people's time in the industrial channels of consumer structures. The other, which still exists, is steeped in the nostalgia of industrial working-class tradition that gives meaning to the "blast furnace" generation. The latter lacks any material support from traditional industry, and this leads to the problem of retraining and a resistance to change without any cultural links to a past that has been transformed into a resource of the present. The two narratives do not clash, but rather run parallel and oblivious to one another. The result of all this is a crisis among traditional communitarian institutions and social networks that once sustained popular initiatives such as neighborhood associations and classic youth groups.

For some, innovation is the objective recognition that this former world and lifestyle is in decline. Others take a more pragmatic functional view, where innovation is a resource that encompasses how they define their lifestyles and future—something that tradition is incapable of doing. There is, then, a divisive narrative, sometimes in silence and in other cases full of complaint. Two worlds run parallel to one another, all the while sustaining a kind of life pact. Innovation implies technological change, the organization of complexity through a network of service companies, and the disappearance of traditional identity symbols—all of which suggest that not everything one wants is attainable and that the discourse of a fluid world has no logical end. The cultural structure exists to point out that innovation is not only handling expert knowledge or managing institutional policy "from above." It is also a question of addressing the impact represented in the manifest split of the cultural structure itself, as well as the paradigm of uncertainty it represents.

From the Industrial Era to the Era of Innovative Knowledge: Strengths and Weaknesses of the Process

The result of all this is that the socioeconomic structure of the Basque Country is experiencing a transition between the disappearance of industrial society and the emergence of a knowledge-based society. No one complete model serves as a reference for the Basque case, which has depended on exogenous and endogenous factors. From a situation in the 1980s, when there was little investment in science, technology, and innovation, Basque society has witnessed a significant increase in public investment in RDI, giving it a privileged position among Spain's autonomous regions. Yet, despite advances, there had been a failure to quell the historical problems that continued to burden new systems of innovation and development.

The timeframe—from the 1980s to the present—in which the Basque system of science, technology, and innovation has been developed should be sufficient to evaluate its achievements and difficulties, taking into account that innovation is not something that is achieved once and for all and that RDI systems are open to innovating on the basis of previous innovation.

To better delimit this first assertion, Basque society has some dynamic assets that address this process: It enjoys a centuries-old industrial tradition and a strong work ethic embedded in its culture. It possesses well-trained human capital in the use of information technology headed by economic agents and business leaders that identify strongly with the region and develop growth strategies from the value placed on personal connections. There is an advanced network of cities and an infrastructure in the throes of transformation and modernization. Its institutions are rooted in civil society, and it has a working administrative strategy that constitutes the heart of the economic development model. Its social welfare is well established and training programs well developed. Investment in formative stages is significant and strategic (and involves training people in new technologies), and there is widespread use of the Internet and cellular phones.

Yet, despite all this, Basque society is not yet a knowledge-based society. For example, there is insufficient technological development and investment in the university system lags behind leading European countries. In addition, it lacks the population mass required to institutionalize a knowledge-based society. The business structure (composed of SMEs) takes a limited role in RDI and cannot fulfill the role of other larger-scale enterprises (such as in the cases of Nokia in Finland or Ericsson in Sweden with regard to the spectacular development of science and technology in their respective countries).

Creating Ikerbasque, Innobasque, the Donostia International Physics Center, and other similar initiatives plugs holes or gaps in the system. Ikerbasque's role is to capture specialized human resources by integrating them into research networks in the Comunidad Autónoma del País Vasco/ Euskal Autonomia Erkidegoa (CAPV/EAE, the Autonomous Community of the Basque Country) and into colleges or various technology centers. Innobasque's mission is to create a new kind of social movement made up of administrative, political, economic, and cultural elites in order to create a collective innovative pedagogy. However, there is still a limited number of qualified people in the CAPV/EAE and therefore one can hardly speak about the importance of the "creative class" in these processes.

There are four basic obstacles to achieving a knowledge-based Basque society: the dimensions of the corporate structure, funding of the system, the institutional framework, and the creation of innovative cultures. Company size is a significant factor in the features of this system. With the proliferation of SMEs, RDI units in companies are also small and lack the force to help companies grow, become more international, and develop technologically. There is a strong link between the size of a business and the scale of its RDI. Therefore, the societies that lead the way in RDI are not just those that have done significant work in urban recovery, but that also have a technical and technological drive that enables them to market their products internationally and occupy a prominent position in leading sectors of the knowledge industries. Figures for the Basque corporate structure reveal the extent of this SME dominance: 93.3 percent of businesses have less than ten employees, and only 0.1 percent have more than two hundred and fifty—although the latter account for 26.6 percent of total employment in the Basque economy.

The financing of a system is always an important element. In fact, the relationship between investment in RDI projects and systemic innovation is clear, so that, for further development, there must be more investment. Data in the Basque case reveal that only 1.47 percent of GDP is invested in RDI, compared with 3.72 percent in Sweden, 3.45 percent in Finland, and 2.54 percent in Germany. Furthermore, the Basque case is also dominated by sectors that do not traditionally invest in RDI, revealing another weakness in the economic framework under investigation here. Similarly, the institutional framework, which is essential in terms of creating innovative scenarios, is also significant. In the Basque case, this is made up of universities, technology centers, and RDI units in companies.

Finally, regarding the creation of innovative cultures, there has been an over-institutionalization of Basque civil society. There are too many public institutions, and people depend too much on public subsidies. The golden rule is that public institutions operate under the criteria of compensating citizens. This has led to the creation of a clientele that is dependent upon the public budget and private initiatives that are estranged from the requirements of the public world, as well as an omnipresent government presence in all public and private activity. The paradox is that institutional strength depends on the over-institutionalization of the administrative framework, as well as the importance of the public budget. Thus, innovative thinking, paradoxically, does not stem from civil society, but rather a result of instrumental action resulting from the structural strategies of public administration.

The result is that innovation, and the culture it favors, are mired in a set of paradoxes that require public institutions to ensure their cultural visibility. Yet, at the same time, success in innovation is risky and inherent to the individual entrepreneurial spirit. The danger is that institutional influence and the public funding of all initiatives extinguish the risk element that innovation demands. What is worse, public funding comes to resemble a buoy that guarantees risk-free innovation. Clearly, the use of public funds through subsidies to protect against entrepreneurial risk is not conducive to a culture of innovation. This is especially true where there appears to be an abundance of public funding or when it is presented as if it were a necessary and natural part of the process of innovation.

Conclusion

Transformational pathways and results have had mixed fortunes in the Basque Country. Countries become knowledge-based societies at different rates and in differing degrees, in accordance with their level of development. Societies and economies reach similar levels of development via diverse rhythms and degrees, experiencing different historical and cultural trajectories, and creating distinctive institutions using disparate forms of social organization. There is no single model or specific route of access to the incorporation of knowledge, just as there is no single way to achieve economic modernization or to build intelligent cities. The world is full of "anomalies" in contrast to the dominant Western-American model.

This calls into question the linear nature (partly dependent on the now-extinct classic evolutionary model) represented in typical versions of modernization and convergence theories, as well as the concepts that negate the difficulties in the current Zeitgeist underscored by a knowledge-based society. The social, cultural, and economic value of the technological paradigm does not deny empirical refutation. The crisis of industrial society does not lead to a knowledge-based or technological society, but rather it is the literal lasting crisis of the transformation that leaves after effects that are difficult to overcome, if not impossible to forget. Yet, compared to technological or social determinism, the knowledge-based society is not a point of arrival or a finite destination, but rather it is a situation or an idealized archetype that different societies would like to resemble.

This is not a case of recreating the convergence theory that so many classic modernization theorists dreamt of, but rather a disjointed reality— one that does not know precisely its point of arrival but does know how to move and in what direction, without thinking of this direction as the point of arrival. Human existence is ephemeral. We are transferring transitional knowledge where social learning spheres are fraught with difficulties and challenges, and we will not necessarily achieve what the official rhetoric proclaims or the technological paradigm sustains. The notion of a society is more convoluted and is conditioned by situations and contexts that situate the problem of contingency at the center of much controversy.

Following the notion of historical sediment remaining in current societies, the meeting of present and future is conditioned by a reading of the past that allows us to see that socioeconomic reconfiguration processes are interdependent. They are made up of invisible threads that connect past, present, and future and that cannot be conceived as lineal modernization processes that lead inevitably to a knowledge-based society. The decline of industrial society is an opportunity for change in the minds of some, but in other societies, it means falling into an inescapable black hole. Social time and its connections do not conform to radical breaks, but rather changes in structures and processes that enable the shaping of other structures built upon differing criteria and constraints upon collective human action. Derivatives or "anomalies" are actually representative of disputes about the differences and limits that allow some to be included and excluded from the networks that shape present and future paths.

There are several paths and "anomalous" roads for reaching some semblance of a knowledge-based society. Yet, there is no mandatory "docking station" where all societies must go. These paths are open to a fluid world and flexible organization in the form of networks. They are traversed by moments of chaos and entropy; disorganization and instability play significant roles in defining feature their existence. Thus, the only way to understand a knowledge-based society is from a wider perspective, devoid of convergence theories or the need to look like something else, but rather in the need to "be by doing" or "do by being." There are no predetermined paths. Ideal types are used here as references points in order to achieve some contrast point in a certain direction toward a horizon, but never as a finishing point.

What is the role of Basque society in the gamble of innovation? Clearly, the size of the society, historical inertia, the structure of businesses, the weakness of key institutions, and the paradoxes of a culture of innovation and human capital inhibit a sustained argument concerning the model of intelligent cities. This is because societies like the Basque Country, with the degree of development and capacity to implement innovative systems, are limited in their ability to become reference points for this model of structural and social development. Societies like the Basque Country depend on the ability to do what they normally do well without trying to reinvent themselves every day. The key for such small societies is to simply do "things well." This is because sudden or rapid changes in the business structure, short-term growth of time and investment in RDI, the emergence of a new institutional system, and a specific culture of innovation are not viable factors in the short or medium term and cannot be created overnight. Quite apart from this is that certain reference points followed might indicate other paths to take and thereby escape predetermined solutions. Certainly, this is not an all or nothing game. On the contrary, one can take many pathways. The problem is which path to choose, and what is clear is that indecision is not an option.

References

Albuty, David and Geoff Mulgan. 2003. *Innovation in the Public Sector.* London: Strategy Unit.

Baumol, William J., Robert E. Litan, and Carl J. Schramm. 2007. *Good Capitalism, Bad Capitalism and the Economics of Growth and Prosperity.* New Haven: Yale University Press.

Beck, Ulrich. 1992. *Risk Society: Towards a New Modernity.* Translated by Mark Ritter. London and Thousand Oaks, CA: Sage Publications.

Beinhocker, Eric D. 2007. *Origin of Wealth: The Radical Remaking of Economics and What It Means for Business and Society.* Boston: Harvard Business Press.

Berger, Peter L. and Samuel P. Huntington, eds. 2002. *Many Globalizations: Cultural Diversity in the Contemporary World.* Oxford: Oxford University Press.

Berkun, Scott. 2007. *The Myths of Innovation.* Sebastopol, CA: O'Reilly Media Inc.

Boekema, Frans. 2003. *Economic Geography of Higher Education: Knowledge, Infrastructure and Learning Regions.* London: Routledge.

Boutellier, Roman, Oliver Gassmann, and Maximilian von Zedtwitz, eds. 2008. *Managing Global Innovation: Uncovering the Secrets of Future Competitiveness.* New York: Springer.

Bowler, Peter and Iwan Rhys Morus. 2005. *Making Modern Science: A Historical Survey.* Chicago: The University Chicago Press.

Department for Innovation, Universities & Skills. 2008. *Innovation Nation.* Government White Paper, presented to Parliament by the Secretary of State for Innovation, Universities & Skills, the Chancellor of the Exchequer and the Secretary of State for Business Enterprise and Regulatory Reform, March. Norwich: The Stationary Office.

Florida, Richard. 2004. *The Rise of the Creative Class: And How It's Transforming Work, Leisure, Community, and Everyday Life.* New York: Basic Books.

Kapstein, Ethan B. 1994. *Governing the Global Economy: International Finance and the State.* Cambridge, MA: Harvard University Press.

OECD/Eurostat. 1992. *Oslo Manual: Proposed Guidelines for Collecting and Interpreting Technological Innovation Data.* Paris: OECD/Eurostat.

———. 1997. *Oslo Manual: Proposed Guidelines for Collecting and Interpreting Technological Innovation Data,* 2d ed. Paris: OECD/Eurostat.

———. 2005. *Oslo Manual: Guidelines for Collecting and Interpreting Innovation Data,* 3d. ed. Paris: OECD/Eurostat.

Phills, James A., Kriss Deiglmeier, and Dale T. Miller. 2008. "Rediscovering Social Innovation." *Stanford Social Innovation Review* (Fall): 34–43.

Rutten, Roel and Frans Boekema. 2007. *The Learning Region: Foundations, State of the Art, Future.* London: Edward Elgar Publishing.

Young Foundation. 2006. *Social Innovation: What Is It, Why It Matters, How It Can Be Accelerated.* London: Basingstoke Press.

4

Socio-Structural Contexts of Social Innovation in the Autonomous Community of the Basque Country

Auxkin Galarraga Ezponda

Translated by Jennifer R. Ottman

Debates about innovation have increased recently, especially in light of the increase in academic approaches that have incorporated the term into their customary language and of its indiscriminate use in business and marketing contexts. With this has come a notable increase in confusion and indeterminacy when trying to examine the phenomenon more closely. Calling for innovation has become a familiar tactic in the face of the uncertainty and complexity of the current historic era of socioeconomic reconfiguration. Nevertheless, the fact that our societies are in need of far-reaching innovations should not lead us to employ the concept as a plea, but rather to theoretically clarify and analytically delimit the object of study and its characteristic traits as a social and human phenomenon.

Research done from the perspective of social and cultural innovation has paved the way for reflection on the sociocultural factors and dynamics present in any process of innovation, going beyond the mere analysis of the effects of technological innovation on society. These approaches remind us that innovation is expressed in different spheres. These include both relational and social components (Von Hippel 1988, 2005; Chesbrough 2006; Lester and Piore 2004). And they incorporate different factors that take on leading roles such as: social capital (Westlund 2006, especially chapter 7), networks, interaction, and diffusion.[1]

Along these lines, numerous sociocultural factors in specific geographical spaces function as sources of and contributors to innovation and even to socioeconomic development.[2] Among these, cities and urban regions—thanks to their density and concentration of people, actors, and resources—host the majority of the interactive learning spaces that nurture innovation.[3] At the same time, several studies of innovation regarding socioeconomic development in developing countries have highlighted the unregulated, bottom-up, and noninstitutional character of some social innovations that are oriented toward improving the quality of life in small communities with insufficient social services.[4]

Also worth highlighting are studies that describe who the innovators are, where they are located, and what their basic characteristics are.[5] Finally, works that analyze the processes of change and reconfiguration across time emphasize human networks and reject perspectives based on exceptionality in explaining change and dynamics of innovation, whether in the technological sense or in the social, cultural, political, and economic

---

1. The classic work by Rogers (1995) proposes that innovation follows a fluctuating path that takes the form of an inverted letter "S" due fundamentally to the drift accumulated in the process of diffusion.

2. See the work of the Centre de Recherche sur les innovations sociales (CRISES), especially Klein and Harrison (2006). On regional innovation systems and the accumulation of resources in global city-regions, see Braczyk, Cooke, and Heidenreich (2003); Lundvall (1992); Edquist (1997); on regional development, see Benko and Lipietz (1992); Amin and Thrift (1995); Veltz (1996); Storper (1997); Scott (1998); Cooke and Morgan (1999); and Beccatini (2004); and on regional and national competitive advantages, see Porter (1990). Himanen (2001) and Saxenian (2007) argue that expanding the culture of innovation is one of the main explanations for why some areas have advanced farther in the direction of a knowledge economy than others.

3. See Soja (2000); Sassen (1991); Drewe, Klein, and Hulsbergen (2008); Moulaert and Scott (1997); Castells (1991); Florida (2005); Scott (2001); Esteban et al. (2008); and Cox (1997) on the idea that due to their density and ability to concentrate resources, urban regions and cities are the places that host most of the dynamics of innovation oriented toward developing a knowledge society.

4. Rodríguez Herrera and Alvarado Ugarte (2008) compile experiences with social innovation in developing geographical areas.

5. Saxenian (2007) describes the trajectory of individuals who immigrated to the United States in order to continue their higher education and who, having acquired valuable academic and work experience, returned to their countries of origin in order to create new companies, while maintaining ties and building collaborative relationships with the influential professional communities in Silicon Valley. Florida (2002) describes the characteristics, behavior, and preferences of what he calls "the creative class."

spheres, where chance and unforeseen events turn out to be even more decisive than rational calculation.[6]

Nevertheless, there continue to be few studies prepared to analyze in depth the relationship between social-structural contexts and social innovation, as well as the difficulties and paradoxes encountered by innovation as it takes its course in specific times and places. In other words, there has been a neglect of the conditions imposed by social structure on the nature and extent of innovative practice. The most common image of innovation is associated with values such as creativity, the ability to learn, flexibility, respect, sustainability, and trust at the same time that it is directly related to factors such as knowledge, the best practices, continuous learning, participation, adaptation, transfer, assimilation, and handling of information.

Even so, there is still much we do not know about the way in which such values and factors are generated and extended among people, due above all to the scant attention paid to social-structural contexts. For this reason, I believe that we need a concept of innovation that relates it directly to social change, processes of structure-building, and the concrete activity of social groups, and in which there is also room for unexpected consequences, complexity, chance, and the unforeseen events that are generated in every human process.

In this regard, I argue in this chapter that innovation neither arises nor develops in a vacuum, but rather in social-structural contexts specific to each geographical space. Along these lines, my objective is to examine the socio-structural characteristics of the Comunidad Autónoma del País Vasco/Euskal Autonomia Erkidegoa (CAPV/EAE, Autonomous Community of the Basque Country) in its particular process of transition to a knowledge society for the purpose of describing the fundamental aspects that currently shape the dynamics of innovation there. This will permit us to determine the decisive elements conditioning the dynamics of innovation and the implications of the interaction between social structure and processes of innovation for the construction of a knowledge society. However, we must understand the relationship between structural change and social innovation.

---

6. Edgerton (2006) and McNeill and McNeill (2003) present the historical view of innovation.

Structural Change and Innovation in the Transition to a Knowledge Society

In an increasingly interconnected world, knowledge, innovation, and the processing of information have become priorities for societies. The areas that currently achieve higher rates of productivity are those dedicated to applied research, development of new technologies, creative industries, and design. High value-added economic activity and wealth generation are currently concentrated in industries that are capable of adapting to the times and that make intensive use of new technologies in the creative industries and in the high-level service sector. These are economic activities that are substantially reliant on highly qualified human capital expected to put its knowledge to practical use, potentially promoting innovation, continuous adaptation, and increasing competitiveness. The socioeconomic structures that these innovative regions have gradually built have caused them to be characterized as knowledge societies.[7] A knowledge society cannot be understood as a fully attained stage of development, but rather as a set of characteristics that some regions are beginning to acquire, although still in partial and relative form.

At a time when the reconfiguration of industrial society appears unavoidable, both public institutions and private businesses, as well as diverse social actors, are turning their attention to what a knowledge society can offer, trying to make its construction, little by little, a reality. For this reason, I believe that the knowledge society is the image that unites the pillars of a new model of development (Galarraga 2007). In this image we find a description of our societies' points of reference with regard both to modes of organization and to issues and methods for action.

It is in the confluence of and dialectic among different factors that different socioeconomic actors are shaped and the emergence of innovative responses to structural change encouraged: an economic structure in which high value-added activities have great weight; the concrete policies implemented by different administrative levels in support of knowledge, innovation, and creativity; the functioning of the infrastructures and institutions that have arisen to stimulate research, knowledge transfer, and innovation in both the technological and the social spheres, thanks to the concentration of human capital; and the culture of innovation.

---

7. The clearest definitions of a knowledge society as used here are those of Stehr (1994), Lamo de Espinosa (1996), Mansell and Wehn (1998), Mansell and Steinmueller (2000), and UNESCO (2005).

Nevertheless, innovation itself is also conditioned by the socio-structural context of which it is a part, with regard both to the possibilities for the emergence of dynamics of innovation and to the context that limits their emergence. In this regard, how do processes of innovation come into being? Where (or in what contexts) does innovation arise? What are the forms that innovation adopts? What are the limits, risks, and paradoxes that it contains?

Ander Gurrutxaga (2010) contributes notably to understanding both the possibilities that the social structure generates and to the limits it imposes on dynamics of innovation. He highlights the fact that social innovation is associated with the expansion of a society's capacity for solving the problems it faces and establishing approaches with which to confront the present and the future. Consequently, it is based on acquired and socialized knowledge, resulting in a social intelligence that shapes itself to fit its specific contexts and circumstances.

In this way, networks, collaborations, knowledge transfers, and interactions that take place among these spheres produce what Gurrutxaga defines as "interactive spaces of learning." In these spaces, social strategies are adopted that mark out the approaches taken by different regions in resolving the dilemmas and situations they face. In this regard, because of their density and concentration of people, actors, and resources, most of these interactive spaces of learning are found in cities and urban regions.[8]

On the other hand, focusing on socio-structural contexts demonstrates that innovation, if it is to find the necessary conditions for its stimulation and development, needs the contribution of a variety of unequally distributed factors—such as knowledge, the ability to learn, skill, experience, creativity, research, and information—but also the transfer, diffusion, transmission, and implementation of all of these across individuals, societies, and generations. As Gurrutxaga writes,

> The social structure of an innovation society . . . aims at a process of diversification, a process in which lifestyle debates and cultural conflicts occupy a central place. The materialization of new social divisions does not draw from the cultural codes that define class, but rather from dif-

8. A recent report by the Young Foundation (2008, 28–29) summarizes some of the most significant sociocultural challenges of the present global historical era, which are present in the majority of European and Western cities and regions, although with differences in their specific manifestations. See also MacCallum, Moulaert, and Hillier (2009).

ferent lifestyles, associated with specific jobs held and the panorama of
expectations, possibilities, and real opportunities, in such a way that
while expectations are democratized, transcending borders and social
divisions, opportunities are subject to and limited by the kind and nature
of work performed. . . . One of the consequences is that an innovation
society facilitates the realization of the dreams of some but denies access
to many others. (2010, 166)

Gurrutxaga notes that the capacity for and the nature of innovation
are directly conditioned by the opportunities offered by the knowledge
society at its present level of development. For this reason, when the vir-
tues of innovation are being praised and proposals are being put forward
to extend the practice of innovation among a society's different actors,
the first thing we must ask ourselves is whether our societies are in a position to be innovative in the direction required in order to transition to a
knowledge society that is sustainable and humane.

Possibilities and Limitations of Social Innovation in the CAPV/ EAE

The deep industrial crisis that began in the early 1980s and lasted until
the mid-1990s was the spearhead of a wide-ranging process of structural
change that has practically completely remodeled Basque society. From
this time forward, the CAPV/EAE has been gradually distancing itself
from those characteristics that defined it as an industrial society in order
to begin a process of intensive socioeconomic reconfiguration.

Following an intensive period of socioeconomic restructuring and
the launch of a variety of strategies to overcome the industrial crisis, the
frame of reference that shapes both public and private sector activity has
shifted to the emerging knowledge societies. Nevertheless, the CAPV/
EAE's transition to a knowledge society has become a tortuous path, in
which overcoming the industrial crisis has also meant modifying some
basic and long-standing social pillars in order to lay new foundations on
unstable and unfamiliar terrain.

In this way, the CAPV/EAE is in the midst of a process of transition to a knowledge society. And it is this very transitional dimension that
is now the CAPV/EAE's principal point of reference for socioeconomic
development, to the point of marking out the priorities as well as the fundamental strategies for confronting the challenges and possibilities of the
new century. At the same time, however, it also means that the CAPV/

EAE still has some way to go in this direction in order to attain the economic, political, and social bases that define knowledge societies. On this transitional path, I am especially interested in the forces and dynamics of innovation that play a part in the CAPV/EAE's process of socioeconomic reconfiguration.

In the first place, we should take into account the CAPV/EAE's (quantitative and qualitative) *relative size* in an increasingly interconnected world. This shows its position in relation to other societies and, above all, provides a significant indirect indicator of its capacity to confront the transition to a knowledge society. Another important aspect is *the regulatory and governance framework* within which the CAPV/EAE is attempting to carry out the institutional and social transition to a knowledge society, and the prominent role of innovation and knowledge generation therein. Finally, I would highlight the relationship between the *skills* of the CAPV/EAE's population and the *opportunities* potentially available to them in their concrete surroundings in order to confront the different stages of life. Here, I will focus on the relationship between citizens' educational level and their access to the labor market and to good jobs.

Although I start with these three basic contexts, these conditions are open to modification because of specific trends, events, and the social innovations themselves created by different actors. In this regard, I believe that the influence of wide-ranging social processes, such as the international financial crisis, climate change, migratory movements, and rampant individualism, deserves consideration.

The CAPV/EAE's Relative Size in the Global Context

The CAPV/EAE is a small (a little more than seven thousand square kilometers in area) although densely populated region, lacking in domestic energy resources and not especially blessed with raw materials, unlike the initial industrial era in Bizkaia. Likewise, the territory's three leading cities (Bilbao, Vitoria-Gasteiz, and Donostia-San Sebastián) are small in comparison to the major Spanish provincial capitals and the larger cities of Europe, with consequently diminished powers to accumulate resources for innovation. On the other hand, these cities are highly connected to neighboring urban areas, to the point of making the Bilbao, Vitoria-Gasteiz, Arrasate-Mondragón, and Donostia-San Sebastián axis an urban continuum that can be considered a single city-region or Euskal-Hiria (the Basque city).

According to data published by Eustat (the Basque Institute of Statistics), the estimated population at the end of 2007 was 2,147,754 people, of whom 15 percent resided in Araba, 53 percent in Bizkaia, and 32 percent in Gipuzkoa. The population structure differs significantly from that of other Spanish and European areas in that the CAPV/EAE has one of Europe's most elderly populations.[9] This is a serious problem on two counts. On the one hand, there is the basic issue of generational replacement.[10] On the other, those regions that have made the greatest progress in building a knowledge society demonstrate a high capacity to attract young people and students, as well as professionals of working age.[11]

However, territorial size and demographic potential do not entirely determine the possibilities of social innovation. They might even be advantages if strategic alliances are successfully forged with other regions and the right choices are made about which networks to join. All the same, the relative size of the critical population mass in the CAPV/EAE should lead it to think carefully about what it is truly capable of doing, renouncing any ambition, for example, to be an innovative leader in every possible field.

As regards the structure of production, even though the tertiary sector is beginning to expand in the CAPV/EAE following the crisis of industrial society, the Basque economy continues to show a markedly industrial character in which manufacturing is more important than in other European regions,[12] something that in principle is a sign of economic solidity.

Applying the Organisation for Economic Cooperation and Development (OECD) classification of economic activities according to technological content and knowledge intensiveness in order to determine the level of development of a high value-added economy in the CAPV/EAE, only 37 percent of jobs in industry as a whole involve high or medium-

---

9. According to Eustat, 18.6 percent of the CAPV/EAE's population was over sixty-five years old in 2008, a percentage exceeded by only Germany and Italy among the twenty-seven member states of the European Union.

10. The percentage of the CAPV/EAE's current population between zero and nineteen years old is low (about 16.5 percent in 2008), and birth and fertility rates are also among the lowest in Europe.

11. This is the case of regions such as Etelä-Suomi (Finland), Baden-Württemberg (Germany), London and Greater Manchester (the UK), Ile-de-France (France), and Noord-Nederland (the Netherlands).

12. According to Eustat, manufacturing-sector activities represented 26.23 percent of gross value added (GVA) in 2007, at current prices, while according to the Spanish National Institute of Statistics (Instituto Nacional de Estadística, INE), in Spain as a whole, manufacturing represented 15.19 percent of total GVA in the same year.

high technology levels, while most industrial jobs are at medium-low or low technology levels. Hence, Basque industry lags behind more technologically minded European regions. That said, high or medium-high technology industrial activities account for a significant share of overall employment. In the production structure of the CAPV/EAE, high and medium-high technology manufacturing maintains a central position in overall employment.[13] Yet at the same time it has plentiful employed and reserve human resources qualified for high-level tech activities.[14] Thus, industry as a whole has not made the leap to a context of high-level technology-intensive and knowledge-intensive activities.

Knowledge-intensive service activities represented 46 percent of total employment in the service sector in 2006, occupying an intermediate position with respect to other European regions with which it is possible to make a comparison. Hence, the bulk of widespread service activities in the CAPV/EAE does not constitute economic activity associated with a knowledge economy. In this context, the limited size of Basque firms[15] continues to be one of the CAPV/EAE's most significant structural traits both when attempting to consolidate the transition to a knowledge society and when trying to increase the dynamism of scientific and technological innovation. This is also one of the priority areas of the Basque government's industrial policy.

According to the Basque economy's international-trade statistics, both exports and imports have maintained a positive evolution since the mid-1990s, evidence of the economy's increasing degree of global interconnection, although with clear decelerations in 2003 and 2008 due to an unfavorable international situation. Nevertheless, it is significant that high tech exports form only a small part of the total exports of CAPV/EAE firms, medium-high tech exports predominant in 2006, for example.

---

13. According to the OECD, manufacturing at a high and medium-high technological level accounted for about 9.20 percent of total employment in the CAPV/EAE in 2006, a truly elevated rate when compared to other European regions.

14. According to the European Statistics Office (Eurostat), 54 percent of the active population was included in the CAPV/EAE's human resources in science and technology in 2008, comparable to that of the regions ranking highest on this indicator, such as the Prague metropolitan region in the Czech Republic (60 percent), the Oslo metropolitan region in Norway (58 percent), Hovedstaden in Denmark (57 percent), Stockholm in Sweden (57 percent), London (54 percent), and Etelä-Suomi (50 percent).

15. According to Eustat, 93 percent of firms in the CAPV/EAE have fewer than ten employees, and 55 percent of workers are employed in firms with fewer than fifty workers on their payrolls.

As regards assessing the CAPV/EAE's relative importance in scientific and technological innovation, we should take into account that it has traveled a long way from the scientific underdevelopment and deindustrialization of the 1980s and now occupies a favorable position in investment and capacity for innovation in the Spanish state as a whole. Here, it is surpassed only by Navarre and the Community of Madrid, the latter of which benefits from the capital-city effect. Thanks to a large increase in spending on and investment in R&D, the CAPV/EAE has come to resemble other European regions, all but reaching the mean level of spending on R&D as a percentage of GDP for the European Union (EU) in 2008 (1.9 percent among the twenty-seven EU member states compared to 1.85 percent in the CAPV/EAE), although still a long way from that of the regions that dedicate the most resources to R&D.[16]

In order to examine the CAPV/EAE's capacity for scientific and technological innovation in greater depth, Mikel Navarro et al. (2008) worked out a typology of the different patterns of innovation in the regions of the twenty-five-member EU on the basis of twenty-one indicators calculated for 2004. Grouping the different European regions into clusters makes it possible to observe each one's positioning and characteristics in terms of scientific and technological innovation. This cluster analysis makes it possible to classify the 188 regions of the twenty-five EU states into seven groups: (1) industrial regions undergoing restructuring with considerable weaknesses; (2) peripheral regions with weak economic and technological development; (3) central regions with an intermediate level of economic and technological development; (4) restructured industrial regions with economic and technological capacity; (5) service regions with a certain degree of economic and technological capacity; (6) technologically advanced industrial regions; and (7) capital regions and regions providing high-level services. The CAPV/EAE occupies a borderline position at the high end of the group 3 regions, but close to forming part of group 4. The CAPV/EAE is in group 3 due to positive economic performance (measured in terms of per capita GDP), but limited scientific and technological development.

This highlights the fact that in today's global networks, different "leagues" are forming according to the capacities that different regions have been able to build up over time. The problem is that there is never

---

16. In intensity of spending on R&D, the CAPV/EAE was placed 55 out of a total of 146 regions in the fifteen-member EU in 2006.

enough room for everyone at the top of the heap, and opportunities to move up in category are not within the reach of every city-region.

Along these lines, if there is a certain correlation between high levels of per capita GDP and the capacity for innovation demonstrated by a region, due to the possibilities for reinvestment and spending offered by the wealth generated, the intense and sustained economic growth displayed by the CAPV/EAE since 1995 and until 2007,[17] situating it among the most prosperous regions of Europe (in terms of per capita GDP), should have also placed it among the European regions with the greatest capacity for innovation. However, the modest efforts of the CAPV/EAE as regards innovation have led to what is known as a "competitive paradox."

According to the Instituto Vasco de Competitividad-Orkestra, after combining levels of per capita GDP (in PPP-€) and rankings on the European Innovation Index calculated by PRO INNO Europe for 2006,

> of the 202 regions considered, 29 surpass the Autonomous Community of the Basque Country in per capita GDP and 54 rank higher on the European Index of Regional Innovation. That is, although the CAPV/EAE practically succeeds in making it into the first quartile of regions, by level of per capita GDP or by regional innovation index, its relative position in terms of per capita GDP continues to be more favorable than in terms of innovation. By comparing the CAPV/EAE with a series of European and Spanish regions chosen for their industrial specialization and their good performance in per capita GDP as objects of comparison for the CAPV/EAE, we can also deduce that, although in general the CAPV/EAE falls in the middle of this reference group, it does somewhat better in per capita GDP than in innovation. (2009, 92)

These findings demonstrate two characteristic processes: that the wealth generated since 1995 has not been reinvested with sufficient solidity in areas that might boost the CAPV/EAE's capacity for scientific and technological innovation, and that the CAPV/EAE's innovation system continues to display some deficiencies and insufficiencies, both in its results and in its functioning. Such shortcomings include the dependence of the system as a whole on public financing; the low level (below that of the fif-

---

17. Per capita GDP has grown exponentially in the CAPV/EAE since 1995, breaking the $30,000 PPP barrier and displaying a growth rate higher than that of other regions with a similar level of wealth.

teen-member EU) of private investment; a lack of spending on university R&D; the low level of spending by public research bodies; the limited size of Basque firms and R&D teams; the shortage of interrelationships among the different actors; the scarcity of individuals with doctoral degrees working for private firms; the low number of patent applications; the lack of a culture of evaluation based on steps completed; and overlapping and direct competition among the variety of actors and agencies that form part of the system. Moreover, there is a lack of clarity on the role and relative importance of the different actors and infrastructures in the innovation system as a whole, especially in the case of the technology centers, cooperative research centers (Centros de Investigación Cooperativa, CICs), and the universities in their articulation with business and with civil society.

The Regulatory and Governance System

The CAPV/EAE's transition to a knowledge society is utterly mediated by the role acquired by public bodies, especially those at the autonomous level. Ever since the CAPV/EAE had to confront the industrial crisis of the 1980s at the same time as it was developing its own institutional structure, intensive public intervention encompassing the economic as well as the political, cultural, and social spheres has resulted in a transition to a knowledge society excessively administered "from above." The outcome has been the configuration in the CAPV/EAE of an over-institutionalized model in which the governing force seems to be the logic of a certain kind of economic, political, and social engineering that seeks to guide socioeconomic reconfiguration toward predetermined parameters.

An initial review of the CAPV/EAE's principal socioeconomic indicators reveals that amid a full-blown industrial crisis, and at a moment in which investment in new sectors and job niches, in education, and in public assistance was more necessary than ever, both Basque and Spanish public institutions took on a commitment to lead the way out of the crisis and tried to see to it that the effects of relative deindustrialization were neutralized to a certain extent. Gradually, beginning in the mid-1990s and continuing until the outbreak of the financial and real-estate crisis in which we are currently entangled, Basque society came to experience surprising economic growth, saw its unemployment rate drop drastically, reached levels of well-being and human development comparable to those of other European societies and regions, improved its citizens' general quality of life, revitalized its cities and towns, and remedied the functioning of public services.

The prevailing logic in the public sector (and one that continues to govern its forms of action) is that of a directive force leading the CAPV/ EAE toward development and well-being. Along this path, the next step imagined by the public sector and by some private actors in the CAPV/ EAE is that of a knowledge society, for which purpose there exists close collaboration—with the public sector in the lead—to take decisive action with regard to the structure of production, the innovation system, the communication and transportation infrastructure, urban renewal, and so on. In this context, the over-institutionalized model constructed in the CAPV/EAE has created its own characteristic vices, incoherencies, weaknesses, and unforeseen consequences that make a true transition to a knowledge society more difficult.[18]

Currently, economic growth and well-being are less dependent on traditional factors such as labor costs, geographical location, and public investment, which have declined in significance relative to quality, the ability to innovate and learn, insertion into global knowledge-transfer networks, the accumulation of human capital, and the incorporation of high value-added economic activities. Therefore, the institutional impetus has turned out to be insufficient as regards encouraging true structural change, because its initiatives must fit the needs and possibilities that exist in the territory, as well as in civil society. In recent years, the over-institutionalization of Basque society has been the most significant obstacle to the expansion of a culture of innovation and change capable of influencing different socioeconomic actors, because it has generated a structural system under the omnipresent direction of the public sector, from the perspective of which the priorities and rhythms of structural change have been marked out.

The process of autonomous institutionalization has been successful, in building stable and competent institutions and providing a framework for the enormous complexity of the CAPV/EAE's institutional system, characterized by its internal division into three historical territories and its emplacement within the overall administration of the Spanish government and within a context of the proliferation of European directives. At the same time, however, levels of institutional density have become extraordinarily high for a territory of the CAPV/EAE's geographical extension and demographic scale, with the existence of various superim-

---

18. For more on the CAPV/EAE's science and technology policy, see Olazaran Lavía, and Otero (2004), Gurrutxaga (2006), and Bilbao-Osorio (2009).

posed administrations such as the municipalities (city halls), the *diputaciones* (provincial governments), and the Basque government, along with a wide spectrum of public associations, foundations, and agencies dependent on these institutional levels, in addition to the powers of the Spanish state and EU interventions.

The system created to develop and manage public policy in the CAPV/EAE is based on relationships between public institutions and civil society founded on the search for political legitimacy and established on the principle of compensation. On the one hand, the administrative system has made good governance and public rhetoric its chief modes of action, constantly seeking its citizens' approval. On the other hand, its persistent presence in all events and initiatives carried out in the CAPV/EAE indicates a growing compensatory tendency, above all in times of socioeconomic crisis and faced with the presence of social problems that have appeared on the political agenda, as well as institutional strategies to promote socioeconomic reconfiguration and the transition to a knowledge society—as in the case of promoting the Basque innovation system, a cluster policy, aid for firms seeking to expand their operations internationally, the private education system, and so on.

With this has come an intense irruption of public institutions into economic and social life, establishing a public economic logic that tries to direct society as a whole along this path. The result is that all activity, even that originating in the private sphere, is subordinate to the approval of public institutions, and this hampers the capacity for innovation, while at the same time encouraging a culture of patronage and compensation.

Skills and Capabilities for Active Participation in the Transition to a Knowledge Society

The CAPV/EAE has one truly significant asset when it comes time to consolidating the construction of a knowledge society: the large number of individuals with secondary or higher education among its citizens. According to Eustat data, the CAPV/EAE ranks around the EU mean and at the level of the most advanced countries in the percentage of the population between twenty and twenty-four years old that has successfully completed at least a secondary education (78 percent in 2008), above the rates in Germany (74.1 percent), the Netherlands (76.2 percent), Spain (60 percent), and Denmark (71 percent), although surpassed by Austria (84.5 percent) and Belgium (82.2 percent). Likewise, the CAPV/EAE is among the EU's highest-scoring regions with regard to the percentage of the population between twenty-five and sixty-four years old that has completed tertiary studies, forming part of the select group of regions in which over 35 percent of the population in this age segment has completed higher education (Eurostat 2009, 119). In addition, it is worth noting that a large part of the population with tertiary education has earned degrees in subjects directly related to science and technology.

The figures demonstrate that from 1995 onward we have witnessed a substantial change in the distribution of the active population. Thus, in 1995, about 44.8 percent of the active population had at most a primary education (without vocational or mixed secondary education), compared to only about 33.6 percent with education leading to a degree or qualification, and the remaining 21.6 percent corresponding to individuals with vocational or nonvocational secondary education. In 2007, the largest group was that of individuals with education leading to a degree or qualification (about 49 percent), while the group with no more than a primary education fell to 29.9 percent, and the intermediate group with vocational or nonvocational secondary education maintained its relative position (21.1 percent).

Taking into consideration a greater disaggregation of the data presented in the 2007 Qualifications Survey of the Active Population (Departamento de Justicia y Seguridad Social del Gobierno Vasco 2009a), economically active individuals with tertiary education, both undergraduate (11 percent) and graduate (18.1 percent), make up a total of 29.1 percent of the active population. This is the only group in which women are a majority. This relative importance is associated above all with undergraduate education, where about 59.2 percent are women, with a notable balancing of the figures in the case of individuals with graduate degrees (50.6 percent women). However, women take the lead once again in the case of those younger than thirty-five, where they constitute 25 percent of this group as a whole.

Nevertheless, among young people there is a worrisome tendency toward a possible dichotomization between the active population with a degree or qualification (postsecondary vocational education and tertiary education) and the active population with no more than primary education. The data reveal that since 2003, the percentage of young people under thirty-five with a degree or qualification has remained stable, while the percentage of young people who have completed only primary education has increased. These figures show that in recent years, and despite educational reforms, many young people have not managed to get beyond primary education or have decided to interrupt their education at this point in order to try their luck in the labor market. Moreover, prior to the international financial crisis, the exit of unskilled individuals into the labor market was a constant in sectors such as construction, the hotel trade (including bars, cafes, and restaurants), and low value-added services. For this reason, the concurrence of an economic crisis and the partial development of a knowledge economy that demands highly skilled workers leads to many people being left on the periphery of the opportunities offered by the socio-structural conditions at this moment.

In general, there continues to be a clear and strong correlation between higher levels of education and lower unemployment rates. At a time of nearly full employment, like 2007, this association is nonetheless nuanced by the improved situation of those groups without any education or with only a primary education. This process is particularly striking among men. At the same time, the differential impact of education turns out to be much greater, in second place, among women. Women's access to higher levels of education constitutes their only guarantee of enjoying lower unemployment, although this is only really effective in the case of women with tertiary education. Indeed, these were the only women with an unemployment rate below 10 percent for all age groups in 2007, taking into account the totality of the potentially active population.

The situation of the population with university degrees turns out nonetheless to be very different. Particularly noteworthy is the still-elevated rate of unemployment among those with graduate education. Although the unemployment rate among this group of economically active individuals improved substantially over the period (from 15.5 percent in 1999 and 11.1 percent in 2003), it was still much higher at 8 percent than the CAPV/EAE mean in 2007. By contrast, the unemployment rate for those with an undergraduate education turned out to be much lower, only about 2 percent. There was a substantial improvement in the situation of this group of university graduates, with a fall in the unemployment rate from 7.3 percent in 2003 and 11.6 percent in 1999. This shows that despite their high-level qualifications, a significant group of the population with graduate education has not entered the labor market on favorable terms, and its education level has not guaranteed finding a job. At the same time, one can also speculate that the skills needed by a sizeable group of Basque firms are to be found at the level of vocational education.[19]

On the one hand, the CAPV/EAE labor market has shown, since 1995, a tendency toward deregulation, flexibility, contractual heterogeneity, and temporary and unstable employment; and on the other, a more limited number of individuals have had access to better, more stable, and more skilled jobs with better working conditions. The data show that economically active men older than thirty-five continue to be those who have the greatest level of access to a stable job (89.6 percent of those older than forty-five and 79.1 percent of those between thirty-five and forty-four years old). Although in somewhat reduced proportions, most women older than thirty-five are in the same situation (82.3 percent of those older than forty-five and 70.3 percent of those between thirty-five and forty-four years old). Meanwhile, less than half of those younger than thirty-five are employed in a stable job (47.4 percent for men and 47.9 percent for women).

Nevertheless, access to stable and technologically modern jobs tends to be greater for members of the economically active population with tertiary education, although in recent years, the largest increase in technologically modern jobs has been among those with secondary education. Breaking down the data by sex and age, the highest rates of stable and technologically modern employment in 2007 were among people older than thirty-five with secondary or tertiary education. Here, most of the people in this age group enjoyed this employment situation, reaching a maximum of 82.7 percent among men older than forty-five with tertiary education. Nevertheless, the figures drop below 50 percent in the case of individuals between thirty-five and forty-four with secondary education (46.6 percent for women and 43.8 percent for men).

In sum, the CAPV/EAE labor market still offers very limited opportunities, above all with regard to stability[20] of employment, but also in the professional profiles in demand. Access to good jobs and jobs directly related to a knowledge-based economy continues to be very complicated for women and young people, who despite achieving high-level qualifi-

---

19. Recent research by Olazaran, Albizu, and Otero (2009) permits a glimpse of the close collaboration between SMEs in the CAPV/EAE's machine-tools sector and the vocational schools located in their areas in order to meet their human-capital needs.

20. Note that the CAPV/EAE is one of the regions with the highest rates of temporary employment in the EU as a whole.

cations, are not guaranteed fulfillment of the expectations generated by their level of education. At the same time, individuals with lower levels of educational qualifications, at the level of primary or nonvocational secondary education, suffer more severely from the limitations and barriers to obtaining a favorable position in the labor market and a good job.

If we add to these tendencies skyrocketing rates of unemployment in the CAPV/EAE since the outbreak of the international financial crisis, the social consequences and implications of transformations in the work world, and new facets of social exclusion, the transition to a knowledge society is advancing by generating new social consequences and, in some cases, doing so without resolving the persistent contradictions of capitalism. Opportunities for an improved quality of life, at least in terms of income, seem to be lacking for at least the 15 percent of the CAPV/EAE's inhabitants who found themselves at "risk of lacking well-being" in 2008, according to the data provided by the most recent Survey of Poverty and Social Inequalities (Departamento de Justicia y Seguridad Social del Gobierno Vasco 2009b). The inclusion of all social sectors is thus among the unfinished business of the transition in the CAPV/EAE.

Conclusion

The structural shift from an industrial society to a knowledge society in the CAPV/EAE has generated a spectacular increase in calls for innovation as a necessity in order to confront a situation of permanent crisis, whether in the economy, the welfare system, the educational system, the environment, the family, or governance. Nevertheless, we are rarely in the habit of considering social innovation as a practice intrinsic to social action and possibly included among the causes of the very same crises I have just mentioned. Innovation is a resource at the disposal of social actors and individuals for confronting the problems they encounter in their immediate environment.

Social innovation is an ambivalent process, plagued by complexity, unexpected consequences, and uncertainty. The innovations that make it possible to advance in the transition to a knowledge society are directly and practically inseparably related to factors such as knowledge, the ability to learn, skills, experience, creativity, research, and information, but also to the transfer, diffusion, transmission, and implementation of all of these among individuals, societies, and generations.

For this reason, in order for social innovations to emerge that can promote the transition to a knowledge society, it is necessary to engage in profound reflection about the conditions available to actors for participating in that process. In the CAPV/EAE specifically, this means the three-dimensional relationship among Basque society's relative size, both quantitative and qualitative, in the global context; the regulatory framework and the character of the system of governance; and the skills acquired and strategies implemented by individuals in order to obtain access to the framework of opportunities they encounter in their particular contexts.

At a time when the transition to a knowledge society entails the construction of a society based on values such as sustainability, human development, democracy, and social inclusion, in addition to the shift to a high value-added economy based on techno-scientific innovation and research, we must consider what factors enable and what factors limit the consolidation of these characteristics. For this reason, it is more important than ever to renounce rhetoric about the dawn of a new era brought forth by innovation in the CAPV/EAE, in order to stimulate profound and impartial analysis of the initial conditions we can draw on in order to consolidate dynamics of innovation that can enable us to advance in the transition to a knowledge society.

References

Amin, Ash and Nigel Thrift. 1995. *Globalization, Institutions and Regional Development in Europe.* Oxford: Oxford University Press.

Becattini, Giacomo. 2004. *Industrial Districts: A New Approach to Industrial Change.* Chentelham: Edward Elgar.

Benko, Georges and Alain Lipietz, eds. 1992. *Les Régions qui Gagnent.* Paris: PUF.

Bilbao-Osorio, Beñat. 2009. *The Basque Innovation System: A Policy Review.* Donostia-San Sebastián: Orkestra-Basque Institute of Competitiveness.

Braczyk, Hans-Joachim, Philip Cooke, and Martin Heidenreich, eds. 2003. *Regional Innovation Systems: The Role of Governance in a Globalized World.* London: University College London Press.

Castells, Manuel. 1991. *The Informational City: Information Technology, Economic Restructuring and the Urban-Regional Process.* Oxford: Blackwell.

Chesbrough, Henry W. 2006. *Open Innovation: New Imperative for Creating and Profiting from Technology.* Boston: Harvard Business School.

Cooke, Philip and Kevin Morgan. 1999. *The Associational Economy: Firms, Regions and Innovation.* Oxford: Oxford University Press.

Cox, Kevin R., ed. 1997. *Spaces of Globalization: Reasserting the Power of the Local.* New York: Guilford Press.

Departamento de Justicia y Seguridad Social, Gobierno Vasco. 2009. *Encuesta de Cualificación de la Población Activa 2007.* Vitoria-Gasteiz: Gobierno Vasco.

———. 2009. *Encuesta de Pobreza y Desigualdades Sociales 2008.* Vitoria-Gasteiz: Gobierno Vasco.

Drewe, Paul, Juan-Luis Klein, and Edward Hulsbergen. 2008. *The Challenge of Social Innovation in Urban Revitalization.* Amsterdam: Techne Press.

Edgerton, David. 2006. *The Shock of the Old: Technology and Global History Since 1900.* Oxford: Oxford University Press.

Edquist, Charles. 1997. *Systems of Innovation: Technologies, Institutions and Organizations.* London: Pinter.

Esteban, María Soledad, Igone Ugalde, Arantxa Rodríguez, and Amaia Altuzarra. 2008. *Territorios Inteligentes: Dimensiones y Experiencias Internacionales.* La Coruña: NetBiblo

Eurostat. 2009. *Eurostat Regional Yearbook 2009.* Luxembourg: Eurostat.

Florida, Richard L. 2005. *Cities and the Creative Class.* London: Routledge.

———. 2002. *The Rise of the Creative Class: And How It's Transforming Work, Leisure and Everyday Life.* New York: Basic Books.

Galarraga, Auxkin. 2007. "De la Sociedad Industrial a la Sociedad del Conocimiento." In *Retratos del Presente: La Sociedad del Siglo XXI,* edited by Ander Gurrutxaga. Bilbao: UPV.

Gurrutxaga, Ander. 2006. "¿Es Posible Innovar? Sociedad Vasca, Universidad e Innovación." In *Las Ciencias Sociales y las Humanidades en los Sistemas de Innovación,* edited by Andoni Ibarra, Javier Castro, and Liliana Rocca. Bilbao: UPV.

———. 2010. *Recorridos por el Cambio, la Innovación y la Incertidumbre.* Bilbao: UPV.

Himanen, Pekka. 2001. *The Hacker Ethic: A Radical Approach to the Philosophy of Business.* New York: Random House.

Instituto Vasco de Competitividad-Orkestra. 2009. *II Informe de Competitividad del País Vasco*. Donostia-San Sebastián: Orkestra-Instituto Vasco de Competitividad.

Klein, Juan-Luis and Denis Harrison, eds. 2006. *L´Innovation Sociale: Émergence et Effets sur la Transformation des Sociétés*. Québec: Presses de l'Université de Québec.

Lamo de Espinosa, Emilio. 1996. *Sociedades de Cultura, Sociedades de Ciencia: Ensayo Sobre la Condición Moderna*. Oviedo: Ediciones Nobel.

Lester, Richard K. and Michael J. Piore. 2004. *Innovation: The Missing Dimension*. Oxford: Oxford University Press.

Lundvall, Bengt-Åke, ed. 1992. *National Systems of Innovation: Toward a Theory of Innovation and Interactive Learning*. London: Pinter.

MacCallum, Diana, Frank Moulaert, and Jean Hillier. 2009. *Social Innovation and Territorial Development*. London: Ashgate.

Mansell, Robin and W. Edward Steinmueller. 2000. *Mobilizing the Information Society: Strategies for Growth and Opportunity*. Oxford: Oxford University Press.

Mansell, Robin and Uta Wehn. 1998. *Knowledge Societies: Information Technology for Sustainable Development*. Oxford: Oxford University Press.

McNeill, John Robert and William H. McNeill. 2003. *The Human Web: A Bird's-Eye View of World History*. New York: W.W. Norton & Company.

Moulaert, Frank and Allen J. Scott, eds. 1997. *Cities, Enterprises and Society on the Eve of the 21ˢᵗ Century*. London: Wellington House.

Navarro, Mikel, Juan José Gibaja, Ricardo Aguado, and Beñat Bilbao. 2008. "Patrones Regionales de Innovación en la UE-25: Tipología y Recomendaciones de Políticas." In *Orkestra Working Paper Series in Territorial Competitiveness*, no. 4.

Olazaran, Mikel, Cristina Lavía, and Beatriz Otero. 2004. "Hacia Una Segunda Transición en la Ciencia? Política Científica y Grupos de Investigación." *Revista Española de Sociología* 4: 143–72.

Olazaran, Mikel, Eneka Albizu, and Beatriz Otero. 2009. *Innovación en las Pequeñas y Medias Empresas Industriales Guipuzcoanas*. Bilbao: UPV

Porter, Michael E. 1990. *The Competitive Advantage of Nations*. London: MacMillan.

Rodríguez Herrera, Adolfo and Hernán Alvarado Ugarte. 2008. *Claves de la Innovación Social en América Latina y el Caribe*. Santiago de Chile: CEPAL.

Rogers, Everett M. 1995. *Diffusion of Innovations*. New York: Free Press.

Sassen, Saskia. 1991. *The Global City: New York, London, Tokyo*. Princeton, NJ: Princeton University Press.

Saxenian, AnnaLee. 2007. *The New Argonauts: Regional Advantage in a Global Economy*. Cambridge, MA: Harvard University Press.

Scott, Allen J., ed. 2001. *Global City-Regions: Trends, Theory, Policy*. Oxford. Oxford University Press.

———. 1998. *Regions and the World Economy: The Coming Shape of Global Production, Competition and Political Order*. Oxford: Oxford University Press.

Soja, Edward W. 2000. *Postmetropolis: Critical Studies of Cities and Regions*. Oxford: Blackwell.

Stehr, Nico. 1994. *Knowledge Societies: The Transformation of Labour, Property and Knowledge in Contemporary Society*. London: Sage.

Storper, Michael. 1997. *The Regional World: Territorial Development in a Global Economy*. New York: Guilford Press.

UNESCO. 2005. *Towards Knowledge Societies*. Paris: United Nations Educational, Scientific and Cultural Organization.

Veltz, Pierre. 1996. *Mondialisation, Villes et Territoires: L'Economie d'Archipel*. Paris: Presses Universitaires de France.

Von Hippel, Eric. 2005. *Democratizing Innovation*. Cambridge, MA: MIT Press.

———. 1988. *The Sources of Innovation*. New York: Oxford University Press.

Westlund, Hans. 2006. *Social Capital in the Knowledge Economy: Theory and Empirics*. Berlin: Springer.

Young Foundation. 2009. *Breakthrough Cities: How Cities Can Mobilise Creativity and Knowledge to Tackle Compelling Social Challenges*. London: British Council.

———. 2007. *Social Innovation: What Is It, Why It Matters, How It Can Be Accelerated*. London: Basingstoke Press.

YProductions. 2008. *Innovación en Cultura*. Madrid: Traficantes de Sueños.

5

Material and Institutional Resources for Innovation in the Basque Economy: An Evaluation of the Basque Innovation System

JAVIER BILBAO-UBILLOS AND VICENTE CAMINO-BELDARRAIN

Translated by Robert Forstag

There is unanimity in the economic literature when it comes to defending the concept of the *innovation system* as the most efficient methodological approach for studying the innovation capacity of any territory. This position has its basis in the characteristics of the phenomenon of innovation, which is inherently both a *systemic process* (since the results of innovation are the product of the collaborative work of multiple institutions that have distinct objectives) as well as a *nonlinear process*, since we cannot identify a sequence of tasks that offers a general and compelling explanation of the introduction of new ideas and processes.

The first of these characteristics forces us to take into consideration not only the behavior of each of the institutions that work within the field of innovation, but also the kind of the relations established among those institutions. The second characteristic (nonlinearity) forces us to both pay close attention to the multiple sources of enriching knowledge that has the potential to constitute the basis of a nation's technical progress, and to take into account the existence of multiple possibilities of inter-institutional interaction regarding technological matters.

This systemic framework involves unclear boundaries when it comes to the practical identification of an innovation system, given the need to include all of those institutions that are capable of playing a role in innovative processes. As a result of the emphasis that various authors have placed upon the leading role of particular institutions, we are faced with "narrower" and "broader" visions when it comes to determining a definition of an innovation system. In the more restrictive proposals, the primary focus of analysis is the institutions and organizations that directly participate in research and exploratory processes (Nelson 1993; Edquist 2005; Lundvall 2007). The broader visions, on the other hand, stress the importance of other elements, such as education, training activities, and even the labor market and financial system, in explaining innovation processes (Cooke, Heidenreich, and Braczyk 2004).

The lack of unanimity in the economic literature when it comes to identifying the key components of a regional innovation system, as well as the lack of precision regarding any causal relationship among those components (Uyarra and Flanagan 2009), introduce an element of ambiguity in the concept that forces us to specify the conceptualization that we are employing in our analysis. We have chosen to analyze the technological sources of the Basque economy on the basis of a restricted conceptualization of an innovation system (the preferred definition within the economic literature). We conceive such a system as the institutional framework that most directly supports the innovation process, and that involves those agents and institutions that carry out activities related to the creation, adaptation, and diffusion of technological information.

Having defined the limits of the scientific and technological system, we propose a sequential study within the Basque context, beginning with a general overview that focuses on a description of the efforts being undertaken and the results that have been attained. We will compare this description to the Spanish, European, and American, using them as reference points to help assess how effective these efforts are. On the basis of this comparison, we will embark upon a more detailed study of the institutional framework of the Basque innovation system with three distinct goals in view: first, to attain a better understanding of the characteristics of each of the institutions involved; second, to determine the degree of coherence of its collective activities; and third, to analyze the content and intensity of the relationships among the different institutions. Finally, we will offer a brief assessment of the scientific and technological policies that are being implemented.

A Comprehensive Description of the Basque Innovation System

The creation of technological capabilities in the Basque economy has until fairly recently run parallel to the same process within the Spanish economy. In both instances, such creation was marked, from the beginning of the twentieth century, by an inability to create technological resources and thus an economic development that was highly dependent on foreign trade. The situation grew considerably worse after the Spanish Civil War (1936–39) and the Franco regime that followed, with the dismantling of scientific institutions and the exile of professors and researchers.

Since the mid-1980s, and parallel to the development of Basque autonomy, technical progress has been accorded an increasingly important role in economic development. This change has been evident in the implementation of policies aimed at fostering the development of the technological potential of the Basque economy—policies that have resulted in a considerable regional improvement in this regard. Clearly, the strong industrial tradition of the Basque economy has made the weakness of its scientific and technological system especially costly in terms of its competitiveness, and has made addressing this weakness all the more urgent. During the 1970s, R&D costs constituted no more than 0.063 percent of the Basque gross domestic product (GDP), and by the end of the 1980s, it had reached 1 percent (resembling the Spanish average). Currently, the percentage stands at 1.85 percent, which is about the average for European countries.

An initial consideration of the characteristics of the Basque innovation system shows how the gap has been reduced between the Basque Country and the European average. One example of efforts to bridge this gap is that the volume of resources dedicated to R&D multiplied by a factor of 3.55 during the period 1996–2008. During these twelve years, the collective GDP of European Union (EU) rose from 1.75 percent to 1.90 percent, while the corresponding rise within the Basque Country was from 1.16 percent to 1.85 percent. Despite these data, Basque efforts to improve R&D activity have still been insufficient, and more work is needed to further reduce the gap between the Basque Country and more developed countries such as the United States (where 2.67 percent of GDP is invested), Germany (2.63 percent), and France (2.02 percent).

Basque businesses play a particularly important role in both financing and investing in R&D. Such leadership would appear to be indicative of the strong commitment on the part of businesses to the process of innovation. Yet the fact that such a commitment has been sustained is evidence of the fact that scientific and technological development within the Basque context has made the innovation efforts of businesses profitable.

Basque businesses finance 56 percent of R&D expenses, a higher level than in Spain or the EU. The strong business leadership as regards investment in R&D, which has reached a level of 81.1 percent of effective R&D, appears to demonstrate an excessive commitment to the distinctively practical R&D traditionally employed within the Basque system. This distinctively "applied" character reveals an interesting technological and business dynamic, but also implies a lack of basic research that constitutes an impediment to progress in the medium term.

In spite of this, since the turn of the millennium, there has been an important channeling of public resources toward basic research in both public centers and in universities for the purpose of supporting the kind of basic knowledge that is absolutely indispensable for participating in the dynamic technology involved in products that have a strong scientific basis. This policy has been limited until fairly recently as a result of a lack of a tradition of basic research. This is because the Basque public university is still very young, and there have been few public research centers financed by the Spanish government in the Basque Country. However, such deficiencies have been addressed, as we note below.

Regarding the results of research, although the data for the Basque economy are significantly better than those for the Spanish economy as a whole, they are still below the European average. The data regarding scientific publications (articles in internationally distributed journals) are somewhat below average within both a Spanish and European context, although the differences are not particularly marked and appear to be decreasing over time. These differences can be explained on the basis of the traditionally weak emphasis on university research, as well as on research regarding R&D activities within the Basque context carried out by public research centers. This situation also appears to be improving, as we will see below, as a result of the recent establishment of both basic and cooperative research centers (CICs, or Centros de Investigación Cooperativa).

In terms of the accomplishments of businesses, patent statistics once again reveal numbers inferior to those of other European countries, yet these numbers are offset somewhat if one takes into account the specific figures for high and medium-high technology products. One can therefore see that innovation within the Basque business sector has emphasized research that aims to foster greater efficiency in production processes, rather than more far-reaching or theoretical ideas that can be patented.

This phenomenon is consistent with an industrial structure that is highly concentrated in the automotive, machine tools, and metallurgical sectors—in which a significant proportion of R&D efforts have focused on the improvement of processes.

The figures for the Basque Country in this regard are significantly better than the Spanish average. European patent applications originating in the Basque Country during the period 2004–8 represent 12.9 percent of those applied for in all of Spain (a figure that would be doubled if the region's relative demographic and economic weight were taken into account). In addition, this trend has grown because patent applications in 2008 represented a 28 percent increase over those in 2004 (Oficina Española de patentes y marcas 2009, 29). When one examines the data for the foreign trade of high tech products—specifically the 2008 coverage rate of 77 percent—one sees that competitiveness in this area is below the European average. However, it is also important to add that if we take into account the trade of high and medium-high technology products, the coverage rate improves to 177 percent.

Finally, one should take account of the EU's European Innovation Index. This is an index created for each of the EU that collapses the measurements made for the twenty-nine most important dimensions of a country's innovation into a single figure (European Commission 2010). The resulting figure represents a highly reliable indication of the technological level of a country or region. This index shows that the economy of the United States has a level of technology that exceeds the average European level by 28 percent, and that the Basque economy has a level 3 percent higher than that of the European average and 33 percent greater than the average for the Spanish economy as a whole. According to the EU's 2009 *Regional Innovation Index*, which analyzes the technological level of the European regions, the Basque Country is classified as a region of medium-high technological development (European Commission 2009).

Within a more specialized context, one should note that the Basque Country was chosen as a branch of the European Spallation Source, the main office of which will be in Lund (Sweden). The home of the Basque branch will be the Scientific Park of the Universidad del País Vasco/Euskal Herriko Unibertsitatea (UPV/EHU, the University of the Basque Country) in Leioa, where the designated team members of the project will work on the construction of a new Linac 4 injector for the Large Hadron Collider in Geneva. Another indication of the Basque commitment to innovation is the 47 million euros secured by Basque universities, businesses, and technology centers in 2007 as a result of the competitive bidding process within the context of the EU's Seventh Framework Programme. This figure represents a 44 percent increase over that of the previous fiscal year (Dorronsoro 2008, 161).

The Basque Innovation System: An Institutional Description

We will now turn to an examination of the current state of technology in the Basque Country and the various institutions involved in its development. Our approach pays especially close attention to the knowledge profile of these institutions, and we will first examine those that work on the level of basic research and thus generate the scientific-supportive knowledge that is the basis of applied development. These university centers and public research centers together comprise the scientific context. We will then proceed to discuss those institutions (technology centers and parks) that collectively constitute the technological infrastructure and that conduct applied research projects, since they aim to provide practical solutions to businesses. Then we will address businesses in their roles as agents that effectuate the phenomenon of innovation and thus generate the kind of knowledge that can be commercially exploited through new products and processes. We will conclude our study by describing the characteristics of the scientific and technological policies that constitute a framework for designing and executing measures that comprise the regulatory conditions that both govern technological activities and that determine public financing levels of R&D activities.

The Scientific Context: Institutions Oriented toward Scientific Research

The scientific context is obviously important in examining those industries that have a strong scientific basis. Universities and public research centers carry out scientific research, and the basic nature of the research they conduct explains the fact that these institutions are primarily financed by the public sector.

An examination of the data reveals the limited role of scientific infrastructure within the Basque innovation system. Universities and the public administration are responsible for only 18.9 percent of R&D efforts, a figure that is significantly below the 35 percent of the EU, and the 24 percent of the United States. This is mainly due to the relative youth of our university system, along with the traditional absence of public research centers in the Comunidad Autónoma del País Vasco /Euskal Autonomia Erkidegoa (CAPV/EAE, Autonomous Community of the Basque Country).

The university is an institution that has a crucially important role to play in the Basque innovation system, given that it will be responsible for carrying out the basic research that will provide the knowledge basis for later applications and experimental development that stem from innovation activities within the economy. The scientific training of the human resources in the system will depend to a large extent on the quality and quantity of basic research. The leading role of universities in this regard will expand to the extent that the scientific content of products that are developed increases. Their participation will be crucial to identifying those areas of economic activity in which we will be able to participate, as well as the extent to which we will be able to do so.

There are four universities in the Basque Country: the UPV/EHU, the Universidad de Deusto, Mondragon Unibertsitatea, and the Universidad de Navarra (Tecnun). Our research shows that the research activities of this academic infrastructure are still somewhat limited in that it falls below the levels of other European countries. Moreover, the UPV/EHU clearly has a leading role with respect to higher education research activities, especially in the areas of experimental sciences and health. In these areas, the UPV/EHU has made a critical contribution to fundamental knowledge that has the potential for future technological applications. In the case of Tecnun, all of its research has focused on technical instruction. The Universidad de Deusto has focused its research on the social sciences, while Mondragon Unibertsitatea has prioritized research in applied technologies, which it has carried out in close cooperation with businesses that form part of the same cooperative structure it is a member of.

Table 5.1. Evolution of RDI spending at the UPV/EHU from 2002–2008

Research Area	2002	2004	2006	2008
Experimental sciences	14,367,603	18,655,092	19,174,523	23,288,301
Technical education	12,698,312	11,414,390	12,804,217	9,814,894
Social and legal sciences	3,758,666	2,903,553	6,290,040	9,050,252
Health sciences	3,618,985	4,056,031	4,413,473	3,706,658
Humanities	3,297,420	1,977,722	5,183,629	4,724,586
Other areas	0	0	941,650	4,195,191
TOTAL	37,740,987	39,006,788	48,807,533	54,779,880

Source: UPV/EHU (2009, 147).

The UPV/EHU will no doubt remain a key player in carrying out the kind of basic research that is so crucial to promoting innovation, as is shown in table 5.1. Even though it is still rather young, the support of the Basque government and a propitious internal dynamic resulted in a 62 percent increase in research in the experimental sciences during the period 2002–8. Within the area of the health sciences, a priority from the economic standpoint, limitations in the human resources available in the UPV/EHU have made it necessary to develop basic supportive efforts in this area through public research centers, which have a greater degree of administrative flexibility and a higher capacity to enlist the collaboration of high-level researchers from other countries.

Public research centers are sponsored by governmental entities and work on basic research in areas that are considered to be of strategic interest for the technological development of the Basque Country—areas that other entities, such as the university, do not sufficiently cover. The lack of a research tradition at the UPV/EHU has made the consolidation of research teams requiring long periods of activity somewhat difficult. New technological developments that have a strong scientific basis, and which underlie the development of new products in the high tech sectors, require a high degree of scientific support that serves as the foundation for the development of practical applications. This kind of basic research is urgently needed in areas such as biotechnology, biomedicine, and new materials. The Basque government has responded to this need since the turn of the millennium by developing a network of centers that will work (preferably at the level of basic research) on areas that are important to the technical and economic development of the Basque Country. These centers have been designed to operate in accordance with the highest standards and follow two different models: basic research centers and cooperative research centers (CICs).

Basic research centers consolidate the development of basic knowledge in areas of technological interest, while CICs work in both the same and other areas, but within an applied context, and try to directly involve other agents, technology centers, and businesses in projects focusing on concrete practical applications.

Basic research centers attempt to make use of the existence of scientific resources in particular areas in order to apply those resources to the development of a knowledge base that can be applied to technology and economy in the Basque Country. The purpose of all of these centers is to carry out intensive training activities, and they include on their respective staffs a fixed number of doctoral students on scholarship. The Basque government has sponsored the centers identified in table 5.2.

Table 5.2. Basic research centers in the CAPV/EAE

Center	Human resources	Research areas
Fundación Biofísica Bizkaia	26 scientists	Biological membranes and other applications
Donostia International Physics Center	57 researchers	Materials physics (condensed materials, polymers, etc.)
Materials Physics Center	34 researchers	Materials physics
Basque Centre for Climate Change	Staff of 20 persons	Climate change
Basque Centre for Applied Mathematics	21 researchers	Applied mathematics
Basque Centre on Cognition, Brain and Language	35 researchers	Neurosciences: cognition, the brain, and language

CICs represent a recent initiative on the part of the Basque government for the purpose of carrying out basic research in specific and highly scientific knowledge areas that are considered strategically important for the economic development of the CAPV/EAE. The seven CICs that have been launched thus far are centers that have an infrastructure that supports the development of research activities through both their own resources as well as resources provided by the various agents associated with the center for the purpose of carrying out their own projects (which are typically more applied in nature). The scientific infrastructure is highly useful in supporting research in those product areas in which technological development requires highly intensive scientific support.

Below is a list of centers that carry out cooperative research:

- *CIC biomaGUNE.* Center dedicated to biomaterials research. This center has a staff of sixty researchers.
- *CIC bioGUNE.* Center dedicated to biotechnology and biomedical research. This center employs 112 people working in various research teams.
- *CIC microGUNE.* Center dedicated to microtechnology and nanotechnology research with industrial applications. This center comprises a total of thirty-four researchers and technicians.

- *CIC nanoGUNE.* Center dedicated to providing leadership in Basque nanoscience research. This center has a staff of thirty-seven researchers working in five different teams.
- *CIC tourGUNE.* This center was conceived as a strategic tool for RDI (research, development, and innovation) within the tourism industry and has a staff of fourteen persons.
- *CIC marGUNE.* Center dedicated to research and development in the area of manufacturing processes. It has a scientific advisory committee of four experts.
- *CIC energiGUNE.* Recently created center dedicated to research to support the development of energy technologies.

These centers promote those lines of research that are considered to be priorities in terms of developing the Basque Country. In addition to carrying out work within their own internal infrastructure, these centers also seek to provide support for other agents within the Basque research network that are interested in the same lines of research. In this way, there is a synergy of resource utilization among workers in the various centers.

Technological Infrastructure

Technological infrastructure is composed of those institutions that work in the most applied areas of research and that directly support the innovation activities of businesses. The increasingly intense dynamics of technology requires an ever-changing knowledge base, and thus there is a growing need on the part of businesses to resort to external sources in order to obtain the particular knowledge required to carry out their projects. Technological infrastructure therefore constitutes those entities that are necessary to facilitate access to knowledge necessary for the purpose of making progress with respect to innovation. The technological infrastructure of the Basque Country is essentially composed of the network of technology centers.

It is never easy to specify in exhaustive detail the technological infrastructure of a country, given that there is always a heterogeneous constellation of institutions carrying out some kind of applied research. Here we want to single out those institutions that, in addition to having a certain quantitative relevance, also have a significant presence within the Basque innovation system in terms of the Basque entrepreneurial framework. It is in this context that we characterize the network of technology centers as constituting the fundamental technological infrastructure in the Basque Country.

Within the context of the technological infrastructure of the Basque Country, it is important to make mention of technology parks, which constitute an organizational framework that encompasses various institutions and agents carrying out technological work, and which play a critical role in our economy.

Technology centers carry out research activities that emphasize applications and that constitute a fundamentally important external reference point for the innovation activities of Basque businesses. They have the fundamental purpose of supporting and promoting technological activities in particular fields and, for this reason, each center specializes in specific areas of applied technology. The centers comprise an institutional framework that is particularly useful in the context of small- and medium-sized enterprises (which have particular relevance in the Basque economy). It is within such a context that technological needs are the most intense in terms of the requirement for new information, given the limited availability of human resources in such businesses. The availability of a network of technology centers is thus critically important to enabling businesses to adapt to the knowledge demands of an ever-changing technological scenario. These centers make available to businesses a series of knowledge resources that could not possibly be generated by the businesses on the basis of their own limited resources.

In the Basque Country, Decree 92/1982 created the institution of sponsored technology centers that governments would later utilize as a basic tool for articulating their technological policies. These centers, while privately owned and operated, receive significant public financing (with the Basque government financing about 50 percent of the operating budget of these centers through both direct financing and generic projects). This strategy makes sense when we consider that the entrepreneurial framework mainly consists of highly specialized small businesses with a scant research tradition that focus on a limited number of activities. Under such conditions, each center can be utilized by a large number of businesses.

The strategy of the Basque government has aimed at strengthening the resources of the centers in those areas most closely tied to the economic activities of businesses. At present, another step forward is currently being taken in the entire network of development centers by organizing them on the basis of two powerful organizational platforms for the purpose of reaching a size that will allow optimal resource utilization and more efficient specialization, avoid duplication of efforts and, through both increased size and accumulated experience, make it possible to not only participate, but to take a leading role in the most ambitious EU projects related to each of their areas of concentration. We will now consider these two large technology platforms.

The Tecnalia Foundation is the result of the merger of six different technology centers: CIDEMCO, ESI, Fatronik, Inasmet, Labein, and Robotiker. In 2008, it had a staff of 1,378 workers and earned revenues of 128.1 million euros. When the merger is finalized during the first quarter of 2011, it will constitute the largest private RDI center in Spain and southern Europe, and the fifth largest on the European continent.

Indicative of Tecnalia's capacities is the fact that it participates in seventy-eight of the projects financed by the EU's Seventh Framework Programme, and that it has a leading role in eleven of these projects, which have a combined dedicated budget of 25.7 million euros. It carries out its activities on the basis of twenty business units that cover every technologically important area in the Basque economy. The pooling of technological resources generated by the merger will facilitate the provision of faster and more efficient innovative responses, the taking on of larger projects that could not otherwise be considered, encourage collaboration on an international level, increase their influence vis-à-vis other institutions, and also help attract researchers from other countries.

The IK4 Alliance comprises seven technology centers: Ikerlan S. Coop, CEIT (the Center for Technical Studies and Research in Gipuzkoa), Tekniker, Gaiker, IDEKO S. Coop, CIDETEC, and Vicomtech. As a result of a Basque government initiative, these centers have begun to integrate their activities for the purpose of forming the second R&D conglomerate of the Basque Country. These centers have been collaborating with one another for some time in order to support the development of research projects that are in many cases interdisciplinary. They are now poised to take the next step—acting as a single integrated platform and thereby obtain all of the advantages that come from greater size (and that we have described above in reference to Tecnalia). Internally, each separate center will develop an area of specialization that will promote optimal performance and that will, above all, avoid duplication of efforts. The technological potential of the IK4 platform can be seen in the fact that it will have a staff of 1,250 people and that it will generate revenues of approximately 80 million euros.

In addition to these centers, there are other entities that are carrying out applied research but that we will not discuss here due to their limited size and technological importance. On the other hand, two larger centers of applied research do deserve special mention. This despite the fact that, because they function within the primary sector and because they are partially financed by Basque government funds, they do not belong among those centers that were previously mentioned. We are referring here to AZTI, which focuses on the fisheries sector and that has a staff of 200 professionals dedicated to marine and food research, and Neiker, which specializes in the agricultural sector and has a staff of 196 people dedicated to agricultural research.

Technology parks are organizational entities that attempt to promote technological development in product fields with a strong scientific base through the geographical conglomeration of different kinds of institutions (technology centers, research centers, universities, and businesses) for the purpose of optimizing interaction among them and thus encouraging the development of new products and processes. The concentration of different kinds of knowledge in one specific knowledge center should ideally work to facilitate the generation of new entrepreneurial projects and attract new businesses seeking to develop their own innovation activities by encouraging interaction. Both physical proximity and an appropriate institutional design may act as catalysts of such relationships, which would otherwise be unlikely to naturally develop.

The Basque Country was in this regard a pioneer within the Spanish context, with the 1985 creation of the Bizkaia Technology Park, designed to promote R&D activities. As a result of the success of this park, technology parks were created in Araba and Donostia-San Sebastián during the 1990s. In 2005, the Garaia Innovation Center was created (headed by the Mondragón Cooperative Corporation and with the support of Mondragon Unibertsitatea and the Ikerlan Technology Center). Together, these entities comprised the Basque Country's network of technology parks.

These organizational structures are very important for the technological activity of the region. R&D activities carried out by businesses, technology centers, and universities located within these parks constitute 30 percent of total R&D expenses of the CAPV/EAE and 50 percent of the R&D expenses of businesses. In the case of Araba, the technology park there accounts for 60 percent of all business R&D carried out within the province.

These parks have been growing steadily and have expansion plans that are currently being implemented: the Galarreta Plan involves an extension of the Donostia-San Sebastián Park to the neighboring territory of Hernani. The Bizkaia Park will be enlarged to include Zamudio and Derio in its original location to the east of Bilbao, and is also to include a westward expansion along the Left Bank of the Nervión River in Greater Bilbao (the Ezkerraldea or Left Bank Technology Park). Noteworthy in this regard is the UPV/EHU Scientific Park in Leioa, where the Spanish branch of the European Spallation Source will be located.

The success of the technology parks reveals the increasing importance of high tech businesses in our region, and also indicates the advantages offered by these organizational structures for business development in these kinds of sectors, in that the parks cluster a critical mass of R&D sources and create spaces that optimize the labor of agents who carry out innovation activities.

Business R&D represents the combined efforts of the entire system, since it involves implementing new solutions for products and processes that have been generated by the system. From a systems point of view, the existence of business R&D calls for both a commitment to innovation on the part of the company interested in innovation as well as a scientific and technological infrastructure that make it possible to carry out the activities that are a part of such a commitment.

Table 5.3. Indicators of business innovation, 2008.

Innovation efforts and results	Basque Country	EU-27	Spain
Business spending on R&D (% of GDP)	1.50	1.21	1.35
Spending on non-R&D innovation (% of business income)	0.187	1.03	0.49
SMEs with innovation (% SMEs)	27.4	30.0	24.6
SMEs with collaborative innovation (% SMEs)	8.22	9.50	5.00
SMEs that introduce product or process innovations (% SMEs)	31.5	33.7	29.5
Sales of new products on the market (% of business income)	9.70	8.60	7.37
Business application of ICTs			
Spending in ICTs (% of GDP)[1]	2.09	2.70	1.40
Businesses with broadband service (% of businesses)	97.2	77.0	92.0
Disposition of corporate websites	63.3	70.0	54.0

[1] Data for the Basque Country from 2006.

Source: European Commission (2009), INE, Eustat.

The data in table 5.3 identify the entrepreneurial framework in which innovation activity has significantly expanded, and which forms a part of business routines. All of the indicators that we group under the heading of "innovation efforts and results" point to the fact that Basque businesses generally lag behind their European counterparts. Nevertheless, Basque businesses are dedicating significant proportions of their budgets to R&D, something which indicates their commitment to engage with dynamic technological processes, as well as the increasing importance of sales generated by businesses offering new products. These data are consistent with the growth of a system that has been developing at a breakneck pace in recent years—a mere twenty years ago, the Basque Country was far behind other European countries—and also show, as one might expect, a heavy concentration of R&D in a limited number of businesses. However, the lack of a research tradition proves a more difficult hurdle when it comes to small businesses.

Of greater concern are the data regarding cooperation among businesses with respect to innovation activities. These data, despite the fact they show a growing trend over time, are still not adequate, and this is hardly consistent with the fact that innovation activities are increasingly multidisciplinary in nature. It is therefore important to remedy this deficiency.

The potential of information and communication technologies as a tool for exchanging information and increasing companies' productivity makes it necessary to discuss the capacity of Basque businesses in this regard. Basque businesses have continued to incorporate these technologies, although they still have a long way to go (especially as regards small businesses). While undeniably the general availability of broadband Internet access indicates a strong commitment to these technologies, those indicators that reference companies' specific behavior offer less grounds for optimism. Such tools as a company website (63 percent), extranet (9.2 percent), intranet (15.4 percent), and electronic data exchange (15.6 percent) are less commonly used than is the case in other European countries (Caja Laboral-Euskadiko Kutxa 2009, 79).

Technology policy has consistently been a strong priority of successive Basque governments, as indicated in the transformations recorded in the Basque system of innovation during the past twenty years. Table 5.4 offers a summary (striking for its high numbers) of the 2010 budget, totaling 221 million euros, which represents an increase of 8.08 percent over that of 2009.

Table 5.4. Principal scientific and technical research projects in the general budget of the CAPV-EAE, 2010 (in thousands of euros)

(Code) Program	Managing agency	Credit 2010	% Total
(5414) Innovation fund	Lehendakaritza-Presidencia	40,000	18.09
(5413) Technology	Departamento de Industria, Comercio y Turismo	119,606	54.10
(5412) Research	Departamento de Educación, Universidades e Investigación	39,770	17.99
(5411) Agricultural-Fishing R&D	Departamento de Agricultura, Pesca y Alimentación	21,702	9.82
TOTAL	General Administration	221,078	100

Source: Government of the CAPV/EAE (2010).

Basque technology policy has been designed in accordance with a systems conception of innovation. There are three features of this policy that should be noted because of both their originality and strategic value.

The policy includes activity aimed at sectoral diversification, and which aim to shift production activities to sectors of high added value that inevitably also have a strong scientific base. The application of life sciences, new materials, and new technological developments derived from nanotechnologies constitute the core of the new activities being promoted. Programs such as ETORTEK and ETORGAI, the promotion of CICs, the financing of basic research centers of excellence, programs oriented toward the launching of technology-based businesses, and programs geared toward incorporating high-quality international human resources have been designed to these ends. The systems perspective—employed in order to implement the various programs in a way that is consistent with the stated objectives—is evident in programs of both the public centers of excellence and the CICs. These programs are aimed at promoting supportive knowledge for new product fields through organizational structures that are specially designed to attract high-level human resources to their facilities; optimize their interactions with other components of the Basque innovation system (technology centers and businesses that work within these new product fields); and facilitate the launching of new technology-based businesses.

Basque technology policy also includes activity aimed at improving the efficiency of the system. In this regard, public sector technological resources (and especially the technology centers) have been reorganized via a policy of mergers that are aimed at attaining a size that allows optimizing use of resources, more efficient specialization, avoiding duplication of efforts, and participating in more ambitious projects. Also important in this context is that activity undertaken for the purpose of strengthening the degree of integration within the system by optimizing relationships—in terms of both quantity and intensity—among the components of the system. Programs aimed at maintenance activities include those of Innobasque (the Basque Innovation Agency) and the Ikerbasque (the Basque Foundation for Science), which both coordinate and promote consistency among the scientific and technological activities of the Basque system of innovation. In a more generic sense, this is an objective that is incorporated in all financing arrangements, although there are differences regarding the specific means for achieving it. Measures involving the consolidation of research groups or increasing the mobility of research staff also represent efforts to improve efficiency.

Finally, the policy includes activity aimed at internationalizing the Basque innovation system. Internationalization is necessary in order to participate in tasks involving technical creation in high tech sectors, and becomes even more urgent when we consider the size of the Basque economy. This internationalization strategy pervades each and every one of the programs: the financing of university research programs; the programs promoting research staff mobility; the merger of technology centers; the organizational structure proposed for the basic research centers; and the CICs. All of these contain elements that are specifically geared toward fostering involvement of the Basque system of innovation in the international system.

An Assessment of the Basque System of Innovation

The Basque system of innovation has expanded greatly since the 1990s, and this has allowed it to approach European standards. In 1970, the system was practically irrelevant (given that spending on R&D that year represented no more than 0.063 percent of GDP). Today, spending on R&D represents 1.85 percent of the GDP, boasts a rich institutional framework, and exhibits a high degree of cognitive consistency among its research activities. In this regard, the policies of the Basque government have been decisive. By way of conclusion, we can identify the main characteristics of the Basque innovation system by using the European system as a comparative frame of reference.

In general terms, the Basque system is still inadequate. The more advanced Europan economies have made more of an effort to promote innovation. It is therefore necessary to accelerate the trend of increasing resources dedicated to R&D if the Basque Country hopes to participate in production activities that are increasingly dependent on scientific knowledge for the development of products and processes.

The Basque innovation system is characterized by the important levels of business spending on R&D, with an important degree of innovation practices within the entrepreneurial framework, as shown by the number of companies that carry out innovation activities. In spite of an improvement in the results obtained, there is still a long way to go in terms of incorporating small businesses in the dynamic process of innovation.

The system suffers from relatively low levels of basic research activity, thereby limiting innovation. Still, it is important to recognize the important progress that has been made, as evident in the establishment of research centers for the purpose of conducting basic research in priority knowledge areas in terms of economic development, such as the life sciences, new materials, and nanotechnologies. However, it remains essential to take greater advantage of the capacities of the UPV/EHU, an institution that should be playing a crucial role in basic research within the Basque Country.

It has achieved disappointing results in terms of innovation. The lack of Basque scientific publications can be explained by the fact that its scientific system is still relatively new. In terms of limited business activities, this can be explained in terms of a technological dynamic that tends to focus on the improvement of processes that are unlikely to be patented.

It does not sufficiently or practically integrate institutions, as shown in limited (in both quantitative and qualitative terms) relationships among the different bodies involved in innovation processes, thereby limiting optimal use of the system's resources. It is therefore necessary to continue to work to integrate all of the system's components, a task that will involve increasing the efficiency of the system, and doing so in a way that enhances cognitive consistency among its activities and that multiplies the number of effective relationships within the system.

The system is the product of a technology policy that has been created on the basis of a systems perspective, and which prioritizes the following objectives: promoting sectoral diversification that focuses on the development of economic applications linked to the life sciences, new materials, and nanotechnology; maximizing efficiency achieved by the system and improving the organization of its components, guiding research activities, and improving relationships among its components; and internationalizing the system.

Resources dedicated to innovation activities should be increased in a way that guarantees the consistency and efficiency of the system, and the following activities should be prioritized: More should be made of the UPV/EHU resources, there should be more small business involvement in the innovation system, and there should be greater interaction among the different components of the system. Intensification of relations within the system should emphasize the participation of businesses (among which there is a great deal of disparity in this regard) as well as universities, which are traditionally self-sufficient, and which have a tendency to isolate themselves from the other institutional components of the system.

References

Caja Laboral-Euskadiko Kutxa. 2009. *Economía vasca: Informe 2008.* Mondragón: Caja Laboral-Euskadiko Kutxa

Cooke, Philip, Martin Heidenreich, and Hans-Joachim Braczyk. 2004. *Regional Innovation Systems.* London: Routledge.

Dorronsoro, Guillermo. 2008. "El sistema vasco de innovación ante los nuevos retos." *Revista Madrid + d.* Monografía 22: 159–66.

Edquist, Charles. 2005. "Systems of Innovation: Perspectives and Challenges." In *The Oxford Handbook of Innovation*, edited by Jan Fagerberg, David C. Mowery, and Richard R. Nelson. Oxford: Oxford University Press.

European Commission. 2010. *European Innovation Scoreboard (EIS) 2009.* Brussels: Pro Inno Europe. European Commission.

———. 2009. *Regional Innovation Scoreboard (RIS) 2009.* Brussels: Pro Inno Europe. European Commission.

Government of the CAPV-EAE. 2010. *Presupuestos Generales de la Comunidad Autónoma Vasca.* Vitoria-Gasteiz: Gobierno Vasco

Lundvall, Bengt-Åke. 2007. "National Innovation Systems-Analytical Concept and Development Tool." *Industry and Innovation* 14, no. 1: 95–119.

Nelson, Richard R., ed. 1993. *National Innovation Systems: A Comparative Analysis*. Oxford: Oxford University Press.

Oficina Española de patentes y marcas. 2009. *Avance de estadísticas de propiedad industrial, 2008*. Madrid: Ministerio de Industria, Turismo y Comercio.

Universidad del País Vasco/Euskal Herriko Unibertsitatea (UPV/EHU). 2009. *La Universidad en cifras 2008–2009*. Leioa: UPV/EHU.

Uyarra, Elvira and Kieran Flanagan. 2009. "La relevancia del concepto 'sistema regional de innovación' para la formulación de la política de innovación." *Ekonomiaz-Revista vasca de Economía* 70: 150–69.

6

Cooperation in Innovation: A Qualitative Study of Industrial SMEs

Eneka Albizu, Mikel Olazaran, and Beatriz Otero

In the context of economic globalization and the growth of competitive pressure on companies, concepts such as "research and development" (R&D), "innovation," and the "knowledge economy and society" have become icons for processes of change in the discourses of political, economic, and social agents. Innovation is also at the basis of the necessary responses to both the current economic crisis and the challenges of the sustainable development paradigm. At the Lisbon summit in 2000, the governments of the European Union (EU) launched the objective of creating "the most competitive and dynamic knowledge economy in the world" by 2010. One of the objectives of the Lisbon strategy was to increase R&D expenditure up to 3 percent of GNP, but, as time has shown, that goal was very unrealistic (in

* This work was carried out thanks to funding received from the Spanish Ministry of Science and Innovation, from the Department of Innovation and Knowledge Society of the Provincial Government of Gipuzkoa (Diputacion de Gipuzkoa/Gipuzkoako Foru Aldundia) and from the Fundación Emilio Soldevilla para la Investigación y el Desarrollo en Economía (FESIDE, the Emilio Soldevilla Foundation for the Development of Management and Business Economics). We wish to express our gratitude to all the companies that took part as informants in this research, and to the following organizations for their collaboration: the Teknika Innovation Center for Vocational Training and Permanent Learning, GBLHI Miguel Altuna IEFPS, GBLHI Bidasoa IEFPS, GBLHI Usurbil IEFPS, the Goierri Vocational Training School, and the IMH/MEI Machine Tool Institute.

fact, expenditure for the EU 27—or twenty-seven-member EU—remained at about the same level between 2000 and 2008 (see table 6.1). Nevertheless, some changes did take place: Both Spain and the Basque Country took some important steps toward increasing their R&D structure, and the latter almost reached European standards (see table 6.1).

Table 6.1. R&D expenditure as a percentage of GDP, 2000–2008

	2000	2001	2002	2003	2004	2005	2006	2007	2008
EU27	1.85	1.86	1.87	1.86	1.82	1.82	1.84	1.85	1.90
Spain	0.91	0.91	0.99	1.05	1.06	1.12	1.20	1.27	1.35
Basque Country	1.43	1.41	1.45	1.42	1.44	1.44	1.47	1.64	1.85

Source: Eustat, Basque Statistics Agency

Before we introduce the issues we explore in this chapter, we will characterize briefly the Basque R&D system. In 2008, the Basque Country spent 1.85 percent of its GNP on R&D, half a point above the Spanish average (1.35 percent). The Basque Country as compared to Spain as a whole has a bigger business R&D sector and smaller university and public sectors. In Spain, the public sector includes both the Consejo Superior de Investigaciones Científicas (CSIC, National Research Council) research council centers and other governmental R&D organizations. Over the years, Basque innovation policies have been aimed at the development of a regional R&D structure based on private (but publicly backed), nonprofit technology centers. As table 6.2 shows, technology centers execute 26 percent of total regional R&D (equivalent to 0.43 percent of GNP).

R&D indicators offer a broad map of the resources devoted to science, technology, and innovation within a territorial unit, but what lies behind the data? And in particular, how do small- and medium-sized enterprises (SMEs) innovate? SMEs are the backbone of the Spanish and European economies (in the Basque Country they amount to 73 percent of total employment), but we know little about the processes of creation and application of new knowledge in such organizations. The size of SMEs strongly limits their capacities for innovation, and therefore cooperation between firms (and between firms and R&D agents) becomes crucial. In this chapter we would like to answer a question that we believe has not been sufficiently addressed: What is the role of cooperation in SMEs' innovation processes?

Table 6.2. R&D expenditure by funding sources and execution sectors, 2007

	Basque Country	Spain	EU27
Gross domestic expenditure on R&D GERD (million PPS)	1,235.0	14,957.8	218,886.9
Percentage of GERD performed by the Higher Education Sector	15.2	26.7	21.8
Percentage of GERD performed by the Government Sector	3.5	18.2	13.2
Percentage of GERD performed by Technology Centers (Basque Country)	26.3		
Percentage of GERD performed by the Business Enterprise Sector (minus technology centers for the Basque Country)	55.0	55.1	65
Higher Education Expenditure on R&D (HERD) as a percentage of GDP	0.25	0.33	0.41
Government Intramural Expenditure on R&D (GOVERD) as a percentage of GDP	0.06	0.22	0.23
Technology Centers' Expenditure on R&D as a percentage of GDP (Basque Country)	0.43		
Business Enterprise Expenditure on R&D (BERD) as a percentage of GDP (minus technology centers for the Basque Country)	0.90	0.71	1.19
Percentage of GERD finance by government	37.6	45.6	33.5
Percentage of GERD finance by industry	58.9	45.0	54.4

PPS = Purchasing Power Standard

Sources: Eustat, INE, and Eurostat

This chapter contributes to the debate on innovation in SMEs that has been revived in recent years. In order to examine these research questions more closely, we take as our conceptual reference the framework of the national innovation system (NIS), which concentrates on the relationship between technical aspects and social aspects (cultural, institutional, and organizational) in processes for the creation and application of new knowledge. The empirical work employed to answer these questions is based on in-depth interviews conducted with forty-seven Basque industrial SMEs, and the opinions of those in charge of innovation in these firms enable us to draw our conclusions.

We will first set out the theoretical framework used for the research, developed from the perspective of innovation systems and, in particular, recent international studies on the influence of the regional environment and cooperation on SMEs' innovative activity. Then we will explain the approach used in our fieldwork and the results of the research. Finally, we will detail our conclusions, linking this up with the initial theoretical discussion.

Regions, Cooperation, and Innovation

The NIS arose in the 1980s via evolutionist and institutionalist economists such as Christopher Freeman, Richard Nelson, and Bengt-Åke Lundvall, who called into question orthodox postulates regarding the role of knowledge as generic, codifiable, costlessly accessible, and context independent (Freeman 1987; Dosi et al. 1988). The perspective went through a major transformation in the 1990s (Lundvall 1992a; Nelson 1993; Edquist 1997), until it acquired great influence, both in the academic and research areas, and in the political realm, within international bodies such as the Organisation for Economic Co-operation and Development (OECD), which is of great importance in scientific and technological policy (Sharif 2006).

The central postulate of the NIS perspective is that social institutions shape economic action in general and innovation processes in particular. Institutions are collections of habits, routines, rules, regulations, and laws that govern the relation between people and shape human interaction (Johnson 1992, 26). Institutions are the "prevailing ways of doing things," modes of coordination that multiply action with a view to obtaining a desired performance within contexts where the actions and interactions of different actors intervene (Nelson 2008, 2). Institutions reduce uncertainty and the search for information that is necessary for individual and collective action and are, therefore, fundamental components in any social system (Johnson 1992, 37). For the NIS perspective, social or socioeconomic change is explained, in the last analysis, by the relations between technology (or "physical technology") and social institutions (or "social technology") (Nelson 2002, 269).

Within the NIS approach, application at a regional level has won large acceptance over recent years (Braczyk, Cooke, and Heidenreich 1996; Cooke and Morgan 1998; Storper 1997; Maskell and Malmberg 1999; Cooke, Gómez, and Etxeberria 1997; Maskell 2001; OECD 2001).

The "regional innovation systems" (RIS) perspective ties in with a growing interest in the importance of the regional environment for innovation, especially with regard to SMEs, and with the growing importance of regional policies that encourage and promote innovation.

From the RIS perspective, innovation is conceived as an interactive learning process within the enterprise and between it and other organizations. In addition, it is a localized process, where specific contextual factors can promote processes of knowledge creation and application. It is believed that an agglomeration of companies represents a saving in transaction costs in relations between firms and favors interactions based on mutual trust and the exchange of noncodified knowledge. Trust, reciprocity, shared values, networks, and regulations accelerate the transfer of information and the development of new knowledge. "Market failures" for the exchange of knowledge between companies can be overcome if purely economic relations are replaced by reciprocal and stable exchange agreements based on trust. Intercompany collaboration networks are particularly important in the case of SMEs, which make up the greater part of the European entrepreneurial fabric.

Recently, different studies have been carried out from the innovation systems perspective, focusing on the influence of the regional environment on SMEs' innovative activity. These studies point out, first of all, that SMEs possess a limited resource base, which limits their possibilities of performing R&D activities and of establishing cooperative relations with other agents. Among the reasons for these limitations are the lack of financial and staff resources, lack of time, lack of technological know-how, and a lack of capacity for searching and selecting relevant information from the outside (Kaufmann and Tödtling 2002; Smallbone, North, and Vickers 2003). Some authors indicate that it is important for enterprises to develop internal competences in order to be able both to establish productive cooperative relations with outside agents and to make use of external information and integrate it with that emerging from within the company (Freel and Harrison 2006; Kauffman and Tödtling 2000; Koschatzky and Sternberg 2000).

Because they are less able to shape and influence the external environment, SMEs innovate reactively as a response to changing circumstances within the field, and not as part of a long-term proactive strategy (Freel 2000; Hassink 1997; Smallbone, North, and Vickers 2003). This reactive, short-term nature of innovation in SMEs hampers cooperation with regional R&D agents (universities and technological centers, for example), which shape their research agenda on a medium- and long-term basis (Hassink 1997). Meanwhile, SME innovation emphasizes a strong market pull (Grotz and Braun 1997; Doloreux 2003, Kaufmann and Tödtling 2002). Studies coincide in pointing to the customer demand pull in SME innovation processes and to the fact that they are often driven by their customers to introduce new technological developments (Hassink 1997; Kauffman and Tödtling 2002, 2003; Gebauer, Woon Nam, and Parsche 2005).

The RIS perspective lays stress on the systemic character of innovation processes. The starting premise is that formal and informal networks between agents (enterprises, government, R&D agents, other agents within the field), in a trust context, make it possible to minimize transaction costs, facilitating the exchange of tacit knowledge of an innovative nature (Cooke, Gómez, and Etxeberria 1997). Similarly, the institutional characteristics of a region and its knowledge infrastructures are believed to offer important basic conditions and may act as a stimulus for the promotion of innovative activities. In this way, the development of different local organizations in order to create "institutional thickness" is emphasized as a significant factor in stimulating cooperation, interactive learning, and innovative activity (Asheim and Isaksen 2003).

In consequence, studies carried out from the RIS angle pay special attention to the analysis of the cooperative relations established by SMEs in their innovation processes and to the geographical ambit within which they are confined. The fact that most of the innovations have a market pull means that for many SMEs cooperative networks are limited to relations with agents within the value chain, that is to say, customers and suppliers (Freel 2000, 2003; Doloreux 2003). As Alexander Kaufmann and Franz Tödtling (2002) point out, just a few lasting selective relations with these agents shape most SME innovation activities. This is particularly true for enterprises that introduce incremental innovations in mature sectors, but also for companies with developments based on scientific advances (Freel 2003; Hassink 1997). These relations are frequently of an informal kind (Fritsch 2001) and, within them, price is not the only determining factor in a commercial operation. The existence of shared values, common norms, and trust between the parties concerned is also of vital importance (Doloreux 2003, 2004; Asheim and Coenen 2005; Hassink 1997; Grotz and Braun 1997).

Significantly, outside these relations produced in the value chain, SMEs hardly have any links with competing enterprises and R&D agents

(Freel 2000; Kaufmann and Tödtling 2002; Gebauer, Woon Nam, and Parsche 2005; Doloreux 2003, 2004; Koschatzky and Sternberg 2000). Special attention has been paid in these studies to the relation with R&D agents, since, within the perspective of "technology supply policies" disseminated throughout Europe during the 1980s, a series of innovation support infrastructures for SMEs were created in different regions (the Basque Country is an important case in this respect). The studies coincide in confirming that R&D structures have a limited impact on SME innovation processes.

The study by Ian Vickers and David North (2000) regarding the role of twelve regional technology centers set up to encourage SME innovation in the United Kingdom highlights the lack of demand from enterprises for their services and the difficulties faced in the self-financing of these centers. Meanwhile, in their analysis of cooperative relations in SME innovation in three German regions, Reinhold Grotz and Boris Braun (1997) conclude that relations between mechanical engineering companies and technology transfer infrastructures are weak. Similarly, Kaufmann and Tödtling's (2002) study of the Upper Austria region shows that SMEs rarely interact with universities, research centers, or technology centers. Finally, Robert Hassink's (1997) comparative study of different technology transfer policy experiences in Europe, the United States, and Japan shows that, among sources of innovation for companies, universities and technology centers play a minor role.

Cooperation with these agents is confined to companies that are larger and/or have greater technological capacity (Koschatzky and Zenker 1999; Kaufmann and Tödtling 2002). Hassink (1997) emphasizes that enterprises that are weaker in terms of technology—the target group for these agents—tend to ignore these R&D infrastructures, while firms with greater capacity for R&D and innovation have recourse to these R&D infrastructures. Likewise, the reactive nature of innovations in SMEs hampers collaboration with R&D agents, whose research horizons function within a longer-term perspective.

The studies also highlight factors where technology supply is concerned that make these relations difficult. These agents do not appear to satisfy the demand from enterprises, and they make a scant contribution toward the resolution of specific company problems and apply new technologies in production processes and new products (Gebauer, Woon Nam, and Parsche 2005). The studies find that what enterprises seek from technology centers is basic technological information, telematic support, and low-value additional services, indicating the need for these infrastructures to be more aligned with these specific SME requirements (Asheim and Coenen 2005; Vickers and North 2000; Gebauer, Woon Nam, and Parsche 2005). Attention is also drawn to the need for R&D agents to have a more proactive strategy (Kaufman and Tödtling 2002; Gebauer, Woon Nam, and Parsche 2005; Vickers and North 2000) and for the technology transfer of these R&D infrastructures to relate to other company areas such as planning, marketing, finances, and human resources (Vickers and North 2000; Hassink 1997).

Despite the limitations of "supply policies" revealed by these studies, they do emphasize that the existence of a regional environment favorable to innovative activity is particularly important for SMEs, because they are more embedded in the regional setting than larger companies (Fritsch 2001; Koschatzky and Sternberg 2000; Koschatzky and Zenker 1999; Kauffmann and Tödtling 2002). In this sense, the conclusions of the study carried out by Andrew Copus, Dimitris Skuras, and Kyriaki Tsegenidi (2008) in twelve (central and peripheral) regions in six European countries are relevant as regards the importance of regional environment in the SMEs' innovative activities. They find that inter-regional differences in innovation rates are the consequence of regional heterogeneity and not of the characteristics of the enterprises themselves.

These studies point out that the region is especially important for tacit knowledge exchange and for the provision of skilled labor, both highly important mechanisms in the innovation processes of small enterprises (Asheim and Coenen 2005; Kauffmann and Tödtling 2003; Grotz and Braun 1997; Doloreux 2003; Gebauer et al. 2005). Nonetheless, not all RIS favor innovative activity in companies. Some drawbacks of RIS that may stand in the way of such activity are the lack of relevant regional actors ("organizational thinness"), fragmentation or lack of collaboration in innovation between agents in the region, and social and cultural "lock in" (Asheim and Isaksen 2003; Kaufmann and Wagner 2005; Tödtling and Trippl 2005; Iammarino 2005). These deficits are produced to a greater degree in peripheral regions, where traditional industrial sectors prevail.

In order to prevent "lock in," these studies highlight the importance of extra-regional links (Fritsch 2001; Koschatzky and Sternberg 2000; Kauffmann and Tödtling 2002, 2003; Arndt and Sternberg 2000; Oinas 2000). They demonstrate that proximity is more important for cooperation with R&D agents than for cooperation within the value chain, where relations with customers and international suppliers are of great relevance (Fritsch

2001; Doloreux 2003, 2004; Koschatzky and Zenker 1999; Gebauer, Woon Nam, and Parsche 2005). In this regard, James Simmie (2002) underscores the importance of combining links at an international level with customers, with local knowledge provided by suppliers, universities, and local transfer agents.

Innovation in Industrial SMEs

In order to analyze the processes of knowledge and innovation generation in enterprises, as well as the relations that exist between enterprises and agents that contribute to innovation, we used a qualitative information-gathering technique: the in-depth interview process. A basic advantage of in-depth interviews is their scope for capturing aspects that define a subject or question (Lee 1999). In this sense, as a qualitative technique, the interview assumes that the interviewees' perspectives will be useful, as well as being able to systemize and made explicit as a part of understanding a problem (Patton 1991).

The fieldwork for this research is based on forty-seven semi-structured interviews conducted with the same number of SMEs in the Basque Country. These interviews took place throughout the first half of 2007 and were held by research team members with technical office directors, R&D directors, and managing directors of these firms, lasting an average of seventy-five minutes.

The SMEs that comprise the sample are characterized by the fact that they belong to various industrial sectors, although those involved in the manufacture of machine-tools and the lifting machinery industry are prominent. In addition, there are a significant number of auxiliary enterprises (principally in the automotive, machine-tools, aerospace, electrical appliances, and lifting equipment sectors). Most of them have between fifty and two hundred employees, except in the auxiliary industry, where the size drops in some cases to as few as fifteen employees. Among the SMEs interviewed, there is large number of family enterprises that are characterized by a greater unwillingness to take risks and that are somewhat resistant to changes. There is also a significant group of companies that are integrated within entrepreneurial groups, thus making the generation of synergies possible, which also materialize within the field of innovation. Finally, this is a sample of companies that, except in the case of auxiliary industry, operate mainly in international markets and, in many cases, find themselves under great pressure from low-cost producers.

The innovation systems framework understands innovation as a complex process that involves cumulative interactive learning. Adopting an evolutionary perspective, most innovations are considered to have an incremental character. In other words, they are novel combinations of already existing knowledge.

This description of innovation is reflected in the interviews conducted. SMEs that manufacture a final product consider innovation as a task of capture, adaptation, development, and implementation in their processes and products of new technologies to be found in the market. But the innovations that are undertaken in auxiliary industry companies are associated, as a rule, with improvements in processes and/or an implantation of new machines that bring about a reduction in costs and obtain increases in productivity with a view to a profitable compliance with the stipulations suggested by their customers (generally, time terms, qualities, and prices). As such, internal activities involving formal R&D (or R&D in the strict sense of the term) have a residual role for most of the enterprises that make up the company sample analyzed.

The innovation systems perspective implies superseding the linear model that conceives of innovation as a sequential process that is initiated with the basic research stage and concludes with the introduction of innovations in the market. The companies with which the interviews took place stress the "market pull" of the innovations they introduce. The pull element in innovations is not the vocation to make technological advances per se, but a question of innovations responding closely to market demands and requirements. Consequently, what triggers the introduction of innovations are customer demands and the need to stay at the level marked out by competitors.

The customer plays a fundamental role in innovative company activity as a source of innovation. Interaction with the customer is also a vital aspect in some sectors, such as machine tooling or aeronautics. In these sectors, the enterprises' strategy involves the establishment of relations of trust and cooperation with customers that transcend the purchase, say, of a particular machine or the securing of a specific order. In these cases, the relation between customers and suppliers is produced within "organized markets" with just a few customers and suppliers (Lundvall 1992b). Among the most important components of organized markets are the exchange of qualitative information, cooperation, and mutual trust. These characteristic elements are liable to lead to lasting and selective relations.

Auxiliary enterprises in general, as well as some companies that have their own product (because of the nature of the sector in which they operate), cooperate far less with customers. In auxiliary industry, customers assert themselves, leaving the companies little room for maneuver, and cooperative and knowledge transfer relations are not empowered. In the remaining cases, the relation is merely commercial or the final customer is not dealt with directly, which means that cooperation with the customer is of little relevance.

The relation with suppliers is also a key element in the innovation processes of the SMEs interviewed. Suppliers provide information and knowledge about the latest technological developments and components available on the market and therefore act as an important "technological antenna" for SMEs. Trust, likewise, is an important component of these relations, since a transfer of company knowledge takes place within them. In this sense, enterprises in which suppliers play a key role in innovation processes underscore the importance of confidentiality on the part of their suppliers. In our study, we were able to verify that proximity is a crucial factor in supplier-customer relations. It is clear that auxiliary enterprises tend to be concentrated near their customers.

The main source of training for innovation flows from technological suppliers. The larger, technologically intense SMEs frequently negotiate with these training packages associated with the purchase of a particular technology. As a result, technology transfer agreements with leading worldwide technology companies were mentioned, where training stages on the supplier's premises were incorporated in which workers from different areas of the enterprise took part. Interviewees recognize that such dynamics have contributed to improving personnel skills in terms of handling technology, as well as favoring people's involvement in the firm.

Cooperation outside the value chain (customers and suppliers) is much less frequent. Specifically, there is no culture of cooperation when it comes to competing enterprises. It was the Basque autonomous government, to be precise, that launched the cluster policy in the 1990s in an attempt to articulate technological demand and to encourage cooperative relations between enterprises in the same sector. The interviews reveal that this has had limited results in stimulating cooperation between firms in the same sector.

The interviews show that there are few examples of inter-company cooperation, beyond the value chain. What is more, practically no innovation experiences are referred to. One exception is cooperation between enterprises within business groups. We can therefore infer that it is also necessary to advance in the area of cooperation and coordination between firms belonging to business groups.

The Basque autonomous government's R&D and innovation policies have essentially been supply policies aimed at the creation of an R&D infrastructure able to provide a service to SMEs within the regional environment (namely, via the technology centers). Along the same lines, programs have been implemented—backed by significant public financing—aimed at encouraging company cooperation with R&D agents.

In this study we analyzed some aspects of the relations between technology centers (the main product of the Basque autonomous government's R&D policies) and enterprises (the targets and beneficiaries of this structure). Cooperation between companies and technology centers—especially in fields where specialized sectorial centers exist—is frequent. The basis for this cooperation is usually the provision of services by centers in different areas (analysis of materials, carrying out of tests, calibration, prototyping, etc.) that fall within the framework of technological developments being carried out by the companies. When the latter consider that the innovation projects directly affect their core know-how, they try to prevent that knowledge from transcending beyond their bounds and tend to develop it with their own resources and capacities or, if they need help, turn to trustworthy customers and/or suppliers.

On other occasions, manufacturers use generic projects that they embark on with technology centers by way of a "technological antenna" in order to get to know the developments and technologies that can be utilized in their field in the near future. These projects frequently tend to arise at the prompting of technology centers.

However, the largest SMEs cooperate the most with technology centers, thereby emphasizing clear discrimination in terms of the size of enterprise. This confirms Arantza Zubiaurre's argument (2002) that medium and large enterprises with more powerful technological strategies have the most access to technology centers. Other factors that positively affect cooperation with technology centers include membership of a business group that can rely on a technological center for the companies in the group or membership of the board of a technology center.

Still, most enterprises, although aware that they are the subject of attention and indirect beneficiaries of regional government policies—in this case, of those directed toward the creation of technology centers for the transfer of knowledge to SMEs—are quite critical of the role of these centers. They point out that technology centers do not take into account their needs, and that the aims pursued by enterprises and centers are different and frequently contradictory. Other motives for complaint are the different work rhythms, price, and the overlap of the centers' areas of action. Then again, the reticence expressed by the enterprises regarding cooperation with competitors is once again expressed with regard to technology centers. There is mistrust about working with technology centers for fear that the latter will disclose knowledge accumulated in the enterprises and that it will reach their competitors. Finally, the enterprises reject outright the idea that it should be obligatory to contract the services of technology centers in order to be eligible for financing from the Basque autonomous government's main funding program for innovation.

Cooperation with the universities is more limited, which was to be expected given the existence of an important network of other R&D agents in the field (namely, the technology centers). Nevertheless, some of the SMEs in the survey use university groups for technological service provision. In addition, relations exist between the enterprises and the universities, through end-of-degree projects (some of these people then go on to join the company).

In the interviews, some cooperative projects with universities are mentioned, with uneven results. The main obstacles for establishing cooperative relations with universities are lack of information about the research being carried out by the university groups and the different rhythms of the projects developed by universities and enterprises. Universities conduct research within a medium- to long-term framework (with more uncertainty), while companies look for results that are applicable in the short term. This is also the case with the technology centers.

One of the discoveries made by this study is the role of vocational training (VT) centers in the SME innovation processes within their field. As noted, VT centers play an important part in the training of skilled human capital for companies, and SME innovation processes are grounded to a great degree in the skill level of their workers. Most of the enterprises therefore maintain a fluid relation with VT centers that send them students for in-house training, many of whom end up being taken on by the company. The VT centers also provide continuous training and demand-driven training for businesses, as well as offering advice and consultancy services to SMEs in the sector. This situation unquestionably contributes to fostering innovation in those enterprises that are equipped with fewer resources for such activity (small and very small firms). The potential role of these agents has not, to date, been sufficiently heeded in R&D policies.

Financial assistance from public programs generally favors companies of larger dimensions and/or greater capacities for innovation. As pointed out, the documentation demanded by these programs requires some degree of planning and formalization of the innovation activities. The scant degree of planning that exists in SMEs impacts negatively on access to public financing programs. As we were able to verify in our study, smaller enterprises with less scope for innovation find themselves left out of public assistance programs. This is frequently due to lack of information, but also because this assistance, given the formalization and documentation required, is better adapted to the bigger enterprises, which have to some degree structured their innovation activity.

Many of the firms that have experience with public financing programs can count on some support, either from within the business group they belong to or from a consultancy or external technology center. Among the reasons put forward by enterprises for not taking part in these kinds of reach-out strategies are: ignorance of the funding that exists, the associated bureaucratic procedures, the fact that the subsidy comes in the form of a loan, deferment of payment by the public administration, and reluctance to disclose information about the firm.

In general, companies view this public funding positively because it helps to overcome the risk and uncertainty associated with these projects. They also consider these programs necessary in order to develop competitive R&D and be able to pass on less cost in the products or services they develop for their customers. However, they do see aspects that could be improved on in the management of these programs, especially in terms of their bureaucracy and its accompanying procedures and the fact that they feel that discrimination is exercised against smaller as opposed to larger enterprises.

Conclusion

The results of this research suggest that industrial SMEs incorporate, develop, and/or adapt new technologies within each industrial field to their own products/solutions and processes. Here we are mainly referring to incremental innovations. The SMEs' innovation efforts therefore are based on creating combinations of already existing (and mainly tacit) knowledge and are, consequently, somewhat removed from formal R&D activities, which have less influence in the sample of companies analyzed.

The innovation systems approach emphasizes the importance of cooperation around R&D for small firms. With things as they are, the capacity of SMEs to engage in R&D and some of their innovative potential lie in their ability to collaborate (or "learn interactively," to use Lundvall's term) with agents in the immediate environment: customers, suppliers, and, to a lesser degree, technology centers, universities, and VT centers.

The relation between customers and suppliers comes to fruition in what Lundvall (1992b) calls "organized markets." Some of the key elements of organized markets are: the exchange of qualitative information, cooperation, and mutual trust. For these elements to appear, it is necessary for selective, stable, and lasting relations to be generated among the actors. Our investigation suggests that this is the main strategy used by industrial SMEs in order to access external technological knowledge. The interactive technological learning process therefore stems from a small set of relations that SMEs establish. Cooperation outside the value chain (for example, with competitors or other companies within the field) is, however, a highly infrequent practice.

In addition to the central role of customers and suppliers as facilitating agents so that a company can acquire knowledge, the role of technology centers is also crucial, especially with regard to the larger SMEs, business groups that have set up technology centers, and enterprises that are on the boards of technology centers. In sum, the research results suggest that the relation between SMEs and technology centers (the main tool in the Basque autonomous government's policies in the 1990s) could be substantially improved upon for SMEs to make effective use of the knowledge these centers possess.

Among the advantages SMEs obtain from cooperation for innovation, mention must also be made of the benefit of their interaction with VT centers. The latter make a significant contribution to human capital training, and one must not overlook the relevance of workers' skill levels in innovation processes. Most of the companies interviewed maintain close relations with VT centers in their district (where such bodies exist). However, regional public policies—that at the time of this writing have been of a disjointed nature between the Basque autonomous government's departments of Education and Industry—have not paid proper attention to this kind of relationship, and it is an area that calls for much improvement.

In general, companies view public funding for innovation programs positively insofar as they contribute to reducing innovation-associated risk and make it possible to cut down the impact that innovation has on product costs in terms of its effect on price. This funding, then, helps to improve business competitiveness, although it is more difficult for smaller enterprises to successfully negotiate the administrative and bureaucratic processes associated with the programs. In any event, given the competitive conditions that currently exist, industrial SMEs are well aware that even when there is no funding, they will have to invest in innovation.

Lastly, our findings generally confirmed those obtained in other studies that analyze the influence of the regional environment on SME innovation, following the RIS approach:

- Low degree of innovation formalization
- Abundance of tacit knowledge and importance of incremental innovations associated with production activities
- Great weight of internal innovation sources
- Importance of cooperation on innovation and R&D
- Few actors involved in the cooperation—especially customers and suppliers—and relations of trust between them ("interactive learning")
- Scant cooperation with other regional R&D agents
- Need for effective public policies but low level of effectiveness of these

It is worth highlighting, however, certain differences in the Basque case, such as the relative importance of external innovation sources in the case of Basque industry, together with the relatively greater importance of technology centers as an R&D agent.

With regard to the first of the questions mentioned, it could be argued that the high skill level of labor, the specialization in market niches, and the trust relationships that exist with customers and suppliers make possible a relatively high level of absorption of outside knowledge. The ability to absorb new knowledge depends on cognitive, cultural, and organizational proximity (Boschma 2004). A company's knowledge base needs to be sufficiently close to the new knowledge so that it can be efficiently communicated, processed, and integrated. The technological "trajectories" and powers of the enterprises interviewed have smoothed the path for them to be prepared for this.

Technology centers as innovation agents have constituted one of the pillars of the Basque department of industry's regional policy for many years—a policy that has been noted by Basque companies. Indeed, because of their number, areas of specialization (linked to some degree to the needs of certain representative sectors of industry), their size, and connections with enterprises via co-financing through public programs, their impact on Basque industrial SMEs is considerable.

In short, the theoretical framework of regional innovation systems (and in particular the concept of "interactive technological learning") is a useful tool for analyzing processes of technological knowledge creation and application in industrial SMEs. The study of the social dimensions of innovation or the social relations and institutions that impact on processes of knowledge creation must be taken into account to complete "supply" policies (or the creation of R&D infrastructures) with a more global vision of the phenomenon of innovation and of the relations between the agents involved.

References

Arndt, Olaf and Rolf Sternberg. 2000. "Do Manufacturing Firms Profit from Intraregional Innovation Linkages? An Empirical Based Answer." *European Planning Studies* 8, no. 4: 465–85.

Asheim, Bjørn T. and Lars Coenen. 2005. "Knowledge Bases and Regional Innovation Systems: Comparing Nordic Clusters." *Research policy* 34, no. 8: 1173–90.

Asheim, Bjørn T. and Arne Isaksen. 2003. "SMEs and the Regional Dimension of Innovation." In *Regional Innovation Policy for Small-Medium Enterprises*, edited by Bjørn T. Asheim, Arne Isaksen, Claire Nauwelaers, and Franz Tödtling. Cheltenham: Edward Elgar.

Boschma, Ron. 2004. "Does Geographical Proximity Favour Innovation?" Paper presented at the 4th Congress of Proximity Economics, June 17–18, Marseilles, France.

Braczyk, Hans-Joachim, Philip Cooke, and Martin Heidenreich, eds. 1996. *Regional Innovation Systems: The Role of Governances in a Globalized World*. London: University College Press.

Cooke, Philip, Mikel Gomez, and Goio Etxebarria. 1997. "Regional Innovation Systems: Institutional and Organizational Dimensions." *Research Policy* 26, nos. 4–5: 475–91.

Cooke, Philip and Kevin Morgan. 1998. *The Associational Economy: Firms, Regions and Innovation*. Oxford: Oxford University Press.

Copus, Andrew, Dimitris Skuras, and Kyriaki Tsegenidi. 2008. "Innovation and Peripherality: An Empirical Comparative Study of SMEs in Six European Union Member Countries." *Economic Geography* 84, no. 1: 51–82.

Doloreux, David. 2004. "Regional Innovation Systems in Canada: A Comparative Study." *Regional Studies* 38, no. 5: 479–92.

———. 2003. "Regional Innovation Systems in the Periphery: The Case of Beauce in Quebec (Canada)." *International Journal of Innovation Management* 7, no. 1: 67–94.

Dosi, Giovanni, Christopher Freeman, Richard R. Nelson, Gerald Silverberg, and Luc Soete, eds. 1988. *Technological Change and Economic Theory*. London: Pinter.

Edquist, Charles. 1997. *Systems of Innovation: Technologies, Institutions, and Organizations*. London: Pinter.

Freel, Mark S. 2000. "Strategy and Structure in Innovative Manufacturing SMEs: The Case of an English Region." *Small Business Economics* 15, no. 1: 27–45.

———. 2003. "Sectoral Patterns of Small Firm Innovation, Networking and Proximity." *Research Policy* 32, no. 5: 751–70.

Freel, Mark S. and Richard T. Harrison. 2006. "Innovation and Cooperation in the Small Firm Sector: Evidence from 'Northern Britain'." *Regional Studies* 40, no. 4: 289–305.

Freeman, Christopher. 1987. *Technology, Policy, and Economic Performance: Lessons from Japan*. London: Pinter.

Fritsch, Michael. 2001. "Co-operation in Regional Innovation Systems." *Regional Studies* 35, no. 4: 297–307.

Gebauer, Andrea, Chang Woon Nam, and Rüdiger Parsche. 2005. "Regional Technology Policy and Factors Shaping Local Innovation Networks in Small German Cities." *European Planning Studies* 13, no. 5: 661–83.

Grotz, Reinhold and Boris Braun. 1997. "Territorial or Transnational Networking: Spatial Aspects of Technology Oriented Cooperation within the German Mechanical Engineering Industry." *Regional Studies* 31, no. 6: 545–57.

Hassink, Robert. 1997. "Technology Transfer Infrastructures: Some Lessons from Experiences in Europe, the US and Japan." *European Planning Studies* 5, no. 3: 351–70.

Iammarino, Simona. 2005. "An Evolutionary Integrated View of Regional Systems of Innovation: Concepts, Measures and Historical Perspectives." *European Planning Studies* 13, no. 4: 497–518.

Johnson, Bjørn. 1992. "Institutional Learning." In *National Systems of Innovation*, edited by Bengt-Åke Lundvall. London: Pinter.

Kaufmann, Alexander and Franz Tödtling. 2002. "How Effective Is Innovation Support for SMEs? An Analysis of the Region of Upper Austria." *Technovation* 22, no. 3: 147–59.

———. 2003. "Innovation Pattern of SMEs." In *Regional Innovation Policy for Small-Medium Enterprises*, edited by Bjørn T. Asheim, Arne Isaksen, Claire Nauwelaers, and Franz Tödtling. Cheltenham: Edward Elgar.

Kaufmann, Alexander and Petra Wagner. 2005. "EU Regional Policy and the Stimulation of Innovation: The Role of the European Regional Development Fund in the Objective 1 Region Burgenland." *European Planning Studies* 13, no. 4: 581–99.

Koschatzky, Knut and Rolf Sternberg. 2000. "R&D Cooperation in Innovation Systems—Some Lessons from the European Regional Innovation Survey (ERIS)." *European Planning Studies* 8, no. 4: 487–501.

Koschatzky, Knut and Andrea Zenker. 1999. "The Regional Embeddedness of Small Manufacturing and Service Firms: Regional Networking as Knowledge Source for Innovation?" Working Papers "Firms and Regions" No. R2/1999. Karlsruhe: Fraunhofer Institute Systems and Innovation Research.

Lee, Thomas W. 1999. *Using Qualitative Methods in Organizational Research*. London: Sage.

Lundvall, Bengt-Åke, ed. 1992a. *National Systems of Innovation: Towards a Theory of Innovation and Interactive Learning*. London: Pinter.

———. 1992b. "User-Producer Relationships, National Systems of Innovation and Internationalization." In *National Systems of Innovation: Towards a Theory of Innovation and Interactive Learning*, edited by Bengt-Åke Lundvall. London: Pinter.

Maskell, Peter. 2001. "Social Capital, Innovation and Competitiveness." In *Social Capital: Critical Perspectives*, edited by Stephen Baron, John Field, and Tom Schuller. Oxford: Oxford University Press.

Maskell, Peter and Anders Malmberg. 1999. "Localised Learning and Industrial Competitiveness." *Cambridge Journal of Economics* 23, no. 2: 167–86.

Nelson, Richard R., ed. 1993. *National Innovation Systems: A Comparative Analysis.* Oxford: Oxford University Press.

———. 2002. "Technology, Institutions, and Innovation Systems." *Research Policy* 31, no. 2: 265–72.

———. 2008. "What Enables Rapid Economic Progress: What Are the Needed Institutions?" *Research Policy* 37, no. 1: 1–11.

OECD (Organisation for Economic Co-operation and Development). 2001. *The Well-being of Nations: The Role of Human and Social Capital.* Paris: OECD.

Oinas, Päivi. 2000. "Distance and Learning: Does Proximity Matter?" In *Knowledge, Innovation and Economic Growth: The Theory and Practice of Learning Regions,* edited by Frans Boekema, Kevin Morgan, Silvia Bakkers, and Roel Rutten. Cheltenham: Edward Elgar.

Patton, Michael Quinn. 1991. *Qualitative Evaluation and Research Methods.* Second edition. London: Sage.

Sharif, Naubahar. 2006. "Emergence and Development of the National Innovation Systems Concept." *Research Policy* 35, no. 5: 745–66.

Simmie, James. 2002. "Knowledge Spillovers and Reasons for the Concentration of Innovative SMEs." *Urban Studies* 39, nos. 5–6: 885–902.

Smallbone, David, David North, and Ian Vickers. 2003. "The Role and Characteristics of SME." In *Regional Innovation Policy for Small-Medium Enterprises,* edited by Bjørn T. Asheim, Arne Isaksen, Claire Nauwelaers, and Franz Tödtling. Cheltenham: Edward Elgar.

Storper, Michael. 1997. *The Regional World: Territorial Development in a Global Economy.* New York: Guilford Press.

Tödtling, Franz and Michaela Trippl. 2004. "Like Phoenix from the Ashes? The Renewal of Clusters in Old Industrial Areas." *Urban Studies* 41, nos. 5–6: 1175–95.

———. 2005. "One Size Fits All? Towards a Differenciated Regional Innovation Policy Approach?" *Research Policy* 34, no. 8: 1203–19.

Vickers, Ian and David North. 2000. "Regional Technology Initiatives: Some Insights from the English Regions." *European Planning Studies* 8, no. 3: 301–18.

Zubiaurre, Arantza. 2002. "Cooperación entre empresas y centros tecnológicos en la política tecnológica vasca." *Economía Industrial* 346: 115–26.

7

Rethinking Bilbao's Regeneration Process: Innovative Strategies in a Global Framework

SANDRA GONZÁLEZ AND ÁLVARO LUNA

Translated by Robert Forstag

The transformation of Metropolitan Bilbao[1] has been evaluated and revaluated from the standpoint of various disciplines and perspectives. In this chapter, we seek to understand this process not as an exceptional case, but rather as part of a complex pattern evident among highly industrialized cities that have attempted to redefine themselves economically, socially, and culturally.

We will first examine the principal models of socio-structural innovation that have been used to understand the transformational dynamics of formerly industrial cities. These models are part of the reductionist framework of the New Economy and have therefore ignored those social and cultural aspects of the urban setting that are most involved in innovation. Such issues must thus be approached within a set of parameters that is more closely related to social and cultural innovation—and therefore more closely interwoven with community development practices in the

---

1. Based on data for 2008, Bilbao, which has a population of 354,180 residents, cannot be understood as a well-defined urban zone that is clearly differentiated from the surrounding area, but rather as encompassing a string of separate municipalities that are both socially and spatially interrelated. That is why we here use both "Greater Bilbao" (understood as comprising the group of municipalities situated along the Nervión Estuary) as well as "the functional area of Metropolitan Bilbao" (referring to all thirty-five municipalities) to refer to the city and its immediate environs.

various social and economic arenas. Secondly, we will address the specific case of Metropolitan Bilbao. Here, an urban setting has constituted the basis for a strategy promoting revitalization and structural change as well as innovations in managing urban development and addressing needs resulting from a process in which physical and economic development, rather than social development, have been prioritized. As a result, reconfiguration and revitalization processes, although specific and embedded in a unique sociopolitical context, also largely reflect a general model of structural change for formerly industrial urban centers.

The Socio-structural Context of the New Regionalism: Expert Knowledge for Reflecting upon Urban Environments

In the late 1980s and throughout the 1990s, transformation and regeneration processes in cities with an industrial past were influenced by strategies associated with the new global economy that involved competitiveness, marketing, and innovation. The main characteristics of this new global economy are based on a unified and interconnected conception of capital flows, the market, information, technology, organization, and business administration, as well as on the internationalization of the notion as the predominant global economic system (Soja 2005). Many of these cities and regions have struggled for a place on the international stage by adopting urban planning during their initial development stages as a strategy for staking out a place on the global map on the basis of infrastructural and esthetic changes. Reconfiguration of the social and spatial organization of these cities required the renovation of their economic, social, and cultural structures, as well as a proper orientation to transnational investment, trade, tourism, and cultural exchange.

The success of urban intervention processes in meeting this challenge has resulted from an adherence to models of combined public and private management that have resulted in the appearance of new institutional structures aimed at administering the city in a more flexible and profitable manner. Although many of these cities and regions have achieved great success in terms of the management and layout of their physical environments, they have been somewhat less adept when it has come to addressing the social and cultural problems resulting from this process.

The different structural change experiences of these kinds of cities shows that although the success of some of their structures was the result of more or less strenuous efforts, it in no way ensured victory with respect to other aspects of society. Adopting good practices and the capacity to innovate are now affected by new uncertainties that require a reconsideration of matters such as education, social welfare, quality of life, balanced territorial development, the environment, and equality issues. If the innovative experience of change demonstrates anything, it is that the greater the degree of accelerated development, the greater the amount of uncertainty generated (Gurrutxaga 2010).

Within this frame of reference, regional and territorial systems of innovation have comprised a base consisting of small- and medium-sized enterprises, with an organizational culture and certain administrative resources in common, and that have focused on meeting all of the expectations and on performing all of the functions related to fostering the socioeconomic progress of each locale. Such activity has often been accompanied by that of other public and private institutions, which have collaborated and cooperated with one another and thereby created dense networks of local and regional development for the purposes of promoting technological-scientific and economic innovation. Some researchers have chosen to term these cities either "global cities" (Sassen 1991) or "global city-regions" (Scott 2001).[2]

This has been the dominant model to which industry-oriented cities in crisis have attempted to adapt. The necessary revitalization of their former industrial spaces, as well as the implementation of a new urban aesthetic, have been the primary elements of a strategy aimed at putting these cities back on the global map. The movement toward a more or less structured service economy, together with a commitment to tourism, a cultural drive, business innovation, and creative industries, have been some of the most common features of attempts to revitalize old industrial cities.

Within this first phase of transformation toward the New Economy, there is a complementary stage of socio-structural changes geared toward the transformation of regional spaces through improvement of their primary urban spaces. Cities as metropolises become objects of innovation themselves, as well as the primary vehicle of progress in a region. Metropolises thus become the principal arenas of operation for the most impor-

---

2. Saskia Sassen (1991) conceives of the global city as an urban space with a heavy concentration of capital flows and economic growth, which functions as one of the principal axes of concentration of power and capital, and which serves as a venue for the transactions of the most important world economies. She has shifted her focus from the activities of cities as such to regional conglomerations of global economic development. See also Scott (2001) and Soja (2000).

tant agents, agencies, and social actors. This approach has been termed "new regionalism," and it is concerned with the most rapid and equitable development of an area, administrative improvement, promoting and defending cultural identities, a commitment to more participatory and representative democratic structures, environmental conservation, and stimulating innovation and creativity (Soja 2005, 59).

Thus, cities have become complex environments in which local and regional elements intersect, and in which innovation processes involve a vast number of social agents, institutions, companies, and organizations, all of which collectively comprise a dense network of cooperation, competitiveness, and support, and which transform cities themselves into the primary protagonists of regional planning and development. This kind of activity has given rise to *collective learning* networks, which are embedded within urban spaces. Such networks share cultural and human codes that are capable of generating innovative sociocultural contexts and institutions (Gurrutxaga 2010, 15). As regards some of these urban spaces, an entire culture of innovation has emerged that is dependent on the conditions and capacities of citizens to address new social and cultural problems (regarding conflict, diversity, climate change, culture, social exclusion, and immigration). While knowledge and innovation explain the success of this new economic development, they also raise questions about the validity of the criteria by which such success is judged. In this regard, a reductionist view of urban and regional growth—a view that is based exclusively on economic criteria—has been prioritized.

Models of territorial development have focused on the instrumental and economic use of institutions. These models have focused most prominently on improved competitiveness and the restructuring of the economic sector of each territory, and have viewed businesses as the sole vehicle of innovation and progress. As a consequence, territorial innovation models have neither paid a great deal of attention to the multifunctional character of the economy, nor overly concerned themselves with noneconomic aspects of the development of individual communities (Moulaert and Nussbaumer 2005).

There are alternative definitions that do address the social, political, and cultural implications of innovation (Athey et al. 2007). For example, social innovation has come to be associated with new procedures aimed at resolving social problems (Young Foundation 2006; Klein and Harrison 2007). Such procedures may be based on any of the different knowledge domains and be applied by different agents. Whatever the case may be, these procedures are oriented toward fostering change in the social logic that they seek to renew (Luna and Galarraga 2010). These kinds of renovations of urban and regional spaces have been most closely associated with sociocultural (education, art, social services, and immigration), socioeconomic (work, employment, and business), or sociopolitical (government, social policies, and planning) needs.

Social innovation may also refer to innovation in individual or community social relationships—an innovation, in the Weberian sense, involving technical and social invention (Moulaert and Nussbaumer 2005, 49). The constellation of social connections and relationships that are undertaken in order to meet a challenge substantially modifies the nature of each individual action undertaken toward that end, as well as the technical, cultural, and economic manifestations of such actions. Such relationships exist within government circles, in companies, in the market, and in different cultural sectors. Each one of these groups interacts internally and externally with other groups, collaborating, competing, and making decisions regarding their surroundings. The decisions they make and the relationships they construct directly affect the transformation of their social context. Without a network of actors integrated within a community, group, or organization, it is impossible to meet the challenge—or even conceive the possibility—of change and invention.

Therefore innovation is a fundamental component in the maintenance and improvement of well-being and quality of life within cities. The capacity to innovate within urban and regional spaces cannot occur in isolated fashion within specific companies and sectors, but must instead originate within media that are territorially interconnected by means of informational and transportation networks and with other media and experiences within the global network (Gurrutxaga 2010).

It is equally important that cities and their surrounding regions pay special attention to the conditions and special characteristics of their sociocultural and sociohistorical milieu. Innovation initiatives that work for one city will not work for other cities, and implementation of a similar kind of measure in two different places needs to be adapted to the specific conditions of each locale. For all these reasons, to reduce urban growth to economic, physical, or labor terms alone overlooks the accompanying distribution and improvement of social benefits implied by such growth (social inclusion, addressing unemployment, and territorial balance), as well as the cultural and economic benefits that might be expected from new creative industries. In many instances, these social and cultural initialives and reforms do not directly impact either the lives of ordinary citizens or the urban communities where they live (Evans 2009; Landry 2000).

The Challenge of Old Industrial Cities

The different concepts employed to characterize the changes that have taken place in old industrial cities have been the subject of heated debate. The post-Fordist interpretation of Allen Scott (1988) stresses the importance of manufacturing industries within the urban setting, with an emphasis on the deindustrialization process that occurred as a result of the decline of Fordism, but that was accompanied by a reindustrialization that was based on the emergence of new industrial forms. In contrast, the postindustrial perspective of Daniel Bell (1973) and Alain Touraine (1971) focuses on the shifting of the economic axis to the tertiary sector, thus promoting the development of a society organized according to the logic of consumption and that represents a radical movement away from the structure and logic of urban industrial capitalism. These approaches do not include the kind of analysis presented here, and use the term "old industrial cities," thereby consciously avoiding any implication of a complete break with industrial processes, and at the same time pointing to the need to understand contemporary city-regions in a fundamentally different way—in economic, cultural, and social terms.

Following the argument of the most prominent advocates of new regionalism, which holds that globalization is an inexorable process in which the local level represents the strategic domain in which the possibilities of having a competitive presence are greatest, cities intervene in their spaces and develop strategies to innovate technology in both economic and social terms for the purpose of competitively differentiating and positioning themselves advantageously in comparison to one another.[3]

In the old industrial cities more than anywhere else, "innovation means accepting the need for transformation, and for converting the transfer of knowledge into the means and vehicle of this objective" (Gurrutxaga 2009, 72). The cases of Pittsburgh, Birmingham, Manchester, and Glasgow (Gómez 1998) serve as an inspiration for Bilbao, which has followed the dominant tendencies of new urban policies in North America

---

3. Competition among cities is revealed by some of the indicators regarding quality of life and degree of creativity. Four important such indicators are Richard Florida's Creative Class Index, Anholt-GMI's City Brands Index, the Euro Creativity Scoreboard, and GaWC's Global City Index.

and Europe, and whose "Guggenheim effect" has led other cities such as Milwaukee, Biloxi, and Boston (Leoné Pucel 2004, 168), to construct museums designed by internationally renowned architects. This process occurs by means of the symbolic global circulation of models utilized "as a dual path to legitimacy": While the local level contributes renovated ideas from the global urban agenda for the city projects themselves, international organizations define the "good practices" of local projects, which end up being removed from the specific context in which they were created (Sánchez and Moura 2005, 33).

It is within this framework of knowledge and practices aimed at reversing the decline of the industrial model that Bilbao finds itself. Within this context, we believe that two factors are of crucial importance: the use of urbanism as an instrument of socioeconomic revitalization, and the emergence of culture as a vehicle of these revitalization processes.

Urbanism as a Strategy for Socioeconomic Revitalization

Focusing more specifically on the common characteristics of formerly industrial cities and on the structural change experienced by these cities during the 1970s and 1980s, the role of city-regions as vehicles of investment flows in the international economy has been supported by the new post-Fordist economy.

This crisis, which occurred as a result of the decline of the Fordist economic model, profoundly modified the urban setting: its physical space, its role, and its form of institutional intervention. This decline had many important repercussions on the physical environment and configuration of cities. Most obviously, this led to abandoned industrial spaces, industrial ruins, deteriorated areas, and contaminated soil. Furthermore, the impact of the crisis was not only felt with respect to the role of cities and their respective regions, but also led to a reconsideration of the forms and purposes of the necessary actions to be taken. In this situation, innovation was more than simply an option: It was instead a necessity in terms of both survival and of reversing a severe socioeconomic decline. Finally, this entire process of structural change has modified how spaces are inhabited by subjects and how these spaces are utilized, represented, and imagined (Lefebvre 2008).

In the face of these important changes, city-regions found themselves required to manage or overcome their industrial legacy and its associated problems. In this regard, a common thread of logic emerged in the strategies employed by cities facing this challenge: namely, the idea that the city needed to be capable of attracting financial and human capital and that the best way to do this was through a commitment to management, intervention, and reconstruction of the city through urban marketing campaigns.

As regards the management of cities, a new model of urban governance was developed that involved collaboration at the various levels of public administration, as well as between the public and private sectors. In addition, specific bodies were created to spearhead this regeneration that were mainly publicly financed, but employed such private-sector criteria as profitability, efficiency, and surplus recovery (Rodríguez 2002, 71).

As regards the intervention model, new urbanism played a key role (Ascher 2004, 72–85). This model led to a specific kind of intervention, which took advantage of abandoned industrial spaces and favored investment in large infrastructure projects in the areas of transportation, cultural and convention facilities, and river clean-up projects. This is where the "flagship projects" designed by famous architects come into play.

Finally, an urban marketing strategy sought to generate a brand for the city by replacing the negative connotations associated with industry (associated with the past, with what was old and outdated, with work, pollution, and production) with more positive associations of a postindustrial era (associated with what was new, with leisure activities, and with consumption). Such marketing campaigns were supported by, and fed off of, the physical interventions that represented a new commitment to the environment, which was now employed as a resource and was rediscovered as a venue for leisure activities (Short et al. 1993, 208–9). And the results of these campaigns were images of cities that were recognizable, exportable, and consumable by both visitors and residents (Muñoz 2008, 68).

Culture as a Vehicle of Urban Regeneration

Although by no means new to urban settings, it was not until the early 1970s that attention began to focus on culture and that the symbolic economy reached its zenith when industry was declining and financial speculation was increasing. Following Sharon Zukin (1982, 1997), the 1970s transformation involved the union of image and product, with images beginning to play a national and even international role. At the same time, the role of the symbolic economy came to represent the city. According to Zukin, "In the shift to a post-postwar economy, who could build the biggest modern art museum suggested the vitality of the financial sector. Who could turn the waterfront from docklands rubble to parks and marinas suggested the possibilities for expansion of the managerial and professional corps" (1997, 12).

The growing incorporation of culture into urban change processes has had a dual aspect. On the one hand, urban policies have incorporated a cultural element. Thus Glasgow, Barcelona, and Bilbao have undergone a culturally based regeneration. Yet here, it has not been culture itself that has made the crucial difference, but the contribution of culture to the urban economy (García 2008, 114). This involved a focus on cultural consumption and its associated practices, with the production and potential involved in cultural activities being correspondingly undervalued (Pratt 2009, 1042). It is this instrumentalization of culture as a consumer good that underlies Richard Florida's (2004) conceptualization of environments that attract the "creative class" as one of their defining features.

We will now proceed to analyze in some detail the specific situation of Metropolitan Bilbao, since we do not want to limit ourselves to abstract models that do not take into account any specific socio-historical context.

The Ongoing Transformation of Metropolitan Bilbao

Prior to undergoing industrialization, the economy of Bilbao was based on trade and maritime activities. Industrialization brought with it the accelerated urbanization of many areas, including the Left Bank of the Nervión Estuary, where many factories were established and most of the workers resided. In contrast, the Right Bank developed at a rather slower pace and was home to the middle and upper classes. Throughout the industrialization phase, central Bilbao continued to expand.

During the 1950s and 1960s, Bilbao witnessed a new wave of industrialization that left it radically transformed. The mouth of the Nervión Estuary, with its large factories involved in metal production, shipbuilding, and chemical plants, became the hub of the city's industry (Cenicacelaya 2004, 18). This industrial conglomeration, as well as its accompanying workforce, was able to absorb the arrival of internal immigrants, and to function as a vehicle of integration during a time when the urban space and the social fabric was undergoing important changes. The clearest example of this was the fact that the municipalities of this metropolitan area doubled and tripled in population within a mere ten years. In addition, environmental and sound pollution was accepted as part of the cost not only of the important socioeconomic benefits of industry, but of the proximity and identification between the population and its industrial base (Pérez 2001, 56).

However, a crisis—at its most severe during the mid-1980s—hit the area in both spatial terms, especially on the Left Bank, and in more widespread generational terms throughout Metropolitan Bilbao. Thus, nearly fifteen years after the process had begun in other European industrial cities, urban decline began to manifest itself in Bilbao in the form of intense social conflicts and decaying urban spaces. Bilbao's worst problem was unemployment, previously nonexistent but that in 1985 reached the highest levels in the European Community: 23.6 percent. This rate was even higher in two Left Bank municipalities: Barakaldo (27.5 percent) and Sestao (30.2 percent). And it was the younger generation hoping to enter the labor market that suffered worst of all, with a 50 percent unemployment rate among this group (Serrano Martínez 2002, 47–52; Pradales 2005; Plöger 2007, 10–14).

Urban Renewal: Moving Forward in the Wake of the Crisis

The process of transformation in Metropolitan Bilbao can and must be understood in terms of the logic of revitalization described above. A number of different studies have analyzed and described the strategies employed by various cities throughout the world to adapt and "creatively" compete in the new contexts and innovative structural spaces. Cities such as Detroit, Pittsburgh, Manchester, and Dortmund had to reinvent themselves following a crisis on the basis of strategies and processes similar to those employed by Bilbao (Amin and Thrift 2001; Sanchez and Moura 2005; García 2008; Plöger 2007).

Within this interpretive framework, several factors can serve as a context for describing the new urban spaces that were supposedly being prepared to take part in the knowledge-based economy. Such factors include high levels of cooperation between local, regional, and national actors and agents (companies, public institutions, universities, and research centers); applying good practices; the quality of governance models; social consensus; the high educational levels of the population; the availability of high-quality educational structures; low levels of social exclusion; establishing a framework of knowledge-based companies and cultural industries; decentralization and local autonomy for municipalities and communities; and good urban, local, regional, and inter-regional transportation systems. These represent some of the goals that old industrial cities are striving for (Gurrutxaga 2009).

In working toward some of these goals, Metropolitan Bilbao has employed strategies that have also been used by other old industrial cities. Yet this transfer of practices and knowledge takes on unique forms within the context of a specific city, and implementing innovative practices within this particular context poses a challenge in itself that necessarily involves innovation and a process in which "transformation occurs in response to need" (Leira 2004, 46).

We will now address the subject of using urban renewal as the principal tool in revitalizing cities by discussing the three elements mentioned above: the new model of urban governance, the new urbanism of projects. undertaken, and urban marketing as a means of reconstructing the image of cities. Thereafter, we will examine the importance of culture as a driving force of the change that has taken place.

The innovation process, at both the macro and micro-social levels, depends on its capacity to act and intervene on the part of different components in the social structure. Focusing specifically on innovations in urban policy, institutional structures have incorporated a competitive management model as well as new instruments, of which two are particularly important: close collaboration, both between the private and public sectors as well as among institutions working toward a common purpose, and the creation of specific bodies to promote the management of urban areas (as in the case of the Bilbao Ría 2000 and Bilbao Metrópoli 30 projects). These agencies are gradually displacing the traditionally oriented administrative departments by (at least in some cases) taking on both the planning and implementation of high-impact projects (Martínez Callejo 2009, 336–40). Such projects are managed according to private business criteria, and their goals are to be self-financing and maintain balanced budgets. However, the strategic and social objectives—such as "regeneration" and "improvement in quality of life"—of such projects do not often meet the criteria typically employed by private businesses (Rodríguez 2002, 95). Three other organizations that function as part of the public administration should also be mentioned: the Society for Industrial Reconversion and Promotion, the Bilbao Urban Renewal Society, and the Bizkaia Business and Innovation Center. Finally, one of the most distinguishing characteristics of the situation in Bilbao is the high level of public investment, which is managed by both the Basque administration and the Spanish government. This not only highlights the leading role of the public sector, but reveals the weakness of private initiative.

Urbanism has been supported by targeted interventions that involve projects where space is used in a way that is, for the most part, radically different from its previous use. Among such projects are those by internationally renowned architects for the purpose of gaining international attention, and include Bilbao airport (designed by Santiago Calatrava), Metro Bilbao (the subway system designed by Norman Foster), the Isozaki Atea (the "Isozaki Gate," two residential and commercial towers designed by Arata Isozaki), and the Guggenheim Museum Bilbao (Frank Gehry). Projects such as these represent urban renewal in the service of an economic logic that has a strong physical component, and that also focuses on intervention in central areas, all within the context of an urban marketing strategy and a logic of self-promotion. These flagship projects have not only put Bilbao on the global map, they have also attempted to strengthen the city's ability to compete with other cities to attract human and financial capital, as well as new visitors and consumers for the purpose of encouraging a new phase of urban growth (Cenicacelaya 2004; Rodríguez 2002).

Turning to the more intangible yet economically important strategy of creating a "city brand," intensive urban marketing campaigns feature spectacular projects by internationally famous companies. One such project is Bilbao Metrópoli 30, which seeks to promote and maintain the innovative, creative, and postmodern image of Bilbao (Larrea and Gamarra 2007, 53) by having the service and tourism sectors project themselves as alternative activities to the industrial model of generating urban wealth. This reconstruction of the city's image has been aided by establishing a new social contract involving both the environment in general and the Nervión Estuary in particular. This social contract has been formalized through both a purification plan for the Nervión and the locating of the Guggenheim Bilbao (a symbol of the transformation process) on the waterside itself (Leira 2004, 37), something that reflected a rediscovery of the estuary as a place to spend leisure time and take walks. This new image, which Bilbao projects to its own residents but also—and more importantly—to outsiders, runs the risk of projecting an overly romantic view that thematizes the city's long period of industrialization. This approach has used iconography as a means of recovering the supposed authentic essence of the city, which allegedly had been "hidden under the smoke of factories and blast furnaces. It is a past that savage industrialism had symbolically robbed the city of, and that the city has now reclaimed" (Muñoz 2008, 192–93).

Culture: Abandoibarra and the Rise of Culture as a Vehicle of Revitalization

Obsolete industrial areas have discovered interesting alternatives to development in the symbolic economy—and more specifically in tourist activities (Moreno 2005, 50–55). In Bilbao, the best example of this is the comprehensive reclamation of Abandoibarra, a project in which the Guggenheim Bilbao plays a leading role, but which also involves such landmarks as the Euskalduna Jauregia Bilbao conference center and concert hall, the Isozaki Atea towers, Calatrava's Zubi-zuri Bridge, and the Sheraton Hotel (designed by Ricardo Legoretta).

Various urban strategies have been employed in the Abandoibarra area to encourage the necessary change. Two of these, the Bilbao General Plan and the Strategic Revitalization Plan, have attempted to reorient this area to the service sector, and here the estuary came to play a crucial role. The General Plan, following the example of the Brownfields in London, identified four "areas of opportunity," one of which was Abandoibarra. At the same time, negotiations were being conducted to construct a Guggenheim Museum in Bilbao, a project that was conceived within a broad regional context and the principal purpose of which was to serve as an economic catalyst.

The "Guggenheim effect" is nowadays widely understood as a process in which cultural installations serve as the catalyst of urban transformation processes and economic reactivation. The Guggenheim Bilbao has been characterized as a culture and leisure waterfront epicenter (Gospodini 2009, 1160) and takes its place beside installations such as the Tate Gallery in London and the Guggenheim Abu Dhabi as cultural magnets whose purpose is to promote the economic reactivation of the surrounding area (Plaza 2008, 506). However, in the case of the Guggenheim Bilbao, the importance of cultural policy in urban revitalization and regeneration represents an ex post facto reading, because at the time the decision was made to build it, what was critically important was reversing the trend of economic decline by any means necessary (Leira 2004).

Outcomes Aside, Rethinking the Model

We will now address some of the limitations and weaknesses involved in this process, from both an urban and cultural perspective, and bearing in mind the importance of a balanced relationship among economic, urban, social, and cultural factors.

Bilbao has succeeded in reactivating its economy by orienting it toward the service sector.[4] While this has been successful in some areas—the Guggenheim Bilbao, the Abandoibarra reform, Metro Bilbao and Eusko Tran (the intra-city tram service), the new airport, the Bizkaia Technology Park, and the Bilbao Exhibition Center—there are still some reservations as to whether the original goals have been fulfilled. This is because the underlying ideas driving the development of any local economy, and the application of these ideas as strategic guidelines for revitalizing economically depressed spaces, do not always represent the most effective or the most appreciated use in the eyes of the majority of the parties involved, especially from a micro-social perspective. There has been a fair amount of criticism of those top-down initiatives that, as a whole, have been rooted in neoliberal development policies. Alternative policies have been proposed that include social development in projects carried out by local actors for the purpose of promoting the social economy (Lévesque, Bourque, and Forgues 2001). In contrast, the regeneration of Bilbao has been carried out on the basis of a model that is, to a great extent, institutional and hierarchical in orientation. Although few people currently question the positive consequences of this model, other kinds of civil society organizations not necessarily connected with those holding political power should have shared the task of revitalizing Bilbao. In any case, there is not one single formula for implementing transformation processes. In addition, innovative societies do not arise as a direct result of either strictly institutional measures or direct public financing.

Another of the weaknesses of this model is the ad hoc nature of its interventions and the lack of an integrated vision of the metropolitan space—a space that is highly integrated both socially and in terms of infrastructure, even though such integration is lacking within the strictly urban space. These territorial imbalances only help bolster the segregation associated with the still existent socio-spatial patronage system.[5]

---

4. Within Greater Bilbao, three out of every four working people are employed in the service sector, with Metropolitan Bilbao having the most employees within this sector (111, 292). According to 2007 data, within this sector, business services (14.4 percent of total jobs) and the commercial services (13.4 percent) are the largest employers. The construction sector employs 10 percent of all workers, and transport/communications employs 9 percent. Industrial activity (mainly involving metallurgy) only employs 5 percent of all workers (Bilbao Lan Ekintza 2008).

5. It was the Left Bank that bore the heaviest brunt of the crisis, and the regeneration process has accentuated an existing socio-spatial segregation (Rodríguez, Martínez, and Guenaga 2001, 162). The socio-structural and urban transformations toward a service-based economy

Finally, there are those who criticize the "branding" of Bilbao—the attempt to insert the city in a circuit of cities to be visited, and to characterize it more in terms of its tourist and cultural interest than in terms of productive activities (Álvarez Mora 1999, 175). This is a postindustrial image that seeks to project attractiveness by prioritizing those on the outside (investors, tourists, and visitors) over those on the inside (those who actually reside in the city).

Following Arantxa Rodríguez (2002, 72–73), as regards the intervention employed in the transformation of Abandoibarra, we believe there are limits to a "valuation urbanism" model, based on the efficiency and maximization of urban opportunities through combining the advantages of recovery (as measured by the launching of large projects), when such a model is extended to an entire metropolitan revitalization. In fact, such a strategy not only depends on heavy public investment, but on the possibilities of a land revaluation that cannot always be the case throughout the whole city, and that prioritizes economic surplus over a gradual regeneration of the social environment.

On the other hand, if we focus on the effect of the Guggenheim Bilbao as a "flagship project," the physical and real transformation of the city has been unquestionable.[6] Beyond the architectural reform, the museums, and the art, the primary elements that have promoted and driven these projects have had to do with tourism, urban renovation, and economic growth based on cultural industries (Guasch and Zulaika 2005; Zulaika 1997).

Despite this success, a number of questions have been raised. In similar fashion to developments regarding the quality of the jobs created in the service sector and in the lack of initiatives for developing a knowledge-based economy comprising companies dedicated to the exclusive production of knowledge, the cultural environment of Bilbao

---

that have occurred in this traditionally working-class space are worthy of study in terms of the practices, representations, and imaginaries of the subjects that live there (González 2010). In addition, this process raises interesting questions regarding the innovation practices carried out there (Gurrutxaga 2010, 169–86).

6. According to data for 2008, 951,369 people visited the museum that year. Thus, the cumulative number of visits to the museum since its opening in 1997 stood, at the end of 2008, at 11,095,201. The economic impact of its activities on the Basque economy in 2008 amounted to 231 million euros. In sum, as a consequence of the spending of those who visited the museum, a total of 210,072,873 euros of GDP was generated. These monies, in turn, generated an additional 28 million euros for the three provincial Basque treasuries and helped maintain a workforce in the Guggenheim Bilbao numbering 4,196 people (Bilbao Lan Ekintza 2008).

is surrounded by structures that offer and exhibit rather than produce culture. In addition, the vast majority of existing cultural institutions in Bilbao—and throughout the Comunidad Autónoma del País Vasco/ Euskal Autonomia Erkidegoa (CAPV/EAE, the Autonomous Community of the Basque Country)—is strongly supported by public financing, in large part due to the fact that the experience of the Guggenheim Bilbao has made institutions appreciate the importance of culture in the city (Plaza, Tironi, and Haarisch 2009). Those cultural institutions that do not receive public financing face numerous challenges in crafting their annual budgets. Within Bilbao, there are cultural structures such as Bilbao Arte (an artistic creative and exhibition center), BilboRock (a concert hall, with practice rooms and a music archive), Bilbao Eszena (a theatrical center with rehearsal and performance facilities), and Social Antzokia (a theater hosting cinema, theater, music, and dance). Although they provide an important and necessary public service in different cultural areas and disciplines, they are still publicly sustained structures that have little socioeconomic impact on the city. In this regard, the number of private cultural entities is few and far between.

The vast majority of these creative industries comprise an average of two to six workers. In accordance with the findings of Graeme Evans (2009, 1030), given the fragility of employment and of the markets involved in these small companies, economic development initiatives for such companies in effect depend on a blind confidence in predictions that creative and knowledge-based economies will grow, thus casting doubt on their role as regeneration and innovation catalysts. This said, it seems fitting to ask whether serving as economic catalysts should in fact be their purpose, or if perhaps their contribution ought to be understood as a basic pillar of any urban environment that is supposedly dynamic and rich in sociocultural resources. Some would agree with the contention that the role of these kinds of industries is not absolutely vital, but rather constitutes a social luxury that is complemented by the cultural life of the city and by the existence of larger cultural structures (museums, theaters, exhibition centers, and concert halls). According to Andy Pratt, "A creative city cannot be founded like some cathedral in the desert; it needs to be linked to, and to be part of, an already existing cultural environment" (2008, 35). Basque culture and the cultural contexts of Basque cities have always been very rich in terms of production. Such production must continue to be supported by cultural and artistic initiatives within the social environment in order to promote a richer culture and greater interdependence between, on the one hand, specific Basque cultural bodies and, on the other, Basque society as a whole.

As regards the sustainability and economic solvency of these supposedly independent industries, the development of creative industry programs and agencies is, to a large extent, dependent on public subsidies and assistance during periods exceeding ten years. Within the European context, these programs and agencies are dependent on the European Regional Development Fund, as well as on assistance from national funds (Evans 2009, 1030).

Within both business environments and cultural sectors, excessive financial support on the part of public institutions not only casts doubt on the supposed success of certain projects, but actually undermines Basque entrepreneurship and the possibility of enriching the entrepreneurial dynamism of the region. From the financial point of view, it is also evidence of reluctance on the part of banks and other financial institutions to support these ideas unless it is through competitions and tenders for the sole financing of social and cultural projects.

Ultimately, the cultural environment of a city, country, or region is much richer and more complex than the intentions and processes reflected in decision-making based on strategic plans, public funding programs, and official cultural strategies (Lash 2002). In this regard, it seems fitting—despite the support of public institutions through strategic plans and projects—to emphasize the social and cultural needs that underlie the urban context, as well as the importance of the social diffusion of its most important practices and deepest meanings. In other words, value should be placed on a balance among economic, cultural, and social dimensions of urban regeneration processes.

Conclusion: The Need for Regeneration with Social and Cultural Components Emphasized as Much as Economic Matters

The process of revitalizing Metropolitan Bilbao has taken place within the context of theoretical models and interpretations that focus on understanding the new aesthetic of cities and their connection to the competitiveness, marketing, and innovation that govern the global economy. Within this logical framework, innovation is seen as a necessary and highly useful tool to be employed in facing problems arising from outdated economic models of industrial cities. Following this framework, city-regions are the new economic and social vehicle of the urban environment, while their development is based on the physical and structural transformation of space, and on a necessary reorientation of economic activity in the direction of services and tourism.

In order to carry out this process, many cities, including Metropolitan Bilbao, have immersed themselves in complex asymmetrical networks of economic relationships in which the ideal models of socioeconomic transformation and the processes of imitating these models have led many cities away from the need to undergo change on the basis of the requirements of their own socio-historical contexts. Urban renewal of the old industrial spaces, along with culture, have been the two primary poles of attraction that have revived these cities. Given that the success of Metropolitan Bilbao has been based on previous models of transformation, it seems fitting to question the consequences that have resulted from these processes, especially in terms of the possibilities for a continued favorable development of the city. The consequences of this socio-structural transformation process reveal other kinds of social and cultural needs that are not being met, many of which are strategically important components of any knowledge-based economy: high-quality educational institutions, quality of employment, and investment in RDI (research, development, and innovation). Others, however, stem from insufficiency that is more social and concrete in nature and, therefore, directly related to problems in the quality of life and well-being of the population: social inclusion, unemployment, territorial development, and new socioeconomic values.

Although some of the strategies for regenerating Metropolitan Bilbao may be considered innovative from the sociocultural point of view, others need improving and require a higher degree of innovative acumen in order to more clearly confront social problems. Thus, Metropolitan Bilbao has needs that are associated directly with local social problems that have not effectively been addressed (Moreno 2005, 712–14). Examples of such problems are social and territorial disparities, the gentrification of urban spaces (Vicario and Martínez Monje 2003), the rising cost of housing, immigration, creating quality jobs, labor mediation, excessive public dependency, and the lack of entrepreneurship on the part of the city's residents.

The visualization of urban and regional growth on the basis of strictly economic criteria is, in the end, insufficient for guaranteeing that socioeconomic problems will be addressed and for fostering improvement in both social well-being and quality of life. Innovation initiatives that work in one city do not necessarily work in others, and although their characteristics may be similar, in the final analysis, it is necessary to tailor them to the specific circumstances of each locale. In order to resolve these kinds of problems, social improvement processes must be focused on those innovation initiatives that more directly address social, political, and cultural issues. Examples of such issues are new strategies of local governance; mechanisms of participation and community development; improvements in education, social services, and employment; support for traditional local culture; and creating integration mechanisms that address the challenges stemming from immigration.

References

Álvarez Mora, Alfonso. 1999. "Bilbao, la definición de una 'imagen' de marca como reclamo competitivo. Crónica de un proceso iniciado." *Revista Ciudades* 5: 151–78.

Amin, Ash and Nigel Thrift, eds. 2001. *Globalization, Institutions and Regional Development in Europe*. New York: Oxford University Press.

Ascher, François. 2004. *Los nuevos principios del urbanismo: El fin de las ciudades no está al orden del día*. Translated by María Hernández Díaz. Madrid: Alianza Ensayo.

Athey, Glen, Catherine Glossop, Ben Harrison, Max Nathan, and Chris Webber, eds. 2007. *Innovation and the City: How Innovation Has Developed in Five City-Regions*. London: NESTA.

Bell, Daniel. 1973. *The Coming of Post-Industrial Society: A Venture in Social Forecasting*. New York: Basic Books.

Bilbao Lan Ekintza. 2008. *Anuario socioeconómico de Bilbao*. Bilbao: Observatorio Socioeconómico de Bilbao.

Cenicacelaya, Javier. 2004. "Bilbao y la urgencia de un urbanismo sostenible." In *Urbanismo en el siglo XXI. Una visión crítica*, edited by Jordi Borja and Zaida Muxi. Barcelona: Ediciones UPC.

Evans, Graeme. 2009. "Creative Cities, Creative Spaces and Urban Policy." *Urban Studies* 46, nos. 5–6 (May): 1003–40.

Florida, Richard L. 2004. *The Rise of the Creative Class: And How It's Transforming Work, Leisure, Community and Everyday Life*. New York: Basic Books.

García, Beatriz. 2008. "Política cultural y regeneración urbana en las ciudades de Europa occidental: Lecciones aprendidas de la experiencia y perspectivas para el futuro." *RIPS: Revista de Investigaciones Políticas y Sociológicas* 7, no. 1: 111–25.

Gómcz, María Victoria. 1998. "Regeneración urbana." In *El malestar urbano en la gran ciudad*, edited by María José González. Madrid: Talasa.

González, Sandra. 2010. "Los espacios en transformación de la Margen Izquierda del Nervión." In *Actas del VIII Congreso Vasco de Sociología y Ciencias Políticas-"Sociedad e Innovación en el Siglo XXI."* Bilbao: Asociación Vasca de Sociología.

Gospodini, Aspa. 2009. "Post-industrial Trajectories of Mediterranean European Cities: The Case of Post-Olympics Athens." *Urban Studies* 46, nos. 5–6 (May): 1157–1186.

Guasch, Anna Maria and Joseba Zulaika, eds. 2005. *Learning from the Bilbao Guggenheim*. Reno: Center for Basque Studies, University of Nevada.

Gurrutxaga, Ander. 2010. *Recorridos por el cambio, la innovación y la incertidumbre*. Bilbao: Servicio Editorial de la UPV-EHU.

———. 2009. "Recorridos por la innovación." In Daniel Innerarity and Ander Gurrutxaga. *¿Cómo es una sociedad innovadora?* Zamudio: Innobasque, Agencia Vasca de la Innovación.

Klein, Juan-Luis and Denis Harrison, eds. 2007. *L'innovation Sociale: Émergence et Effets sur la Transformation des Sociétés*. Québec: Presses de l'Université de Québec.

Landry, Charles. 2000. *The Creative City: A Toolkit for Urban Innovators*. London: Earthscan.

Larrea, Andeka and Garikoitz Gamarra. 2007. *Bilbao y su doble*. Bilbao: Martxoak, 18.

Lash, Scott. 2002. *Critique of Information*. London and Thousand Oaks, CA: Sage.

Lefebvre, Henri. 2008. *The Production of Space*. Translated by Donald Nicholson-Smith. Oxford: Blackwell.

Leira, Eduardo. 2004. "Bilbao: Balance provisional de una importante transformación urbana." In *Urbanismo en el siglo XXI. Una visión crítica*, edited by Jordi Borja and Zaida Muxi. Barcelona: Ediciones UPC.

Leoné Pucel, Santiago. 2004. "'Global Frisson': La transformación de la imagen de Bilbao." *Revista Internacional de Estudios Vascos* 49, no. 1: 159–69.

Lévesque, Benoît, Gilles L. Bourque, and Eric Forgues. 2001. *La nouvelle économie sociale*. Paris: Desclée de Brouwer.

Luna, Álvaro and Auxkin Galarraga. 2010. "Sociedad, Cultura e Innovación Social: El Proceso de Transformación de Bilbao." *Actas del VIII Congreso Vasco de Sociología y Ciencias Políticas-"Sociedad e Innovación en el Siglo XXI."* Bilbao: Asociación Vasca de Sociología.

Martínez Callejo, Javier. 2009. *Bilbao: Desarrollos urbanos 1960/2000. Ciudad y forma.* Vitoria-Gasteiz: Servicio Central de Publicaciones del Gobierno Vasco.

Moreno, Judith. 2005. *Bilbao: Declive industrial, regeneración urbana y reactivación económica de un espacio metropolitano.* Bilbao: Instituto Vasco de Administración Pública.

Moulaert, Frank and Jacques Nussbaumer. 2005. "The Social Region: Beyond the Territorial Dynamics of the Learning Economy." *European Urban and Regional Studies* 12, no. 1: 45–64.

Muñoz, Francesc. 2008. *Urbanalización. Paisajes comunes, lugares globales.* Barcelona: Gustavo Gilli.

Pérez, José Antonio. 2001. *Los años del acero. La transformación del mundo laboral en el área industrial del Gran Bilbao (1958–77): Trabajadores, convenios y conflictos.* Madrid: Biblioteca Nueva.

Plaza, Beatriz. 2008. "On Some Challenges and Conditions for the Guggenheim Museum Bilbao to be an Effective Economic Re-activator." *International Journal of Urban and Regional Research* 32, no. 2 (June): 506–17.

Plaza, Beatriz, Manuel Tironi, and Silke N. Haarisch. 2009. "Bilbao's Art Scene and the 'Guggenheim effect' Revisited." *European Planning Studies* 17, no. 11 (November): 1711–29.

Plöger, Jörg. 2007. *Bilbao City Report.* CASEreport 43. London: Centre for Analysis of Social Exclusion (CASE). At sticerd.lse.ac.uk/dps/case/cr/CASEreport43.pdf.

Pradales, Imanol. 2005. *Estructura social del empleo en la CAPV: Transformación del trabajo y zonas de empleo.* Vitoria-Gasteiz: Servico Central de Publicaciones del Gobierno Vasco.

Pratt, Andy C. 2008. "Creative Cities?" *Urban Design* 106: 35.

———. 2009. "Urban Regeneration: From the Arts 'Feel Good' Factor to the Cultural Economy: A Case Study of Hoxton, London." *Urban Studies* 46, nos. 5–6 (May): 1041–61.

Rodríguez, Arantxa. 2002. "Reinventar la Ciudad: Milagros y espejismos de la revitalización urbana en Bilbao." *Lan Herremanak* 6, no. 1: 69–108.

Rodríguez, Arantxa, Elena Martínez, and Galder Guenaga. 2001. "New Urban Policies and Socio-spatial Fragmentation in Metropolitan Bilbao." *European Urban and Regional Studies* 8, no. 2: 161–78.

Sánchez, Fernanda and Rosa Moura. 2005. "Ciudades-modelo: Estrategias convergentes para su difusión internacional." *EURE* 31, no. 93: 21–34.

Sassen, Saskia. 1991. *The Global City: New York, London, Tokyo.* Princeton, NJ: Princeton University Press.

Scott, Allen J., ed. 2001. *Global City-Regions: Trends, Theory, Policy.* New York: Oxford University Press.

———. 1988. "Urban Theories and Realities." In *Metropolis: From the Division of Labor to Urban Form.* Berkeley: University of California Press.

Serrano Martínez, José María. 2002. "Red y Sistema Urbano de las Capitales de Provincia en España a comienzos del siglo XXI: Fases de crecimiento demográfico y significación territorial." *Cuadernos Geográficos de la Universidad de Granada* 32: 43–71.

Short, J. R., L. M. Benton, W. B. Luce, and J. Walton. 1993. "Reconstructing the Image of an Industrial City." *Annals of the Association of American Geographers* 83, no. 2 (June): 207–24.

Soja, Edward W. 2005. "Algunas consideraciones sobre el concepto de ciudades región globales." *Ekonomiaz* 56: 44–75.

———. 2000. *Postmetropolis: Critical Studies of Cities and Regions.* Oxford: Blackwell.

Touraine, Alain. 1971. *The Post-Industrial Society, Tomorrow's Social History: Classes, Conflicts and Culture in the Programmed Society.* Translated by Leonard F. X. Mayhew. New York: Random House.

Vicario, Lorenzo and P. Manuel Martínez Monje. 2003. "Another Guggenheim Effect? The Generation of a Potentially Gentrificable Neighbourhood in Bilbao." *Urban Studies* 40, no. 12 (November): 2383–2400.

Young Foundation. 2006. *Social Innovation: What It Is, Why It Matters, How It Can Be Accelerated.* London: Basingstoke Press.

Zukin, Sharon. 1997. *The Culture of Cities.* Oxford: Blackwell Publishing.

———. 1982. *Loft Living: Culture and Capital in Urban Change.* Baltimore: Johns Hopkins University Press.

Zulaika, Joseba. 1997. *Crónica de una Seducción: El Museo Guggenheim de Bilbao.* Madrid: Nerea.

8

Art and Social Innovation in the City

Natxo Rodríguez Arkaute

Translated by Jennifer R. Ottman

In recent years, cities have certainly been sensitive to a succession of cultural policies. In most recent cases, when new contemporary art facilities have been proposed, the beneficial effects these will supposedly bring to the city in question in many different areas have been stressed: from the creation of new tourist attractions or the renewal of decayed urban spaces to the search for distinguishing characteristics in a context of growing inter-city competition. This cultural battle between cities has been on view recently in an extraordinary way in the competition for the award of the European capital of culture title in 2016, with sixteen candidates from the Spanish state. These supposed effects, as a rule, do not generally center in the first instance on what might be supposed to be their primary function: invigorating and strengthening the cultural fabric of the locality. Such activity in the sphere of cultural policy around the turn of the millennium is more a case of a very specific stereotypical understanding of both culture and models of creating a city.

Until not long ago, cities were traditionally envisioned as geographical and cultural spaces, in gradual construction along urban lines, as centers for the concentration of people and services. Within this logic, the possible effects of artistic practices on a city's future have generally been posed in terms of dialogue and tension between artists' work and the city, the streets, or public spaces. Seen from this perspective, there are basically two ways in which art and the city could relate to one another and engage in dialogue: artistic interventions in urban spaces and the spaces designated for art in a city. As we will see later, however, early twenty-first-century cities are in the process of moving beyond this physical conception of the city toward a more complex, less strictly spatial model, translating the concept of the urban itself into another idea of the city. As a consequence, the role of contemporary artistic practices and the system of art at issue in the new urban context, as well as their probable effects, also need to be envisioned along quite different lines.

In the traditional city, understood as a geographical area with a high concentration of people, industry, and services, artistic interventions consider the urban space as a place of presentation-representation, where these actions may play an antagonistic or critical role (tension) or may also take place with a greater or lesser degree of complicity. As regards tension in the urban space, for example, certain manifestations of graffiti evidently take place without permission and in forbidden locations, and there are certain more critical artistic interventions. Where complicity is concerned, although this may not be the most appropriate term, we could look at the whole complex revolving around what we understand as "public art," usually having to do with all possible varieties of sculpture in the urban environment. In both cases, with some exceptions, this presence of art in the urban environment has more of an effect on the city's surface layer—on how it is perceived aesthetically—than on its social or spatial configuration.

Furthermore, examining the presence of art in the urban environment leads us inevitably to look at the infrastructure and facilities dedicated to artistic practices. Yet even taking into account that these facilities, as the current museum paradigm dictates, need architecture in order to be present in the city, it is the museum (a hegemonic protagonist) that sets itself up as the most visible element within the system of art. It also enjoys an ever more frequent presence within the urban fabric, at the same time that—precisely because it is an instance of architecture—it appears as a resource with great potential for transforming or altering that fabric. Hence, from the perspective of an ever more extensive utilization of culture as a resource, and with architecture as its tool, institutional policies for contemporary art today consist almost exclusively in the creation of facilities of this kind, amplifying their protagonism and their effects on the city to a greater or lesser degree according to the interests of the moment, even the interests of each new administration. In the context of the Spanish state, and more specifically in the case of the Basque Country, the majority of museums and art centers designed since the mid- to late-1990s, whether already open or still to be opened in the near future, have originated in good measure in considerations of this kind. Somehow, the idea of the city as a physical location appeared to have been transcended, and it came to be understood, at least initially, as a symbolic political and economic space, only to end up with plans for urban and economic renewal in which museums became the principal vehicles, at the same time that architecture passed into the realm of ideology.

An Inherited Model

The Guggenheim Bilbao turns out to be a paradigmatic example of all this, where almost nobody now denies the success of an initiative that without any doubt has consolidated itself as the driving force of revitalization in an area that had been depressed on many different levels. Any evaluation made of what has already become a model leads to positive results. For example, a study published by the Visual Artists Association of Catalonia (Associació d'Artistes Visuals de Catalunya, AAVC 2006, 165) analyzing the economic impact of the visual arts in Spain, argues that "practically the entire growth in visitor numbers to Bilbao since the creation of the Guggenheim is due to the opening of the museum, greatly facilitating the calculation of its impact (it is merely necessary to quantify the economic effects of the growth of tourism on the city)." In fact, the administrators of the museum themselves, interviewed and mentioned in the study, declare that the Guggenheim Bilbao has contributed to the urban development of the area and to endowing the city with a new tourist attraction.

Nevertheless, the success of the Guggenheim phenomenon in Bilbao is relativized if we consider other indicators. The AAVC report also takes into account the cultural effect on the urban fabric as another indicator. However, at least in this study, it is not such a determining one since, as the title indicates, it is more concerned with the economic dimension of museums' impact. Even so, the report refers to what it calls the "cultural objective," which it characterizes as the "provision of a location for an existing artistic collection (already in the city or recently acquired) that lacks an appropriate space for its exhibition, or creation of a space that invigorates artistic production in the area" (2006, 163). It does so after arguing for the generous fulfillment of other objectives such as the "tourism objective"— "improvement of the city's position in the tourism market, making the museum a key factor in attracting tourists" (2006, 163)—and the "urban-planning objective," expressed as the "desire to revitalize the municipality's historic center or to invigorate a specified urban area through the creation of a prestigious item of cultural infrastructure" (163). It turns out, as a result, that the objectives of the Bilbao art museum "extend beyond the cultural sector" (Esteban 2007, 37). This is the understanding of Iñaki Esteban upon observing that the Guggenheim "miracle" in Bilbao satisfactorily performs a variety of functions. It performs an urban-planning function through its significance at the level of the revitalization and clean-up of its surroundings, extending its aestheticizing influence to the rest of the city. It also fulfills an economic function because it attracts tourists and fosters new businesses, as we have seen above, with a significant impact on economic activity in its urban context.

Nor should we forget its political function, accumulating a great deal of symbolic capital in favor of the institutions, the city, and the region that promote it. Nevertheless, as in the AAVC report, for Esteban the cultural function "is missing," and he believes that for the Guggenheim Bilbao this function is more "a mechanism of self-legitimation, of self-justification, of prestige" (2007, 73). The Guggenheim at the time it was planning to locate in Bilbao, according to the AAVC study, did not suppose that the creation of the museum would invigorate the artistic activity of local creators. "The difficult situation of local artists is, as a result, another crucial aspect of this phenomenon. Fundamentally, in a Krensified museum, local representatives lose intellectual control over deciding what is or is not quality art, in addition to financial control over their own resources and institutional control through which to promote a specific type of art by purchasing and exhibiting it. Local artists have been completely marginalized from the centers that determine the fate of their careers" (2006, 163).

In this situation, the Guggenheim Bilbao's overwhelming success in such significant fields as urban planning, economics, and even politics has made it the model to be imitated in many cultural policies being implemented today. This "Guggenheimization" of the museum has become a pattern to be followed, as if it were the only possible model and no others existed.

But let us not focus so much on the specific case of the Guggenheim Bilbao, aware as we are that under current circumstances it represents a phenomenon difficult to repeat, and instead pay more attention to the model drawn from its experience, insofar as this provides a "how-to manual" for many current cultural policies. We find ourselves at present, as a result, confronting an inherited model that clearly answers to a program of managing culture as a resource. Culture is assigned value as a tool for urban reordering and revaluation, for attracting tourists or generating new businesses and creating jobs, while other more socially oriented considerations about culture have no place and are relegated to secondary status.

The Digital Urban Context

Evidently, this vision of culture, linked to economic issues in a utilitarian way, distances itself from its more social dimension and poses many problems due to the recurrent banalization and commercialization of artistic practices in a dynamic in which culture is progressively being turned into spectacle.

In any event, by translating these reflections into the framework of the city and the idea of social innovation, analysis of the current hegemonic models for managing contemporary art enables us to expand debate and reflection on these models. If we agree to observe the city as a living organism in constant movement, it is beyond doubt that certain decisions on the management of cultural policy have a corresponding impact on the city's morphological and conceptual development. As a consequence, other different models of cultural management and other decisions in the sphere of cultural policy will affect the metropolitan organism in different ways and as a function of different interests.

If the early twenty-first-century city can no longer be understood with reference to its physical nature alone, since it is in the process of evolving in a very lively way toward new, less strictly spatial forms, translating the concept of the urban itself into another idea encompassing much more than the traditional city, any new proposal must take into account that "the urban is not only a geospatial category, but rather, above all, a territory in permanent construction and expansion, exceeding the physical limits of what has traditionally been considered a city" (Sotelo Navalpotro and Sotelo Pérez 2010, 15). In the same way, due especially to the full-scale invasion of the latest digital technologies, the city must be understood differently. As a consequence, the role of contemporary artistic practices and the system of art, with all the actors involved in the new urban context as well as their possible effects, also need to be envisioned along quite different lines. In the context of contemporary cultural production affected by radical technological changes, we must rethink contemporary art and creation, the diffusion and distribution of cultural products, and access to them, in quite a different way. The very notion of an author has been "tainted," and the historical barrier between producers and consumers is ever more diffuse.

Social Innovation in Culture

In this situation, models like that of the Guggenheim Bilbao can be understood in terms of innovation, from the moment in which they have entailed a significant transformation of Bilbao's urban and economic fabric, in addition to also constituting a change in the way of understanding cultural policy. Even the very idea of a museum has been turned upside-down, and it is a different matter to reflect on what a museum signifies as a facility and as a project before and after an experience as far-reaching as the one that the city of Bilbao has lived through. These processes of innovation additionally bring with them economically quantifiable returns, with which the formula of innovation appears to be effectively fulfilled.

Nevertheless, this is not a complete reading of the situation, because many authors have lately been expressing a concern, which I share, about this interpretation of what innovation entails, since it brings with it serious problems when it comes time to transfer it to the world of culture. According to Juan Freire, "innovation, when understood as a process associated solely and exclusively with the economic and business sphere, is not enough to guarantee social development. . . . At the same time, conventional political action does not seem to be producing any comprehensive solutions either, and is looking for solutions based on actively involving citizens in the 'construction' of the city" (2009a, 18–19).

From this perspective, understanding culture in terms of social benefits and development, the collective and horizontal construction of the city leads us to consider the concept of social innovation as a new terrain in the universe of innovation, one not contemplated in the traditionally necessary linkage of innovation with economic return: "Social innovation is the name given to all those market processes that arise in order to respond to needs of a social nature, or to innovations that are going to have a significant impact not only on the market, but also in the social sphere" (YProductions 2007, 40).

These problems of fracture between one kind of innovation associated exclusively with economic return and another that aims at benefits of another kind are also evident in the cultural policies launched by assorted governments. For Javier Echeverría (2008, 610), "social innovation, in contrast, must refer to social values, for example a society's well-being, quality of life, social inclusion, solidarity, citizen participation, environmental quality, healthcare, efficiency of public services, or educational level."

As a result, taking into account the paradigm of innovation in its more social dimension, assigning value to its social rather than commercial returns, it is appropriate to rethink contemporary cultural policy and artistic practice, as well as their repercussion on the construction of the city, along other lines. Our task is to think in other formulas, different from the ones we have inherited, and to be conscious that these new ways of acting may give shape to a new model (or models) of the city.

Other Models for Managing Public Cultural Policy

We have already seen that certain recent cultural policies have demonstrated culture's tremendous transformative potential. This capacity does not disappear even if the urban context changes, as indeed it has. It can still be exploited, taking into account that the most recent changes raise a variety of crucial issues that need to be considered:

- The cultural policies that we have inherited are basically shaped by economic considerations, for which reason cultural and social objectives have been relegated to a secondary or tertiary level.
- The economic context has changed, and many of these policies were envisioned in a previous (very different) local and global context.
- The city as a public and collective space must once again be reclaimed from the perspective of citizen reempowerment.
- From the perspective of a more social conception of innovation, "other" ways of doing things open up new possibilities.
- The digital world and ever-wider access to technological tools enable the recovery of collective dynamics of work, participation, and decision-making.

Considering innovation as a positive value, provided always that we take the more social view of it, these points act as fundamental axes from which we can envision other cultural policies and other models of cultural management—in our case in relation to artistic practices and with reference to some ideas that should be taken into consideration that are indicated below.

Social Creativity

The example of Bilbao has been mentioned several times as a paradigmatic case, but it is surely Barcelona that for some years has been *the* case study, with multiple readings analyzing cultural policy and the city. As a result, "seen through this prism, a considerable number of cultural policies (implemented with special vigor during the years in which Ferrán Mascarell was councilor for culture in the Barcelona city hall and director of the ICUB, the Institut de Cultura de Barcelona [Barcelona Cultural Institute]) have favored festivals, events, and fairs over more-slowly developing cultural projects that were able to give voice to, as well as provide benefits for, the city's social and cultural fabric" (YProductions 2008, 109–10). While these words highlight the case of Barcelona as a clear example of turning culture into spectacle, it is no less important that it is precisely other, slower processes, with less-immediate results, that are relegated to a lesser status, even if they are more socially and culturally productive over the long term.

All these activities that tend toward spectacle also tend proportionately toward the neglect of social creativity—a neglect that eventually becomes an inability to bring together all the knowledge that in an urban context is no longer generated in the traditional and hegemonic places in which it has in the past been found: schools, museums, universities, television, and so on. In order to bring together this creative and hence innovative potential, it is necessary to promote other, more horizontal, relationships between the different parts, stimulating a flow of relationships in all directions.

Juan Freire (2009a), for example, proposes some ideas for fostering environments conducive to creativity and innovation. In his opinion, in the sphere of education "there needs to be a radical change in the models of learning," taking advantage of the knowledge that circulates through networks and originates in informal sources and developing communicative and collaborative abilities. He also proposes dynamics based on providing incentives in place of subsidy policies; invigorating the public space as a place for relationship and communication, with direct citizen participation in its government, in the face of "politicians' and government officials' obsession with control, which reduces the options for use"; making use of the meaningful contributions of digital culture (hackers, open-source software, and so forth) in matters having to do with new tools for collaboration and organizational models; and promoting the existence of new spaces of creation of a more horizontal and less monop-olistic nature than the museum—in addition to another crucial aspect, flexible intellectual-property policies aimed at protecting and developing the common good.

We can pause here to take a look at how the subject of the city as a focus of social creativity is perceived and treated in the Basque Country from the perspective of its various governments, because in fact, a variety of institutional proposals coexist that talk about innovation linked to cre-ativity and culture. In practice, each of the three capital cities of the Comu-nidad Autónoma del País Vasco/Euskal Autonomia Erkidegoa (CAPV/EAE, Autonomous Community of the Basque Country)—Bilbao, Donos-tia-San Sebastián, and Vitoria-Gasteiz—is trying in a different way to fos-ter a model of the city as an active pole of creativity and knowledge in the name of innovation. These proposals deserve a more extended analysis, but everything seems to indicate that they follow the utilitarian path of view-ing culture as a resource and not so much as a sincere acknowledgement of the city as a social space for collective creativity. Bilbao, for example, presents itself in this way at the 2010 Shanghai Universal Exposition, with the slogan "From Industrial City to a Knowledge City": "Museums and art institutions (Museum of Fine Arts, Bilbao Art . . .). The choice for art is very much linked to the change in Bilbao's model of urban and economic development. . . . Art in the city. Dalí, Chillida, Oteiza, Valdés, Koons, and Borgoise, among others, have poured out their creativity throughout the city" (Bilbao Guggenheim Shanghai World Expo 2010, 35, 47).

Vitoria-Gasteiz and Donostia-San Sebastián also present themselves as innovative cities: "Vitoria-Gasteiz needs to maintain a high level of competitiveness and become an active leading element with a view to pro-moting ideal conditions, attracting intensive knowledge-related activities and creating opportunities for employment and for the development of people, as well as creative and talented professionals" (Vitoria-Gasteiz website). Donostia-San Sebastián, for its part, as one of the four axes of its strategic plan, "City of Creativity and Innovation," aims to "convert Donostia-San Sebastián into a magnet of creativity and innovation for cultural production by strengthening the publishing and audiovisual sec-tors, as well as the creative arts sector, with special attention to the applied use of new technologies" (Donostia-San Sebastián 2006, 43).

It is not by chance, as a result, that the three cities have turned to their respective cultural or arts centers as the vehicle of their short-term policies: Donostia (Tabakalera, the International Contemporary Culture Centre), Vitoria-Gasteiz (Artium, the Basque Museum-Centre of Contemporary Art), and Bilbao (Guggenheim Museum Bilbao). While Donostia-San Sebastián has as an objective "that in 2013 the Tabakalera Center is triumphing as an international center of visual culture" (2006, 73), Bilbao significantly links its entire project to the Guggenheim Bilbao, and Vitoria-Gasteiz illustrates its institutional webpage "Vitoria-Gasteiz: City of Innovation" with an image of the Artium Museum.

Complexity of the City

A city is an ever more complex social organism, due not only to economic flows that increasingly escape all control, but also to increasingly global migratory movements and to the expanding social possibilities offered by the latest digital technologies and the routinization of access to digital networks: "A center that wants to relate sustainably to its surroundings should adopt an ecosystem-oriented attitude and not try to cover indiscriminately and monopolistically everything 'that moves' and could fall under the heading of culture" (Carrillo 2008).

It is appropriate to ask, as a result, to what extent these urban policies are capable of promoting a creative ecosystem and enriching the urban cultural fabric, as well as of providing a vehicle for social creativity, as they take action on the basis of infrastructures that, by vocation or by delegation from the institutions under whose umbrella they fall, tend toward monopolistic behavior and face difficulties in adapting to today's urban complexity.

Networked City

On the other hand, a large part of the knowledge and the artistic creation produced in cities today does not correspond to the canonical models of only a decade or two ago, when the institutional models now operating in cities were designed. How, then, should we approach all this intangible cultural production, of diffuse origin, in which the line between producers and consumers is unclear? How should we bring together those artistic practices that merge with the social and all the new ideas about the concept of culture in its more collective dimension?

If we add to this the consequences of the full-scale invasion of the city by new technologies, we find that "urban digital platforms are reheating a now-old debate about citizen participation, a concept that is as manipulated as it is important" (Freire 2009b, 18). In the same way, these technologies are reactivating ancient dynamics of collaboration and giving new meaning, by way of open-source software, to ideas such as liberty and autonomy. The new hybrid city that is emerging from the fusion of the classic metropolitan infrastructure and the integration of information-technology tools and networks into daily activities opens a space for new ways of organizing and distributing knowledge.

Nevertheless, at the same time that this flow of knowledge and new artistic practices entails an incredibly rich source of cultural common good for the benefit of all, the management of that commons is facing new restrictions. Restrictive intellectual-property policies are becoming a problem for the free circulation of knowledge and, as a result, for social creativity. For Emmanuel Rodríguez,

> intellectual-property and industrial-property legislation plays a crucial and perhaps irreplaceable role, insofar as it enables businesses to take ownership of continuing and complex processes, and moreover, of pro-cesses that extend into the future. Ownership of a product or process of innovation is similar to holding shares in an entire field of possibilities, that is, a kind of monopoly over a fragment of the future, over which they will have not only significant control, but also an entire monopoly in terms of economic profitability. (2007, 204)

In the same context and for similar reasons, the traditional concept of authorship, focused on the individual of genius, is also being questioned, and all intellectual-property policies that stem from this way of thinking are tending to become obstacles to creativity. With the excuse of protect-ing artistic production and one very specific type of author, restrictive management of intellectual property is becoming a method for busi-nesses and cultural institutions to set up barricades around what is public and appropriate for themselves what should be common. This too can be blamed more than on anything else, in many cases, on museums that under the pretext of acting as custodians of everyone's shared heritage, subsidized with public funds, block many "uses" of this heritage, to the detriment of a truly open and free common good. As a result, a flexible intellectual-property policy and an active sense of responsibility for pro-tecting and enriching the public domain are desirable, understanding the public domain as the source from which collective culture progressively draws nourishment and to which the entire community contributes to a greater or lesser extent. In this sphere—that of the public domain and of the kinds of knowledge that are common to all—"Copyleft," which in other areas may be proposed as "an" option, should be established as "the" option, precisely because it is directed at the enrichment of the common good and because it takes into account the rights of creators, and also those of users, at the same time that it proposes more open ways of distributing and accessing artistic creation.

Artists as a Source of Innovation

Finally, amid the debate on the possibility of innovation in art and the chiefly semantic consequences of the different combinations of the two terms, art and innovation (innovative art, innovation in art, innovating through art, and so on), it is indeed pertinent to talk about the possibility of innovating in art. This is possible, moreover, on the margins of the market, moving beyond the idea of novelty on which it continually feeds. If creativity and innovation are sources of value in almost any sphere of the contemporary city, the collective of artists—whose primary raw material is creativity—can be an inexhaustible source of creativity and innovative thinking for society's benefit. Nevertheless, the integration of artists into working groups and decision-making at the municipal level should not necessarily bring with it the umpteenth turn of the screw in the aestheticization of the city and politics, as Walter Benjamin (1968) warned. Entirely to the contrary, it should serve to definitively install creativity and innovative thinking in its more social aspect as part of the contemporary city's design.

It is possible to innovate in art, if we believe that artistic practices today cannot be differentiated from their context and that it is in this dialogue with their context that their ability to make a difference resides. This capacity for social innovation, in addition, will be greater to the extent that it succeeds in distancing itself from the market and the economic macrosystem (the case of the innovation-oriented readings of a phenomenon like the Guggenheim Bilbao) and orienting itself toward the framework of the social and the collective, where the added value of artistic projects is not exclusively economic. Innovation in the system of contemporary artistic production goes beyond the paired terms of discourse and artistic forms and affects the entire system of production, diffusion, and access. In other words, innovation in the field of art is possible, and its benefits are quantifiable not only in the meta-artistic space, but also in other social arenas, leading me to believe that, as Pau Alsina proposes, "Cultural innovation should be linked to investment in research, instead of to processes that lead to turning culture into spectacle. That is, it should be seen as investment in something that generates benefits over the long term, instead of thinking in the short term" (quoted in YProductions 2008, 90–91).

The great majority of the cultural projects we now have were envisioned in economically favorable times. Even the Guggenheim Bilbao, although it was not exactly designed in the context of an economic boom, did fit comfortably into a scenario with abundant economic resources, as has been the case until now. If we consider the cultural model that we have is a consequence of that economic model, which now urgently needs to be abandoned, we also need to think about recovering the idea of sustainability for art and culture as well. In times when "changing the economic model" is on everyone's lips as the only solution for getting out of a crisis, it might be useful to talk about "changing the cultural model" as well.

References

AAVC (Associació d'Artistes Visuals de Catalunya). 2006. *La dimensión económica de las Artes Visuales en España*. Barcelona.

Benjamin, Walter. 1968. "The Work of Art in the Age of Mechanical Reproduction." In *Illuminations: Essays and Reflections*, edited and with an introduction by Hannah Arendt. Translated by Harry Zohn. New York: Schocken Books.

Bilbao Guggenheim Shanghai World Expo 2010. 2010. *Bilbao en Expo Shanghai 2010: Una oportunidad para las empresas*. Bilbao: Promobisa.

Carrillo, Jesús. 2008. "Reflexiones y propuestas sobre los nuevos centros de creación contemporánea." Lecture, Laboratorio del Procomún, Medialab-Prado, Madrid, February 21.

Donostia-San Sebastián. 2006. *Plan Estratégico*. Donostia-San Sebastián: N.P.

Echeverría, Javier. 2008. "El Manual de Oslo y la innovación social." *Arbor: Ciencia, Pensamiento y Cultura* 184, no. 732 (July–August): 609–18.

Esteban, Iñaki. 2007. *El efecto Guggenheim*. Barcelona: Anagrama.

Freire, Juan. 2009a. "Ideas sobre los entornos para la creatividad y la innovación." Paper presented at the conference "Ciudades Creativas en la Sociedad de la Imaginación," Cáceres, November 12–14.

———. 2009b. "Urbanismo emergente: ciudad, tecnología e innovación social / Emerging Urban Planning: City, Technology and Social Innovation." *Paisajes Domésticos / Domestic Landscapes* 4: 18–27.

Rodríguez, Emmanuel. 2007. "La Riqueza y la Ciudad." In *Producta50: una introducción a algunas de las relaciones entre la cultura y la economía*, edited by YProductions. Barcelona: CASM.

Sotelo Navalpotro, José Antonio, and María Sotelo Pérez. 2010. "Los imaginarios urbanos (una visión sintética desde el medio ambiente): El trabajo de campo." *Apuntes de Medio Ambiente* 10 (February): 15–16 and 25.

Tellitu, Alberto and Iñaki Esteban. 1997. *El milagro Guggenheim. Una ilusión de alto riesgo*. Bilbao: Ed. Diario El Correo.

Vitoria-Gasteiz website. At www.vitoria-gasteiz.org/we001/was/we001Action.do?idioma=en&nuevaPag=&uid=6e611b5e_12157645218__7f ab&aplicacion=wb021&id=&tabla=contenido.

VV.AA. 2007. *Aprendiendo del Guggenheim Bilbao*. Ed. Guasch Anna María and Zulaika Joseba. Barcelona: Akal.

YProductions. 2008. *Innovación en cultura. Una introducción crítica a la genealogía y usos del concepto*. Madrid: Traficantes de Sueños.

———, eds. 2007. *Producta50: una introducción a algunas de las relaciones entre la cultura y la economía*. Barcelona: CASM.

ZEMOS98, eds. 2005. Creación e Inteligencia Colectiva, Asociación Cultural Comenzemos Empezemos. Sevilla.

Zulaika, Joseba. 2001. "Los centros de arte como revitalizadores del tejido urbano." *Inventario*. Special Edition, no. 7: 67–78.

9

Ikastolas as a Social Innovation Phenomenon: A Case Study

Marce Masa

Translated by Robert Forstag

Ikastolas are schools that provide comprehensive instruction in Euskara, the Basque language. My central contention in this chapter is that these schools meet one of the definitions of social innovation proposed by the Young Foundation (2006). It was on the basis of this definition that Javier Echeverría (2010) devised a framework for carrying out applied studies (or case studies). Within the context of this "restricted perspective" of social innovation phenomena, the history of Ikastolas has until the present time made it possible to draw a number of important conclusions: The movement to promote these schools emerged among specific segments of the civil society (specifically, within the "third sector"). Its values, underlying motivations, and objectives within a socio-structural context perceived as unsatisfactory place it fundamentally within the social realm. Within this axiological code lies one of its primary innovations—namely the search for a place within the dualistic private-public educational structure. And finally, a new reading of its six decades of history is now possible—one that identifies three basic stages of the entire process of social innovation: invention, implementation, and diffusion.

The choice of Ikastolas as an object of study is due to my interest in the analytical capacity and the interpretive limitations of the public-private dichotomy within an analysis of the daily reality of the Basque Country (Masa 1999, 2000). Ikastolas are a clear example of the limitations of the public-private duality, as it has been conceived in recent times (Unceta and Masa 2010).

The New "Social Tendency" in Studies of Innovation

Innovation is emblematic of modern societies, which are ipso facto societies of knowledge and innovation. The logic of this triumph is based on the elective affinity—in the sense used by Max Weber, following Goethe (Howe 1978; González García 1992)—that exists between knowledge and innovation, on the one hand, and wealth and quality of life (or well-being) on the other.

One result of the innovation imperative is an amplification of its meanings (Godin 2008), and this process of extending the definition of the term has both advantages and disadvantages. With respect to the latter, innovation may become a controversial concept that "gives everyone the impression that they are talking about the same thing, when in fact they are referring to different phenomena" (Albornoz 2009, 10). On the other hand, one of the advantages has to do with the recent "social tendency" (Echeverria 2008a, 82; 2008b, 611; and 2010) in studies of innovation. This is a term that represents an effort to move beyond the Joseph Schumpeter's economism model and its interpretation. This model of innovation focuses on businesses as vehicles of innovation, given that they are the organizations that are capable of applying inventions that are typically generated on the scientific and technical plane and that, in doing so, contribute value (albeit solely on the basis of economic motivations).

This model, which focuses on improving the competitive position of companies, has until now been dominant in the development and promotion of institutional innovation policies. There are, however, some exceptions. The British government, for example, has promoted new forms of nonentrepreneurial innovation in bodies such as NESTA (the National Endowment for Science, Technology and Arts) and the Young Foundation, on the basis of its premise that "social innovation refers to new ideas that work in meeting social goals" (Young Foundation 2006, 11).

The Restricted Perspective of Social Innovation: Opening a Line of Investigation

The British perspective has reinforced the revaluation of the social character of innovative phenomena and has also, to a certain point, allowed a repositioning of the principal role of the social sciences within this field—

namely in terms of a consideration of whether certain innovations not only arise, but then subsequently succeed. In other words, the question is whether and how a given innovation comes to plant deep roots within a particular social context, or among some of the social agents within that context. Fernand Braudel captured the spirit of this scientific-social context when he wrote that, "Every invention that presents itself has to wait years or even centuries before being introduced into real life. First comes the invention and then, very much later the application, society having attained the required degree of receptivity" (1992, 335).

Embracing the idea that a broad-based notion of innovation (Gurrutxaga 2010, 336) is fitting and proper for a social science, this social understanding of innovation leads to certain interesting reflections regarding theoretical and methodological effectiveness. Society, in the general sense, cannot be conceived as merely a passive receptacle of innovations by entrepreneurial agents. Instead, societies themselves (along with their component agents) are themselves capable of innovation mechanisms in accordance with their specific axiological assumptions (Von Hippel 2005). We therefore run the risk of entering into an infinite spiral of trying to discover hidden innovation. Such a broad perspective leads us to address critical issues, especially when the silent or hidden social processes have had a high explanatory value throughout history (Braudel 1958). It might even require a rethinking of the definition of what is actually "social," since by limiting its "scope," it also limits the "scope" of the term "social innovation" itself.

In a way, it is paradoxical that after a period during which the social conception of the idea of innovation dominated, a new problem emerged: that of demarcating the very concept of social innovation and, along with it, the wide variety of studies involved in such an enterprise. In fact, the Young Foundation itself (2006, 18) maintains that individuals, social movements, and organizations all have the capacity to be socially innovative agents, a broad-based viewpoint that is also reflected in NESTA's most recent declaration (Murray, Caulier-Grice, and Mulgan 2010).

It may be that this "wider perspective" is more suggestive, but I agree with Echeverría (2008b, 617; 2010) that if the goal is to consolidate a line of investigation in the area of social innovation, it is best to specify exactly what the term means, as well as the scope of what it entails. This is how what might be called a "restricted perspective" (or "demarcated perspective") of social innovation arose. This represents the choice of lines of analysis already embraced by the third edition of the *Oslo Manual*. Here it states that even though innovation might be present in many different sectors of a society (for example, public services, health, and education), the authors make a conscious choice to concentrate solely on "innovation in the business and enterprise sector" (OECD/Eurostat 2005, 7–8).

This restricted perspective is based upon an interpretation of contributions by NESTA and the Young Foundation. Even though they both extend the authority to carry out innovation to a variety of agents (and therefore to a variety of values, motivations, and purposes that channel innovative action), Echeverría proposes concentrating on the "third sector" (social movements, nongovernmental organizations, associations, etc.), or on more or less structured social frameworks within civil society (Echeverría 2008a, 88). This demarcation was instituted on the basis of the Young Foundation's definition of social innovation (2006, 11) as "innovative activities and services that are motivated by the goal of meeting a social need and that are predominantly developed and diffused through organisations whose primary purposes are social."

This is the "turn toward the social" or "social tendency" that has become common in studies of innovation. Thus, while "companies are the key agents of business innovation (just as governments and administrations are, in the case of innovation in the public sector) . . . there are other kinds of social agents that also generate innovation, even though such innovation is neither political nor profitable, but instead meets and satisfies needs that are social in nature" (Echeverría 2008a, 89). Clearly, this perspective displays a preference for a "bottom-up" rather than a "top-down" model, given that the sources of innovation are seen as not being limited exclusively to the political, economic, scientific, and technological bodies where decisions are made, but also within the moderately formalized frameworks of civil society.

Social innovation processes in the third sector—or, in a social scenario that is removed from the logical process of what might be termed either public (the state) or private (the market)—present two important characteristics. First, nonentrepreneurial social agents try to implement innovative practices and strategies for the purpose of resolving social questions that they themselves perceive as unsatisfactory in terms of the realities of daily life (Gurrutxaga 2010, 16). That is why there is a certain measure of uneasiness and discontent inherent in these social innovation phenomena that are catalysts at both the conceptual and practical levels (Young Foundation 2006, 12).

In addition, in most instances, social innovation does not represent a fixed strategy that has been determined in advance, since "innovation does not always aim at 'achieving something,' but rather takes place as a result of improvisation or because 'it works'" (Gurrutxaga 2009, 72). The role played by uncertainty and chance in innovation processes represents a long and winding road rather than a straight line (Rogers 1995). Ander Gurrutxaga has addressed this issue, and he maintains that it is necessary to rethink the nature of change and innovation (2007, 2010; Gurrutxaga and Unceta 2007, 2008).

Finally, and in accordance with the logic of basing a line of research on this restricted perspective, Echeverría proposes a schema of three phases that represent the minimum number of steps that any social innovation process has to traverse whenever it occurs within the third sector: invention, development or implementation of the original proposal, and the social diffusion of the innovations in various arenas. As Echeverría explains (2010, 4):

> Social innovation processes also have a minimum of three phases. The first involves the emergence of a novel idea, the invention, which requires social creativity in a way analogous to that of technological or artistic invention. . . . But ideas in themselves are not enough. They have to be implemented, in other words developed, in the form of proposals that are able to address concrete problems. Finally, the social diffusion of these ideas is necessary, and this is the task that often proves to be the most complicated of all. . . . For a social innovation to succeed, it needs to go through three phases. Nice ideas are not enough.

In sum, it would appear that the specific label attached to innovation depends not only on the character of the agent who puts it into practice, but on the values, purposes, and axiological code that guide the actions of those who carry it out. In Weberian terms (Weber 1978, 18), one can speak of social innovation when the agents who carry it out are considered social in the sense that the underlying rationale of their activity is not primarily economic. Instead, the rationale should be determined by values—in this case, social values—without losing sight of the analytical character or ideal aspect of this differentiation of values.

This chapter attempts to consolidate a line of applied studies regarding social innovation on the basis of this restricted perspective. I believe it is possible, by means of a case study, to reread Ikastolas as paradigmatic instance of social innovation, not only in terms of their origins, values, and purpose, but also in terms of the strategies they have implemented in order to assure their survival until the present time.

The Ikastolas: Reconstruction of the Key Aspects of a Paradigmatic Process of Social Innovation

I am aware of the fact that I am leaving out a number of important issues in the present discussion of the Ikastolas. Some of these issues have been addressed in previous works regarding these schools. Many others— perhaps the most important—may be found not only in these works but also, and most importantly, in the recollections of those who personally experienced and were a part of (Ferrarotti 1986) this socially innovative movement.

As Max Weber pointed out, this kind of selectivity is the prerogative of social science (1978, 4)—a discipline in which, to a large extent, social facts are placed in the service of an analytical model. In this particular instance, such a procedure may lead to an interpretation of a phenomenon that is more complex, because Ikastolas transcend the frontiers of the merely educational and linguistic (Gurrutxaga 1985, 264; Unceta 2003, 327). In other words, they have come to be conceived as a "total social fact" (Mauss 1999)—a multidimensional reality (Arpal, Asua, and Dávila 1982).

One should also underscore the fact that this approach to the Ikastolas has not been made within the context of educational innovation. There is a vast bibliography regarding the variety of ways in which educational innovation is manifested (de Haro 2009, 72): technologically, the particular educational levels in which it is applied, and the various institutional settings in the different countries or regions where it occurs (Smith 1986; García 1996; Hannan and Silver 2000; Fidalgo 2009). I will not be discussing the Ikastolas from this perspective, but rather from a point of view in which educational aspects are conceived within a larger social context, given that this movement's innovations are social rather than educational.

The Ikastola phenomenon may be considered a paradigmatic example of the concept of social innovation for the following reasons: It arose within civil society; it has promoted a social meaning of Euskara that differs from how it was previously perceived; it constitutes a response on the part of citizens to a demand that had not been satisfied within the prevailing social and political context (teaching the younger generation the Basque language—and teaching them *in* Euskara); it has motivations, purposes, and values that are inherently social in nature (specifically, within the educational or socializing context, in its broadest sense); and, finally and most importantly, because of its innovative nature in the sense that it constitutes a challenge to or a reconsideration of the public-private educational dichotomy, and instead proposes a tripartite educational division: public, private, and social/popular.

A Challenge to the Public-Private Dichotomy: Toward a Third Educational Space

Analyses of Ikastolas typically characterize them as constituting a "movement" (Arpal, Arsua, and Dávila 1982, 45; Basurco 1989, 139; Onaindia 1994, 11; Fernández 1994, 99; Dávila Balsera 2003, 33). The term "movement" refers to all of those social practices that emerge within a local setting that transcend the public-private dichotomy. Accordingly, there is a social or even "popular" scenario in which there exists a set of practices and strategies "alongside" (Maffesoli 1996, 86–87) public and private activity. The importance of these practices and strategies within the structure of daily life is abundantly clear (Agamben 1996; Masa 2000).

It is within this alternative scenario, which is usually understood within the context of civil society, where the social or popular movement of the Ikastolas is to be found. But what is innovative about this movement is not merely its location, but rather the fact that this third sector institution by its very nature and founding principles challenges the public-private dichotomy (Remy 1973) or tandem (Flaquer 1984) that is typically characteristic of education.

The public-private dichotomy is very important in all of the aspects of social life in Western cultures (Arendt 1998; Masa 1999). On a strictly educational level, the nation-state initially imposed this dichotomy through its creation of public school systems (Archer 1979; Boli, Ramirez, and Meyer 1985) as a means of guaranteeing citizens access to basic education. The fact that education was embraced as something of a strategic concern by the nation-state implied that nonpublic education was ipso facto private in nature. The nation-state's successful intervention in this regard has endowed the current differentiation between public and private education with its modern meaning. This differentiation represents a reorganization (and therefore a redefinition) of structures and practices that had in fact already been in existence (Lerena 1983).

The kind of innovation represented by the Ikastola movement is the search for a place within this dichotomous logic, and it is for this reason that some authors have premised their analyses on the "claiming of a third educational space" (Unceta 2003, 343), or on its status as an "educational alternative" (López-Goñi 2003). In what follows, I will reflect on the history of Ikastolas in terms of this social innovation (its search for a place in the public-private structure of education). For this purpose, I will rely in large measure on Echeverría's aforementioned three-phase schema (Echeverría 2010).

How it Began (the Inventive Phase): A Response to Unsatisfactory Social Circumstances

Any innovative action naturally flows from a concrete interpretation of the social reality. The following extract produced by the Confederation of Ikastolas (Ikastolen Elkartea)—the result of internal reflection on the proposed content of the forthcoming Law of Basque Public Schools (1993)—reflects in paradigmatic fashion the new understanding of the prevailing context of dissatisfaction that led to the birth of the Ikastolas:

> Ikastolas were created as a result of a *popular initiative*, given the fact that the alternatives (whether private or public) that were previously available *did not meet the needs and demands* of an important sector of individuals and groups, and of the collectivity of the Basque people as a whole—a people that had considered Euskara to be an essential component of its identity. At that time, schools were instruments of acculturation and colonization. The Ikastola was thus created as an educational alternative that included those components that fundamentally define a people—namely, their language and culture. (Euskal Herriko Ikastolen Elkartea 1988, 7)

As is the case with any instance of social innovation, it is difficult to identify the precise moment of creation, since it is always possible to cite antecedents—in this case, the *etxe eskolak* (home schools) created in Donostia-San Sebastián in 1946, spearheaded by Elbira Zipitria (Dávila Balsera 2003, 33). Similarly, there is territorial and regional variation, and (as is to be expected) different applications among specific schools within the Ikastola phenomenon. Nevertheless, one can still say in general terms this social movement emerged in the early 1960s due to the widespread dissatisfaction with the prevailing social structure among certain sectors of the Basque population (Giddens 1984). This social discontent, which contributed to the creation of an intersubjective framework of social relationships, production mechanisms, and social reproduction (Pérez-Agote 1984, 1987) in the strictly educational sphere, came to form "the most innovative sociolinguistic movement in the history of the Basque nation" (Onaindia 1994, 11).

This dissatisfaction with the shape that education was taking in the Basque Country as a result of the initiatives of the Franco dictatorship—a dissatisfaction that also encompassed the internal weaknesses of the system (specifically, the inadequate operating budget foisted upon the system by the educational policy of the regime)—led not only to the creation of the Ikastola movement, but to the particular characteristics of the Basque educational system as a whole that have endured until the present time. In the words of Alfonso Unceta:

> The Basque educational system has characteristics that place it beyond the public-private dichotomy. The strong presence of religious orders, together with the fact that the Ikastola movement emerged and developed during the second half of the twentieth century, at a time when Franco's regime (and therefore a particular public manifestation of the nation-state—the national schools) lacked legitimacy, are crucial factors to understanding the importance of private initiative in education, as well as its role in the specific form that the educational system took on later during the current period of autonomy. (2003, 117)

Stages of Implementation

The invention of this system was followed by the most distinctive stage of any innovative process: its implementation. The conviction that accompanied the initial idea—namely, that innovation was considered necessary in the face of the urgent need to respond to the demands of the environment in a new and creative way—in some ways logically follows from the characteristics, conditions, and limitations of the socio-structural context in which it arose. As part of this clash with the prevailing reality, conflicts arise within any movement or organization, as debates take shape regarding the right way to translate innovative proposals into the daily life that one seeks to transform, without vitiating their spirit.

Most of the existing literature characterizing the development of the Ikastola movement in terms of distinct stages is often somewhat outdated, given that it tends to focus only on a specific period of its development, most particularly its initial development within a democratic context (Arpal, Asua, and Dávila 1982, 45; Basurco 1989, 143). But the Ikastola movement has existed since the 1960s—and since the 1980s within the context of a democratic system. Taking this into account, and on the basis of the primary innovative element of the Ikastolas being its challenge to the public private dichotomy in education so reflective of modernity, I would distinguish four principal stages that together comprise what can be thought of as the institutionalization process of the Ikastolas.

Beyond the Public-Private Dichotomy in Education

Félix Basurco has written that improvisation, the precariousness of resources, self-administration, and self-financing were the primary characteristics of the movement during its initial phase (1989, 145). During that time, the movement received important support from the church (Gurrutxaga X. 1987, 87; Onaindia 1994, 11), and also drew on its own strategic platform (Unceta 2003, 297) in order to implement the idea of innovation beyond the public-state framework imposed by the Franco regime. The idea was to establish an educational space through the intensive creation of schools, attracting both students and faculty at the beginning of the process, and by instituting organizational structures afterward (throughout the 1960s and early 1970s).

Originally, the innovative Ikastola movement was based on individual and group commitment and activism as a means of addressing the urgent educational demands of the population for education in Euskara. This implied a de-emphasis on the equally important need to articulate a common organizational strategy that transcended each particular school and locale. Yet the organizational dimension of the Ikastola movement gradually took on increasingly greater importance. The movement looked to Catalonia for inspiration in this regard, and exchange and summer school programs were initiated. It was also during this stage that roles were increasingly differentiated within the Ikastolas, with parents expected to provide the educational means and teachers responsible for providing instruction. A certain amount of tension arose as a result of this division of labor. Finally, in 1969 the Federation of Ikastolas of Gipuzkoa and the French Basque Country were established, followed by those of Araba (1974), Navarre (1976), and Bizkaia (1977).

Initial Integration into the Public-Private Conceptualization of Education: The General Education Law and Its Definition of "Nonstate Public Schools"

Various different readings of the educational process in the Spanish state are in agreement in concluding that its institutionalization was not formalized until the enactment of the General Law on Education and Financing, which formed part of the 1970 educational reforms (Viñao Frago 1982;

de Puelles 1999). The "Villar Palasí" law helped modernize the Spanish educational system, where the differentiation between public and private instruction had historically played a central role. This law also had a profound effect on the Ikastola movement, in that the state regulatory framework now made it possible to (among other things) significantly improve the facilities of schools already in existence and to create additional schools. Having said that, there was internal debate within the Ikastola movement over whether it was worth attempting to join the public-private educational structure.

This initial integration of the Ikastola movement into the public-private framework of education set the stage for what could be considered one of the most important events in its history: the full recognition on the part of the Spanish state of Ikastolas during the transition to democracy. Following the pattern of the teaching system that had been instituted in Catalonia the previous year, the Ministry of Education's Royal Decree 1049/1979 of April 20 (which regulates the incorporation of the Basque language into educational institutions in the Basque Country) the Ikastolas were recognized as "nonstate public schools." They have since that time served as centers of reference for the study of Euskara, a status that brings with it specific financing, and which was gradually acquired through "regulations regarding the official status of Ikastolas."[1]

Within the logic of the public-private dichotomy, the designation "nonstate public schools" is worth examining in more detail. In terms of legal regulations, this designation reflects a social reality that took shape in the Basque Country during the final twenty years of Franco's dictatorship: a movement capable of establishing effective educational strategies (through its schools) that was outside of both the public (state) and private (religious, entrepreneurial) framework, and that was rooted in specific sectors of the population or of civil society. In this sense, it was actually public in the sense that it was part of daily life and of the people's common experience: in a word, "popular," in the root sense of the term meaning "of the people."

Second Integration into the Public-Private Logic of Education: The Law on Basque Public Schools

This initial public recognition of Ikastolas involved a gradual integration of the movement into the public-private framework of the prevailing edu-

---

1. *Boletín Oficial del País Vasco*, January 24, 1980.

cational system. In the early days of the transition to democracy in Spain, Ikastolas were left to occupy a "third educational space" that was neither public nor private, but this laissez faire attitude had a strategic objective: to supply elements that would facilitate the construction of a new postdictatorship educational system, not only for the new Spanish state, but for the new Comunidad Autónoma del País Vasco/Euskal Autonomia Erkidegoa (CAPV/EAE, Autonomous Community of the Basque Country).

There was a variety of institutional activity in this regard during the early phase of the CAPV/EAE: For example, decision-making authority in educational matters was transferred from the central state to the CAPV/EAE,[2] and an official registry of Ikastolas was created in 1980, in line with the wishes of the Basque government. Similarly, law 15/1983 of July 27 created the Euskal Ikastolen Erakundea (the Basque Institute of Ikastolas), and a legal status for Ikastolas was likewise approved. Finally, constitutional law 9/1985 of July 3, regulating the right to education, was also important as part of this wider process. This process involved above all the general transfer of a significant number of Ikastola students to public schools that were better equipped (but less crowded in terms of student enrollment). It took place especially in Gipuzkoa during the early 1980s, and in effect constituted a move toward incorporating Ikastolas into the public sphere, for while they did not disappear, their role was now strictly limited to primary education.

These changes, in turn, led to another important development in the process of integrating Ikastolas into the public-private educational schema: the Basque Public School Law 1/1993 of February 19. This incorporation of the Ikastolas into the public sphere would thus appear to be the logical outcome of a progressively implemented integration process that began with the creation of the new democratic and autonomous structure of the Spanish state.

The impact on the Ikastolas of gradually coming to terms with the public education system, where the security provided by a public institutional framework (Dávila Legeren 2003) once again assumed great importance, was significant, especially given their precarious economic condition (Mateos González 2000, 103). During a period of a little more than ten years, then, the institutionalization of the Basque autonomous public administration gradually took shape. In educational matters, this

---

2. Royal Decree 2808/1980, September 26.

perhaps represented an opportunity to assert public authority and put an end to the Ikastolas' anomalous situation. After all, despite enjoying public financing, in practice they continued to constitute a third educational space in a manner consistent with the way that the movement had consistently identified itself.

The strategies and intentions behind the Basque Public School Law were set against a highly complex backdrop: Given the number of actors involved, it was in fact a far more nuanced picture than it may appear from this descriptive summary. Be that as it may, this moment represented an opportunity to resolve the ambiguity (Mateos González 2000, 90) inherent in the public-private-social (or "popular") triad that had been effectively embraced by the Ikastola movement for the previous thirty years and to replace that schema, for all practical purposes, with the public-private duality of an educational system representing the new structure of the CAPV/EAE (as well as being consistent with parallel developments in all modern states). This development also seemed to transcend the apparently irreconcilable differences between political adversaries (nationalists and constitutionalists) regarding the place of the Ikastolas. Both of these tendencies were represented in the Basque government at that time.

Consolidating Its Status as an Educational Service Provider: Prioritizing Innovation Beyond the Public/Private Dichotomy

The Basque Public School Law represents a turning point in the Ikastolas' history. I would contend that the Ikastola movement has, since the law was passed, embraced in varying degrees the public-private dichotomy in the structure of the Basque autonomous educational system that constitutes the law's framework. Yet this assumption by no means implies the disappearance of a structural characteristic of the movement that has always constituted one of its distinctive and innovative features. In fact, the Ikastola movement continues to carry out its activities in a way that transcends the logic of the public-private dichotomy—or perhaps that even utilizes it—as a means of evolving a system that is more closely tied to or rooted in social and community participation. But the question of creating its own or a "third" space tied to legal regulations within its specific social context, and the accompanying political and ideological affinities that form the substratum of Basque society, seem to have been relegated to secondary importance in terms of the day-to-day functioning of the Ikastola movement.

It would now seem that the Ikastola movement is more concerned with conceiving educational innovation as an aspect of social innovation. Thus, since the enactment of the Basque Public School law, Ikastolas have tended to emphasize their role as "pedagogical services" agencies. By this, they mean that every Ikastola offers a complete educational, learning, and support structure as part of its general educational mission, whether related to instruction and learning or more general support processes. These supportive elements include internal and external communication, legal-economic stability, and administration in the broadest sense (Euskal Herriko Ikastolen Elkartea 2009).

During the Third National Conference of Ikastolas (1996), held approximately three years after the Basque Public School Law entered into force, the change in strategic priorities reflected by the placing of primary emphasis on the educational function of the movement was evident in the following statement, which refers to the years 1992–94, when the Basque Public School Law was being formulated:

> Although what was achieved during these years has been immensely productive, these achievements have been obscured because of economic, administrative, and legal problems. The Ikastola Federations have now adopted as a common principal function the implementation of activities within the field of education. . . . The Confederation of Ikastolas must focus on carrying out high-quality work that is part of the *Euskaldun* [Basque-speaking] project, not only on behalf of the Ikastolas of each territory, but also on behalf of other Ikastolas, as well as of other schools that, while not Ikastolas, want to be considered Basque schools. (Euskal Herriko Ikastolen Elkartea 1997, 17)

This new orientation represents a "reinforcement" of the educational/pedagogical dimension that had been present ever since the Ikastola movement was first conceived. In fact, during the 1960s and 1970s, "during a time of marked institutional stagnation, Ikastolas represented places where experimentation in new organizational and pedagogical forms was happening, and where new functional models were being defined. This is a dimension that has most strongly reinforced the social aspect of the movement, which is perceived as a vehicle of a new system of rules, pedagogical procedures, and cultural content" (Unceta 2003, 340). Jesús Arpal, Begoña Asua, and Pauli Dávila had long before expressed a similar point of view when they said, "The Ikastola has involved the practice . . . of improvising, transferring, and *innovating* within the context of modern education, with its bureaucracy, state structures, and specifically defined functions" (1982, 49).

In 1960, a publication unit was formed that would eventually become Saioka, the publishing company responsible for Ikastola-related material. However, Xabier Garagorri was mainly responsible for the innovative character of the learning materials and processes of the Ikastolas. Through his input, and within the context of the growing influence of the Gipuzkoan Federation of Ikastolas during the 1980s, a more professional working environment was generated within the Ikastolas. The Confederation of Ikastolas (Ikastolen Elkartea), created in 1987, helped impart the new "pedagogical services" philosophy to other federations and centers throughout the Basque Country. This philosophy constitutes an "Ikastola educational model" (Unceta and Masa 2010) that requires a close connection, in terms of both content and methodology, between what each Ikastola needs, on the one hand, and the educational service that the movement as a whole (through the separate federations or through the Confederation of Ikastolas) is able to offer it, on the other (Euskal Herriko Ikastolen Elkartea 1999).

The Specific Means of Social Diffusion

In this instance, it is not easy to differentiate between (following Echeverría's model) the implementation phase (phase 2) and the diffusion phase (phase 3), because these two processes overlap in the history of the Ikastolas.

Be that as it may, it is possible to distinguish at least three kinds (or fields) of social diffusion: the specific importance (in strictly educational terms) that Ikastolas have assumed; the external diffusion of the Ikastola model to other educational and pedagogical agents; and a more qualitative diffusion (that perhaps most closely resembles "social diffusion" in the strict sense of the term). Yet the Ikastola case also appears to involve a fourth kind of diffusion that is internal in character. I have hinted at this above but am unable to explore it in more detail due to the lack of important and primary sources, especially regarding the present situation.

Beginning with the first kind of social diffusion, the specific influence of the Ikastola phenomenon historically, from a strictly educational point of view, is obvious. Arrien (1992, 225) points out that, between 1960 and 1975, 144 Ikastolas were founded in Araba, Gipuzkoa, Bizkaia, and Navarre as a result of the combination of efforts of the organized movement and the General Law on Education. During the 1983–84 academic year (the first for which Eustat, the Basque Institute of Statistics has official data) 65,151 students were enrolled in Ikastolas in the CAPV/EAE, a figure that represented 12.3 percent of the total number of students enrolled, and 33 percent of students enrolled in private schools. Thereafter, during the academic year just prior to incorporation into the public sphere (1992–93), 65,808 students were enrolled, which represented 15.1 percent of total students enrolled and 39 percent of students enrolled in private schools.

The impact of the process of incorporation into the public sphere following implementation of the Basque Public School Law in 1993 was unquestionably very important. Of the 105 schools in the Confederation of Ikastolas during the 1992–93 academic year in Araba, Bizkaia, and Gipuzkoa, 54 were incorporated into the public sphere. This meant that slightly more than half of the schools ceased to be a formal part of the Ikastola organization. Nevertheless, from that time until the present, the number of schools affiliated with the Confederation of Ikastolas has remained steady. As of the academic year 2009–10, a total of fifty-eight Ikastolas were affiliated with the confederation in the CAPV/EAE: eight in Araba, twenty-two in Bizkaia, and twenty-eight in Gipuzkoa. This translates into a total of 3,320 teachers and 39,186 students, or almost 11 percent of students enrolled in all of the CAPV/EAE (359,203) during this same academic year. These percentages are not significantly less than those cited above for the academic years 1983–84 and 1992–93.

The persistence and vitality of the movement in recent years is even more evident if one takes into account the entire sphere of activity of the Confederation of Ikastolas, and not only its functioning within the CAPV/EAE. Thus, as a whole, the confederation comprises a total of one hundred schools: the fifty-eight in Araba, Bizkaia, and Gipuzkoa indicated above, plus fifteen in the Federation of Ikastolas of Navarre and twenty-seven in the Federation of Ikastolas of the Northern Basque Country (Seaska). These numbers translate into approximate totals of 48,146 students and 3,500 teachers. There is no question as to the success of the social diffusion of this innovative phenomenon, its importance, and its comprehensive integration into the daily life of the Basque Country, irrespective of whether it is conceived as a public, private, or independent enterprise.

The transfer of knowledge with respect to the various educational innovations generated by the Ikastolas would constitute the second kind of social diffusion. This transfer took place in both public and private schools, and both within and outside of the Basque Country. The Ikastola educational model has continued to have an important impact, not only on other schools, but also on publishing companies and other groups linked to the extensive educational network. Efforts have been made to identify a set of good practices on the basis of the activities that have been carried out in the schools affiliated with the Confederation of Ikastolas, the body primarily responsible for promoting these diffusion activities. In this regard, one paradigmatic example seems to be the multidirectional character of the innovations, as opposed to the unidirectional approach dominant in educational circles, and in which innovations are expected to arise only from within businesses and to be promoted only through the institutional policies that sustain them.

I previously indicated that another of the arenas of social diffusion of the Ikastola phenomenon was more qualitative in nature and might perhaps most properly fall under the category of "social innovation," given that it is oriented toward residents of the Basque Country. Thus, even though the term "Ikastola" continues to be an important part of the people's lives there, its daily use may be growing more and more divorced from the symbolic value that has typically been attached to the Ikastola movement.

There are currently two uses of the term "Ikastola," and the different conceptualizations inherent in each of them would appear to merit more considered analysis. The first of these represents a "market use": an image that creates the a priori possibility of a more or less successful strategy in a market, such as that of Basque education that is undoubtedly competitive. An example of this, and apart from the regulatory obligations that were involved, is the fact that, in the process of their incorporation into the public sphere, some Ikastolas have continued to identify themselves as such, despite belonging to the public network (in which schools are typically termed an *ikastetxe* or *eskola*). Within the private network of schools some institutions call themselves Ikastolas even though they are not officially part of the movement.

The second use of the term "Ikastola" is centered more closely on time-honored common usage in the sense identified by Alfred Schutz (1973). Among some segments of the Basque population, what may be occurring is a confusion or melding of the terms "Ikastola" and "school" (*eskola*). Such a fusion of terms would, rather paradoxically, make some logical sense in terms of the etymology of the neologism Ikastola ("*ikas-ola*," meaning "place of study"). This specific kind of social diffusion of the term "Ikastola," which occurs on a daily basis, might also be seen as an indicator of the relative success of the public-private dichotomy of the educational system in the CAPV/EAE. In other words, part of the Basque population habitually uses the term "Ikastola" even when it is not, in a legal or historical sense, applicable to the school (whether public or private) being referred to. From a social standpoint, it is important for these collectives that students receive their schooling in a school generically referred to as an Ikastola precisely because it is located in the Basque Country ("Because here/there, we/they go to the Ikastola."). Thus, "going to the Ikastola" or "being part of the Ikastola" has a variety of meanings within the current context of the Basque Country, and in each of its current meanings incorporates the nearly univocal sense that was identified nearly thirty years ago by Arpal, Asua, and Dávila (1982, 44).

References

Agamben, Giorgio. 1996. "El pueblo y su doble." *Archipiélago* 24: 79–82.

Albornoz, Mario. 2009. "Indicadores de innovación: las dificultades de un concepto en evolución." *CTS. Revista iberoamericana de ciencia, tecnología y sociedad* 5, no. 13 (November): 9–25.

Archer, Margaret Scotford. 1979. *Social Origins of Educational Systems*. London: Sage.

Arendt, Hannah. 1998. *The Human Condition*. 2nd edition. Chicago: University of Chicago Press.

Arpal, Jesús, Begoña Asua, and Pauli Dávila. 1982. *Educación y Sociedad en el País Vasco*. Donostia-San Sebastián: Txertoa.

Arrien, Gregorio. 1992. *Las ikastolas de Bizkaia, 1957–1972: Sus orígenes y organización*. Donostia: Eusko Ikaskuntza.

Basurco, Félix. 1989. "La normalización de las ikastolas: breve historia y estado de la cuestión de la escuela pública vasca." In *Historia de la Educación. Revista Interuniversitaria* 8 (January–December): 139–165.

Boli, John, Francisco O. Ramírez, and John W. Meyer. 1985. "Explaining the Origins and Expansion of Mass Education." *Comparative Education Review* 29, no. 2: 145–170.

Braudel, Fernand. 1992. *Civilization and Capitalism: 15th–18h Century*. Volume 1. *The Structures of Everyday Life*. Translated and revised by

Siân Reynolds. Berkeley and Los Angeles: University of California Press.

———. 1958. "Histoire et sciences sociales: Le longue durée." *Annales: Histoire, Sciences Sociales* 13, no. 4 (October–December): 725–53.

Dávila Balsera, Paulí, coord. 2003. *Enseñanza y educación en el País Vasco contemporáneo.* Donostia-San Sebastián: Erein.

Dávila Legeren, Andrés. 2003. "Seguridad y sociedad ectópica. De la bonalización de la seguridad a la segurización implicada." Ph.D. diss., Universidad del País Vasco/Euskal Herriko Unibertsitatea, Leioa.

de Haro, José. 2009. "Algunas experiencias en innovación educativa." *Arbor* 185: 71–97.

de Puelles, Manuel. 1999. *Educación e ideología en la España contemporánea.* Madrid: Tecnos.

Echeverría, Javier. 2008a. "Aportaciones preliminares a los estudios de innovación social." In *Textos y pretextos para repensar lo social. Libro homenaje a Jesús Arpal,* edited by Ignacio Mendiola. Bilbao: UPV/EHU.

———. 2008b. "El manual de Oslo y la innovación social." *Arbor* 732: 609–618.

———. 2010. "Giro social en los estudios de innovación: el ejemplo del Reino Unido." Paper presented at the 8th Basque Conference on Sociology, Bilbao, February 10–12.

Euskal Herriko Ikastolen Elkartea. 1988. *La Ikastola. Carácter y estructura.* Zarautz: Euskal Herriko Ikastolen Elkartea.

———. 2009. *Las ikastolas, presente y future.* Report for the 6th Conference of Ikastolas.

———. 1997. "Ikastolen III. Batzarra." *Ikastola Aldizkaria* 62: 8.

———. 1999. *Sketch for the normalisation of ikastolas in the educational system.* Internal Document.

Fernández, Idoia. 1994. *Oroimenaren hitza. Ikastolen historia 1960–1975.* Bilbao: Udako Euskal Unibertsitatea.

Ferrarotti, Franco. 1986. *La storia e il quotidiano.* Rome: Laterza.

Fidalgo, Ángel. 2009. "¿Qué es la innovación educativa?" At innovacioneducativa.wordpress.com/2007/01/09/%C2%BFque-es-innovacioneducativa/.

Flaquer, Lluís. 1984. "Tres concepciones de la privacidad." *Sistema* 58: 31–44.

García, Carlos Marcelo, dir. 1996. *Innovación educativa, asesoramiento y desarrollo profesional.* Madrid: Ministerio de Educación y Ciencia.

Giddens, Anthony. 1984. *The Constitution of Society: Outline of the Theory of Structuration.* Berkeley: University of California Press.

Godin, Benoît. 2008. "Innovation: The History of a Category." Working Paper No. 1. *Project on the Intellectual History of Innovation,* Montreal: INRS.

González García, José María. 1992. *Las huellas de Fausto: La herencia de Goethe en la sociología de Max Weber.* Madrid: Tecnos.

Gurrutxaga, Ander. 1985. *El código nacionalista vasco durante el franquismo.* Barcelona: Anthropos.

———. 2007. "Cambio, innovación, complejidad y orden global." In *Retratos del presente: la sociedad del siglo XXI,* edited by Ander Gurrutxaga. Bilbao. UPV/EHU.

———. 2010. *Recorridos por el cambio, la innovación y la incertidumbre.* Bilbao: UPV/EHU.

———. 2009. "Recorridos por la innovación." En *¿Cómo es una sociedad innovadora?* Bilbao: Innobasque, Agencia Vasca de Innovación.

Gurrutxaga, Ander and Alfonso Unceta. 2007. "Hacia una historia comparada de la innovación: cambio, complejidad y globalización." *Revista de Historia Contemporánea* 32: 133–164.

———. 2008. "Innovación, incertidumbre y cambio social." In *Textos y pretextos para repensar lo social. Libro homenaje a Jesús Arpal,* edited by Ignacio Mendiola. Bilbao: UPV/EHU.

Gurrutxaga, Xabier. 1987. "La normalización de las ikastolas: una cuestión pendiente." *Cuadernos de Alzate* 6 (April-September): 83–103.

Hannan, Andrew and Harold Silver. 2000. *Innovating in Higher Education: Teaching, Learning, and Institutional Cultures.* Buckingham; Philadelphia, PA: Society for Research into Higher Education and the Open University Press.

Howe, Richard Herbert. 1978. "Max Weber's Elective Affinities: Sociology Within the Bounds of Pure Reason." *American Journal of Sociology* 84, no. 2: 366–85.

Lerena, Carlos. 1983. *Reprimir y liberar: Crítica sociológica de la educación y de la cultura contemporáneas.* Madrid: Akal.

López-Goñi, Irene. 2003. "Ikastola in the Twentieth Century: An Alternative for Schooling in the Basque Country." *History of Education* 32, no. 6: 661–676.

Maffesoli, Michel. 1996. *The Time of the Tribes: The Decline of Individualism in Mass Society.* Translated by Don Smith. London and Thousand Oaks, CA: Sage.

Masa, Marce. 2000. "Antes de la política: la estructuración de lo cotidiano en el País Vasco." *Inguruak. Revista Vasca de Sociología* 28 (December): 153–162.

———. 1999. "Privatización y socialidad. La estructuración de lo cotidiano en el País Vasco." Doctoral Thesis. UPV/EHU, Leioa.

Mateos González, Txoli. 2000. "Ikastola eta eskola publikoa euskal nazionalismoaren diskurtsoan." *Inguruak* 26, no. 3: 85–103.

Mauss, Marcel. 1999. *Sociologie et anthropologie.* Paris: Quadrige, Presses Universitaires de France.

Murray, Robin, Julie Caulier-Grice, and Geoff Mulgan. 2010. *The Open Book of Social Innovation.* London: The Young Foundation and NESTA.

OECD/Eurostat. 2005. *Oslo Manual: Guidelines for Collecting and Interpreting Innovation Data*, 3d. ed. Paris: OECD/Eurostat.

Onaindia, Mario. 1994. "La Escuela Pública Vasca y la construcción nacional." *Cuadernos de Alzate* 20: 9–63.

Pérez-Agote, Alfonso. 1987. *El nacionalismo vasco a la salida del franquismo.* Madrid: Centro de Investigaciones Sociológicas.

———. 1984. *La reproducción del nacionalismo: El caso vasco.* Madrid: Centro de Investigaciones Sociológicas. English version: 2006. *The Social Roots of Basque Nationalism.* Translated by Cameron Watson and William A. Douglass. Reno and Las Vegas: University of Nevada Press.

Remy, Jean. 1973. "La dichotomie privé/public dans l'usage courant: fonction et genèse." *Recherches Sociologiques* 4: 10–38.

Rogers, Everett M. 1995. *Diffusion of Innovations.* New York: Free Press.

Schutz, Alfred. 1973. *The Problem of Social Reality.* Edited and introduced by Maurice Natanson. Preface by H.L. Van Breda. The Hague: M. Nijhoff.

Smith, L. M. 1986. *Anatomy of Educational Innovation: A Mid to Long Term Re-study and Reconstrual.* New York: Falmer.

Unceta, Alfonso. 2003. "La producción del sistema educativo en el País Vasco: la lógica público-privado." Tesis Doctoral. UPV/EEU, Leioa.

Unceta, Alfonso and Marce Masa. 2010. "Ikastola: From the Community to the Knowledge Community: Leaning and Organizational Changes." In *Knowledge Communities*, edited by Javier Echeverría, Andoni Alonso, and Pedro J. Oiarzabal. Conference Papers Series 6. Reno: Center for Basque Studies, University of Nevada, Reno. (In Press 2010).

Viñao Frago, Antonio. 1982. *Política y educación en los orígenes de la España contemporánea*. Madrid: Siglo XXI.

Von Hippel, Eric. 2005. *Democratizing Innovation*. Cambridge, MA: MIT Press.

Weber, Max. 1978. *Economy and Society: An Outline of Interpretative Sociology*. Volume 1. Translated by Ephraim Fischoff et al. Edited by Guenther Roth and Claus Wittich. Berkeley and Los Angeles: University of California Press.

Young Foundation. 2006. *Social Innovation: What Is It, Why It Matters, How It Can Be Accelerated*. London: Basingstoke Press.

10

The Distinctiveness of the Social Services System in the Autonomous Community of the Basque Country

Lola Simón Alfonso

Translated by Laura Bunt-MacRury

This chapter examines the evolution of social services in the Comunidad Autónoma del País Vasco/Euskal Autonomia Erkidegoa (CAPV/EAE, Autonomous Community of the Basque Country). Since its launch, with the first law concerning social services (and in tandem with recent second- and third-generation laws), the CAPV/EAE welfare model has been transformed by a complex process of adaptation along with the changing social reality itself as a consequence of major modernization.[1]

Social policies since the early 1990s have been influenced by a number of socioeconomic and cultural factors, resulting from the contingencies of each era and social situation since that time. Furthermore, in the Basque case, the uniqueness of the social assistance models in each province of

---

1. The concept of social services in the Basque case is equivalent to both general social assistance (welfare) and individual social services. This is derived from the Social Services Law that takes its definition from the *European Social Charter* adopted by the Council of Europe in 1961. Specifically (Council of Europe 1981), social services are "services which, by using methods of social work, would contribute to the welfare and development of both individuals and groups in the community, and to their adjustment to the social environment" (Article 14). A subsequent publication of the Council of Europe defines it as "all agencies whose mission is to provide a support and personal assistance to individuals, groups, and communities in order to facilitate their integration into the community and not services that address only to ensure some level of life through the provision of benefits in cash or in kind" (Council of Europe 1980).

the CAPV/EAE (Araba, Bizkaia, and Gipuzkoa) prior to the implementation of collective modern legislation has been conditioned, to a large extent, by the philosophy and resources emanating from the sphere of social assistance. This explains why the process of homogenizing social assistance policy is still incomplete, in spite of the collective laws.

Another important factor to consider is the process of administrative decentralization that emerged at the mercy of "neo-localism" in public administration. As a result, social care has been particularly important within the sphere of social policy by way of municipal services and programs. In the case of the CAPV/EAE, a further difficulty exists in relation to the specific nature of its administrative framework and powers as regards social services.

The Emergence of a New Reality for Social Action (1970–80)

In the 1980s, a social services system was established that exceeded many of the basic expectations associated with basic welfare and laid the groundwork for the creation of a modern system of protection based on social assistance as distinguished from previous welfare measures. From its initiation, the Basque government established as a priority the need to organize and encourage public services to limit discretionary actions and ensure equal access to resources. Bolstering an adequate network of basic social services—or primary care—was the defining element of this policy and guaranteed care for unspecified marginal groups, or any groups in situations of dire need that lacked the influence to lobby for their demands.

Faced with the manifest obstacle of different social realities and provincial approaches, a major planning effort was undertaken concerning healthcare provision. The aim was to prioritize services and resources according to medium- and long-term objectives, in lieu of focusing on the short-term demand for services by certain pressure groups. From the start, the contribution of social actors was taken into account and assessed. Indeed, the mixed social services model has always been based on cooperation between social initiatives and public institutions.

In 1982, the first law concerning social services during the democratic era launched a mixed social services model. Among its aims was to emphasize the structure of a collective system based on the recognition of a series of social rights (as opposed to the discretionary measures of the previous era) and the recognition that services must be assimilated to fit a particular social environment.

The evolution of the social services system since the early 1990s has been a constant process of adaptation and remodeling of a model that ensures uniform coverage, as well as basic and collective organizational structures and functioning based on the principle of citizenship (regardless of province or municipality of residence). At present, however, it is an unfinished process, fraught with great difficulty, especially in relation to both the prior structures and particular operational modes of each province as regards social assistance and the administrative organization of the CAPV/EAE, in which the *diputaciones forales* (provincial administrative and governmental bodies) have a major influence in the shaping of public policy. Therefore, both prior to the 1970s and 1980s, and during the political change associated with the creation of the CAPV/EAE, as regards social policy there remained three different kinds of welfare models and strategies in Bizkaia, Araba, and Gipuzkoa.

In Bizkaia, there was a working model of residual charitable care, characterized by a scarcity of public resources that limited assistance for the poor, orphans, and the elderly. At the same time, the lobbying of social initiatives was marked by a strong political discourse, confrontation, and mistrust of authority. Although a pioneering and visionary approach to social health—via psychosocial units—was launched, more traditional methods of social assistance were still in use, involving fragmented associations (especially regarding disabilities).

In Araba, and specifically in Vitoria-Gasteiz, pioneering community structures were created based on collaboration between government and citizens: civic centers, based on a functionalist model. Their success is the result of genuine involvement in and a real commitment to social services as a public service on the part of the Vitoria-Gasteiz city hall and the provincial government of Araba. Community centers are diverse meeting places, with multidisciplinary teams integrated in decentralized local neighborhood services, serving the community and with a vocation for public service.

Finally, as regards Gipuzkoa during this time, the provincial government's role in social assistance stood out, as did the existence of a strong associative framework. Specific social initiatives were especially important in work and care-related services, particularly regarding disability.

With regard to the distinctiveness of administrative organization in the CAPV/EAE, one should bear in mind the critical role played by the provincial governments in both passing legislation and managing resources within the administrative framework of the autonomous community. This role has been strengthened by a special system of regional financing structured through the "fiscal pact" (*concierto económico*). In practice, the provincial governments have major financial resources, which allow them to substantiate and determine the budget revenue for the joint bodies of the CAPV/EAE via the Basque Council of Finance. In addition, the provincial governments also administer much of the financial resources potentially available to city halls and other local bodies. The allocation of budget funds is linked to activities previously approved by the provincial governments, which has consequences for (among other things) social assistance initiatives.

Legislative Regulation of Social Services in the CAPV/EAE

In every society, certain social policy measures have a dual dimension regarding both the need for social cohesion and stability, and, more obviously, politicized tactics and strategies that promote a specific model of social identity, as well as courting the electorate.

Thus, at root, social policies reflect a strategic approach framed within a standard European social model. They are, therefore, a preferred intervention mechanism for public authorities that, by means of transferring revenue and services, guarantee minimum parameters of social well-being for all citizens. In short, they facilitate social integration and cohesion, which, in turn, guarantee a certain stability to social and economic systems and, presumably as a consequence, result in greater development and wealth of a particular society. Furthermore, the tactical approach in fomenting social policies also reflects, in part, the need to enhance the image of the public administration itself and/or improve popular perception of political authority.

All these issues were central—as regards the relations between the three administrative levels—to homogenizing and planning an egalitarian social services system for the Basque population. In practice, the provincial authorities enjoy greater decision-making and financial power to the detriment of the other two administrative levels, despite the importance of basic or joint social services, municipal supervision of such services, and the need to adapt these services fairly to the current social situation. This is why joint efforts are emphasized as a basis for social integration and local development.

Finally, one of the defining elements of the Basque assistance model is the role of private initiatives. All successive legislation concerning social services, without exception, has taken into account the important role traditionally played by nonprofit social initiatives in the context of social action, as well as the growing presence of private business within this field.

The Rise of the Social Services System: The Law of 1982

Throughout the history of the social services system in the CAPV/EAE, there have been a number of competing and conflicting interests among the different institutions that make up the Basque administrative framework. These institutions include autonomous bodies with authority in the CAPV/EAE as a whole, decision-making bodies within the provincial authorities, and municipal authority as represented by city halls (the latter of which represent the primary demand for social assistance). Decentralization, equity, and universality are essential principles of social services laws that, in practice, may come into conflict with the interests of these different administrations and political parties.

The Social Services Law of 1982—the first collective law in force throughout the CAPV/EAE—was faced with the enormous difficulty of putting in place a system based on three divergent realities, alongside the existence of fragmented, weak, and often contradictory resources and social services. Moreover, the particular administrative setup of the CAPV/EAE made this situation even more complex. The law was intended to embody a standard that would lay the groundwork for addressing and overcoming the complex situation in order to establish a public system of social services. The 1982 law, and others that followed, identified a series of principles that placed responsibility for the effective running of social services on the public authorities, whether such services were public or private. The law also established the collective public nature of these social services. In other words, regardless of their public or private nature, these services were put under the control and planning of the Basque public administration, which, in turn, operated along specific strategic lines in the sphere of social assistance.

The spirit of these different laws, from their inception to the present day, has sought the development and consolidation of a social services system based on the principle of citizenship. Moreover, provision has been made for the inclusion of social services within a wider network of services so as to enable integrated and coordinated action. In short, these laws have sought to make social services one more feature of a welfare system aimed at the entire population. By means of covering the most basic needs, it would thus guarantee the principle of equal access to social resources within the various systems of social protection.

The initial law also reflected the need for decentralization—making the municipality or district (as opposed to the province or the autonomous community as a whole) the basic frame for administering these services—and was also based on the principle of solidarity. Its aim, ultimately, was to bring to an end legislative and administrative fragmentation, thereby aiding better planning and coordination of services. Subsequent legislation adapted social services in the CAPV/EAE more closely to these founding principles—an as yet unfinished process of constant renewal.

In 1982, the Basque government was aware of the shortcomings of the first social services law. The Basque Country was still in a transitory period regarding its own administrative organization, and the Law on the Historic Territories—which would clearly demarcate the powers of the provincial authorities in relation to the authority of the new autonomous Basque government—had still not been enacted. In reality, this first law was more of an attempt to lay the groundwork for a new organizational model regarding a modern and public social services system based on the principle of citizenship.

In sum, the 1982 law was important for both giving social services the same status as that of health and education and for clearly defining the different responsibilities of the various institutional levels. It achieved the latter by means of the basic principles of decentralized management and centralized planning, a feature that kept in mind the role of the provincial authorities.

Decentralized management as a core principle of action concerning the dissemination of resources involved giving an important role to the city halls within the area of social assistance, and this is how the law conceived this responsibility. However, the reality of the time meant that the goal of integrating municipal authority into the social services system was not initially possible. This was due to the fact that city halls were extremely heterogeneous, with most towns having few inhabitants. Further, most lacked the self-financing resources to integrate the provision of social services into their powers on an equal basis. Although some of these difficulties—especially regarding financing—remain today, the administrative structure of the *mancomunidad/mankomunitatea* (a district composed of different municipalities) now provides for a basic network of social services throughout the CAPV/EAE. Consequently, it also guarantees access to a series of basic community resources regarding social assistance, regardless of residence in a particular municipality.

When it came to applying the 1982 law, it suffered from different levels of adherence, mainly as a result of the tendency of the Basque provincial governments to marginalize the Basque autonomous government—when logically the latter should have exercised maximum authority in the CAPV/EAE. Finally, in 1996, a new social services law was passed that addressed the legal shortcomings of the 1982 law, which had been recognized as a transitory measure.

The Adaptation of the Social Services System to a New Social Reality and Its Legislative Development, 1996–2001

Between the passing of the 1982 law and well into the 1990s, because of a series of economic crises, as well as significant cultural transformations and changes to the traditional family structure, new legislation and social measures were needed to meet changing social requirements. Consequently, a wave of new legislation was passed concerning social assistance, with a number of new measures introduced: more resources for people at risk of social exclusion, a new social services law, and a clearer delimitation of authority regarding social assistance among the different administrative levels of the CAPV/EAE. These were all responses to the challenges stemming from significant socioeconomic change in Basque society, as well as attempts to improve the joint action of the three different administrative levels involved in providing social services.

The financial crisis, prompted by an economic collapse during the period 1975–85 and the subsequent industrial downsizing, resulted in unemployment becoming a major structural problem in the Basque Country, with jobless rates rising from 5 percent in 1975 to 24 percent in 1985.[2] Although these rates fell in the 1990s, they remained at about 16 percent, and in the last quarter of 1998 was over 17 percent, a situation that was particularly acute in Bizkaia where it exceeded three percentage points of the total average.

Moreover, the normative fragmentation of the labor market ended stability and security for a growing number of groups. Consequently, the

---

2. For more information on the Basque economy, labor market developments, and the situation in Bizkaia in particular, see Araujo et al. (2001). On the labor market situation and its relation to vocational training, see Basterretxea et al. (2002).

social services system had to assume an increasing role in covering certain basic needs that the social welfare system no longer covered because of job insecurity and public assistance regarding this. It was during this era that a major phenomenon known as *the new poverty* emerged, leading to greater awareness of the processes of social exclusion, the vulnerability of large segments of the population, and their lack of "employability."[3] Examples of measures taken at the time to address the new social and economic situation included specific plans to combat poverty that provided resources such as a "minimum social insertion income" and "social emergency grants." Here, proof of need went hand in glove with the implementation of social rights.

Demographically, natural population growth became stagnant. In 1996, the relative size of the population over fifty years of age was slightly over 32 percent, with the highest increase in the group of people over seventy-five years of age.[4] In addition, forecasts predicted an increasing aging of the Basque population, as reflected by the evolution of the dependency ratio in the CAPV/EAE, which reached a value of 16 percent in 1986, as compared to 21 percent in 1996. This progressive aging of the population resulted, in practice, in the updating and expansion of institutionalized resources and home residences. Likewise, a community-based home help service—first implemented in the period 1983–85 and intended for people with some degree of dependency yet still living in their own homes—was consolidated during this period. Provision of this service was mainly conditioned on the income levels of those requiring it, and it was estimated to

---

3. New poverty is also known as *unskilled poverty* (Paugam 2002) and is defined by a precarious employment situation, low income, poor quality of housing, bad health, and fragile family ties. This perspective focuses on the multidimensional nature of poverty and takes into account a combination of factors related to the lack of economic resources, as well as the personal, cultural, educational, and relational influences present (Pérez Yruela, Sáez Méndez, and Manuel Trujillo 2002). Moreover, poverty associated with structural factors, as related to the process of social exclusion, is a persistent phenomenon over time, even despite significant economic improvement in society. In other words, there are population centers predisposed to many difficulties that hinder short-term improvements in society. In sum, a multidimensional approach is necessary regarding those sectors of the population in a structural situation of poverty. Ibáñez (2002) argues that when addressing how to tackle poverty, factors that are not usually considered so much—such as its emergence, development, and reproduction—should be taken into account in order to help us overcome seeing it in merely individual terms. Thus, the concept of poverty today goes beyond the notion of a lack of material goods and is instead related to the minimum living conditions associated with an acceptable life in a given society (Susín Beltrán 2000).

4. Data corresponds to the year 1996, see Eustat (*Euskal Estatistika Erakundea* / Basque Statistics Institute), www.eustat.es/idioma_i/indice.html.

cover the needs of 3 percent of the population over sixty-five years of age in 1994 (Institución Ararteko 1996).

The entrance of women into the workplace was another factor to be considered during the restructuring of social assistance. Although the female labor force figures were still low compared with the European average, the female participation increased from just over 32 percent in 1985 to just over 40 percent in 1995. In practice, the increasing employment of women and new cultural and family patterns altering their traditional roles meant that those household care services that until this time had been typically carried out by women had to be restructured. Thus began a process that addressed the need to implement and develop so-called individual care services in order to complement and replace the care role of dependent household members, traditionally carried out by women. With the advent of the social services system, the home help service was extended.

In addition, more general legal factors were also important in affecting reform of the social services law, especially following the implementation of the Law of the Historic Territories, the basic regulation governing the institutional framework of the Basque Country.[5] This established the need to adapt organizational and financial dimensions of the division of powers between *foral* (provincial) and common (autonomous) institutions in the CAPV/EAE to management, assessment, and participatory bodies, as well as delineating responsibilities in the financing of social services.

Law 5/1996 of October 18 concerning social services described itself as a care model aimed at helping people enter both society and the workplace through a "specific system distinct from that of social welfare, but likewise one of universal, guaranteed, and public responsibility that, besides protecting individuals and groups, should contribute to promoting economic development in the CAPV/EAE and employment, especially for those groups that find it most difficult to enter the labor market." This law ultimately served, specifically, as the basis for planning both general and specialized social services.

---

5. Law 27/1983, November 25, 1983, on relations among the common institutions of the autonomous community and *foral* bodies in its historic territories, which provided for the deployment by the historic territories (the three provinces) within their territory, of "legislation of the common institutions" (Art.7c.l.). In practice, this meant giving a prominent role to the provinces in the institutional organization of the CAPV/EAE, a role that was reinforced by the fiscal pact.

Although ultimate responsibility for social assistance remained with the public authorities, the legislation also recognized the importance of social and private initiatives. Title 5 of the law established the rules for private participation as supplementary to public initiatives. Although it recognized the participation of private, profit-based initiative within the field of social assistance, under the same conditions of efficiency and quality, nonprofit bodies would be prioritized in any collaboration with the public authorities. In any event, when carrying out any aspect of social assistance, these bodies would have to comply with a series of precautionary administrative measures ensuring a minimum level of quality in the provision of services. As a guarantee, private centers and services would require prior administrative authorization before they could open and function. The law also established the need for the public administration to homologate private centers and services as a preliminary step to signing any collaborative agreements. For practical purposes, the law considered all officially recognized public or private resources, services, activities, and facilities as part of one single social assistance system.

The Basque parliament retained the legislative capacity over, as well as the power to delineate areas of authority in, carrying out any program provided in the CAPV/EAE as a whole, such as the law against social exclusion. The provincial governments would implement social services legislation, as well as establishing, marinating, and managing specialized social services. One new aspect of the law was the obligation of municipalities with more than twenty thousand inhabitants to have an emergency service. It also emphasized the need to decentralize services, including the possibility of delegating authority regarding benefits or services arrangements among public administrations. However, there had still been no prior territorial readjustment to eliminate the heterogeneous nature of municipalities and provide for effective planning. Moreover, the municipal authorities were still hampered in their self-financing and therefore relied in great measure on the *foral* (provincial) authorities, the latter retaining the power of awarding discretionary grants.

The new law maintained the Basque Social Welfare Council, first established by decree 93/1983 of May 9, which created five council committees to address different areas: the elderly, the disabled, basic social assistance, childhood and youth, and other marginalized groups. Currently, it continues to be an advisory body comprising representatives of the Basque government, the three provincial governments, city halls, labor unions, system users, social assistance volunteer workers, and professionals working in the field of social services. Its functions are limited to giving advice and developing proposals and initiatives by the Basque government in the field of social services, as well as drawing up mandatory reports regarding these activities. The law also provided for the existence of provincial and municipal social welfare councils. The final delimitation of powers within this complex Basque institutional framework came five years later, by mans of decree 155/2001, which was preceded by an agreement between the Basque government, the provincial councils, and the Association of Basque Municipalities.

It is worth pointing out the leading role of the Basque provincial authorities in maintaining and developing social services. They ensure the existence of facilities and services for specific groups through specialized social services, with particular emphasis on the attention and care of dependent people. These provincial bodies have the authority to manage and sufficient financial resources to cover the maintenance and development of social assistance. Moreover, provincial authority resources cover benefits designed to meet basic income and social emergency aid, although this is technically the responsibility of the Basque government. This lends a certain rigidity and inefficiency to the system, especially since demand for such services falls within the local realm among municipalities, and city halls provide direct professional intervention.

The Need for Stability and Universality in the Social Services System: The Law of 2008

This law was the most recent attempt to adapt the social services system to the new reality. Its aim was to bridge the differences between areas that remained and to strengthen the character of the law in regard to acknowledged individual rights. To be sure, access to certain benefits—such as those covering basic income and social emergency aid—was by now guaranteed thanks to the efforts of the Basque government, which was responsible for social inclusion programs. Initially, the distribution of allocated resources for social inclusion was based on a proportional system in general relation to the socioeconomic situation and population size in each province. However, since the 1990s, the Basque government has been perfecting the system by calculating a more effective distribution of resources based on the specific socioeconomic characteristics of demand in each province and municipality. In fact, there has been a more equitable distribution of allocated resources as a result of detecting and targeting pockets of poverty—

areas where there is a greater risk of social exclusion—and delineating the characteristics of the most vulnerable groups with real needs.

There remain differences, however, in both access to and funding for the rest of the services among the provinces because of the different kinds of management and levels of funding by the provincial governments. Thus, the distribution of powers between the provincial and municipal authorities does not fit the new requirements, with the added aggravation of municipal reliance on external funding to implement services demanded by citizens. The reality was that social services lacked an effective strategic planning for the entire CAPV/EAE, which the new law sought to address. In an attempt to resolve the discrepancies among the interests of the various governments and parties that govern them, the Institutional Social Services Authority was created with the task of directing cooperation and coordination between three administrations. This would, it was hoped, ensure unanimity of access to Basque social services and the harmonization of all programs and resources. The new law also recognized the need for a performance portfolio, binding services for all, and a common system for collecting information (and its subsequent translation into a social services map) when attempting to understand the reality of social assistance and in order to be able to develop appropriate planning and management in line with the real demand, as well as guidelines arising from this strategic management in order to achieve greater guarantees of basic benefits.

The reform of the law on social services was, first and foremost, necessary because of the need to adapt it to recent legislative developments with the passing of the Charter of Social Rights (ensuring the personal right to social services as a right of citizenship). This would be possible provided that, in practice, the development of social services policies was similar to that of other welfare policies (education, social welfare, employment, and health) through management and coordination bodies that might effectively oversee the activity of the three authorities involved.

Secondly, since the turn of the millennium, a series of issues have emerged as a result of the Law on Dependency.[6] Compliance with the requirements of the law regarding the provision of certain services and

---

6. Actually, this is Spanish Law 39/2006, of December 14, on promoting personal autonomy and attending to people in dependent situations. It was a necessary yet insufficient measure to cover the needs of the targeted population, as well as being badly structured in terms of coordinating health and social matters.

resources by social services required taking into account the needs of the community—or rather, the real demand, according to factors such as population structure, density and potential evolution, family structure, and the basic quality of life associated with certain socioeconomic conditions. The significant increase of people with limited autonomy and its upward trend due to an aging population highlighted the need for a legislative response to this situation and the consequent adjustment and restructuring of social resources.

Concerning care, because of advances in acknowledgement of the need for equality between men and women, exclusionary practices pertaining to either gender had to be eliminated. Additionally, it was also necessary to meet the need that had arisen to both ease and reinforce the social and familial support network by encouraging greater democratization in the family structure and the abandonment of the traditional allocation of the role assigned to women as solely responsible for family care.

Moreover, the neo-localist trend in social policy underscored the central role of municipalities in the field of social assistance, which, in turn, affected the need for the reformulation of social services. In reality, it sought to satisfy the community-based demands for the social benefits related to social assistance by means of social inclusion, public health, and socio-educational programs. In turn, an attempt was also made (insofar as possible) to avoid institutionalizing those people with a certain degree of dependence through the development of new resources, intermediary services, and family support, as well as the strengthening of those resources already present (such as those introduced by the dependency laws).

The law therefore established in its preamble regarding the Basque social services system, "a system of public accountability and universal coverage, targeted toward the entire population." In any event, the system would be based on:

> The need to strengthen collaboration with the third sector, the support of informal support networks, the promotion of organized participation by people themselves affected, the creation of opportunities for cooperation and coordination among systems (social and community based, social and work based, social and housing based, socio-educational, socio-judicial, sociocultural, or others) and the development of social policies that enable access of all people to full citizenship, thereby promoting social justice and addressing the structural causes of exclusion.

Another key dimension of this new social services legislation was the separation of the traditional division of responsibilities between municipalities and provincial authorities with regard to basic and special social services. The new version of the legislation contains a series of services aimed at specific sectors of the population and semi-institutionalized people, which strictly speaking are considered specialized services within the scope of community or primary care services. These services and resources were already managed by city halls and functioned largely through cooperative agreements with welfare departments of the respective provincial governments. In this way, a wide range of functions assigned to primary care social services were developed that enabled a community-based approach to social intervention. Specifically, a catalogue of services was listed that included: an information service, generalized assessment, diagnosis and counseling, a home help service, a socio-educational and psychosocial intervention service, a caregivers support service, the duty of promoting social participation and inclusion in the field of social services, a phone-care service, a day care service, a night service, boarding and foster homes, assisted living, and community housing.

Ultimately, it strengthened the relationship between government and social initiatives. While the 1996 law regulated the supportive role of the third sector, the more recent social services law of 2008, while taking into account social and private initiative, focused on stabilizing all this activity. Specifically, it established an agreement between the social services and the public authorities concerning the provision of services referred to in the catalog of benefits and services of the Basque social services. By including the principle of public accountability, citizens were still guaranteed access to services and benefits provided by the social services. Moreover, special relevance was given to the role of managing social initiatives, although always under the supervision of and within the boundaries set by the public administration.

Conclusion

The complex Basque institutional framework has led to a constant remodeling of social assistance policy. One of the main concerns in this area was the need to overcome provincial inequalities, especially by recognizing individual rights to social services. Currently (2010), after more than a year of being in force, the Inter-Institutional Social Services Authority has been set up according to the law as a meeting point for the three public administrations responsible for the process of convergence in social assistance that ensures equal access to resources and social benefits for all people (regardless of residence). In order to achieve this, it was necessary to establish and maintain a portfolio of benefits and services depending on the needs of the moment. However, as this was constituted for the first time on March 30, 2010, more time is needed to determine its effectiveness.

Also worth noting is the trend toward the increasing importance of health care programs and resources in the context of social protection. These are intended to alleviate the pitfalls of the labor market and their effects on personal autonomy and quality of life. The rigid and precarious nature of working conditions, coupled with changes in family structures, has also had an impact on care operations. It is now believed that community action is ideal for addressing any problems of social displacement, vulnerability, and exclusion that may arise.

In any event, this comprehensive and ambitious approach to social assistance, was framed in a fully assistive and corporatist model under the guise of a false universalism.[7] In practice, and due to limited economic resources, this will result in a system of protection with important weaknesses underscored by the involvement of the third sector and private initiatives (López Basaguren 2007).

The presence of the third sector and private enterprise, in principle, enriches open and plural societies. The impetus of private sector participation in the field of social assistance can open a range of potentialities with respect to detecting social needs and organizing an active civil society that is accountable to and inclusive of its members (Ascoli and Ranzi 2002).

This will always be the case if their participation is engrained within the frame of cooperation and accompaniment of business activity as a fully developed social service. The difficult balance between public accountability in the management of services and private participation would be a guarantee of this. In other words, it would be based on the extent to which the existence of private initiative meets the criteria of normal-

7. Corporatism is the structuring of social protection by combining two different systems together. Thus, protection is linked to employment status and the implementation of social policies is carried out by a duality in the so-called welfare system between the social welfare and social assistance systems. The latter is subsidiary in nature and designed for those who cannot access the former because of their employment status. This model has been presented as an alternative to capitalism and communism, and is prevalent in those countries influenced by Catholicism, although with significant differences between those found in Germany and in the so-called residual corporatism in Spain (Simón Alfonso 2000).

ity and solidarity, and that such private involvement are not principally supplementary in the face of the lack of coverage of basic needs offered by public authorities).

In the case of the CAPV/EAE, a sense of participation in social initiatives has been instrumental in illustrating the uneven development of coverage of social assistance among the three provinces. With the exception of Araba, and only until recent times, the role assigned to the private sector responded to the need for a shift in demand toward the private due to lack of government resources to cover such needs (Ascoli and Ranzi 2002). Indeed, this has been used as a deterrent to public access to certain services (e.g., home help service, day care centers, and housing), when, in fact, the demand itself (on the part of a certain part of the population) shifted to the private sector and the informal sector. This all occurred despite the fact that financing is based on public money provided by a tax system that is supposed to redirect funds to its populace.

The 2008 law provides a model of care and intervention centered on a community-based approach that adapts its activity to local community characteristics and to the attentive development of the social environment whenever possible. The model, however, suffers from a lack of adequate funding for its objectives, and from the imposed task of filling the gaps left by the social welfare system. A poignant example is the meaning of the dependency law concerning reform of the social services laws, which proposed universal coverage of the needs of "passive classes" of people with a certain degree of dependence. In this case, social services are allocated the task of ensuring a range of community social and health resources primarily for this group of people. And once again, demand falls on the municipalities.

However, in the Basque case, the provincial governments have great financial muscle, as well as the authority to distribute resources for the elderly and people with disabilities. Thus, there is a duplication of conflicting resources and measures that looks more like competition among the different public authorities than streamlining resources to fit the right demand.[8] In the European context, the problem of coverage for dependent

---

8. Another method of dealing with the provision of care is the notion of dependent insurance or long-term social welfare care. In the pioneering case of Germany, insurance has been compulsory for all workers since 1995, with funding provided by the payments of social welfare contributions by workers and employers, thereby aiming to cope with the costs of healthcare for family dependents or disability for a minimum period of six months (Simón Alfonso 2000).

persons has been solved by a pragmatic combination between insurance and social welfare systems, which includes universal coverage. This example should be taken into account if the goal is to achieve greater equity and effectiveness in the use of social resources regarding dependency.

References

Araujo Andrés, Imanol Basterrextea, Ana González, Lola Simón, and María Saiz. 2001. *Situación del empleo en Bizkaia: Estrategias para afrontar el paro.* Bilbao: UPV, Servicio Editorial.

Ascoli, Ugo and Constanzo Ranzi, eds. 2002. *Dilemmas of the Welfare Mix: The New Structure of Welfare in an Era of Privatization.* London: Kluwer Academic /Plenum Publishers.

Basterretxea, Imanol, Ana González, María Saiz, and Lola Simón. 2002. *Colaboración entre centros de Formación profesional y empresas en la Comunidad Autónoma Vasca.* Bilbao: UPV, Servicio Editorial.

Council of Europe. 1981. *European Social Charter.* Strasbourg: Council of Europe.

———. 1980. *Les services sociaux.* Strasbourg: Conseil d'Europe.

Ibáñez, Hilario. 2002. *De la integración a la exclusión: Los avatares del trabajo productivo a finales del siglo XX.* Santander: Sal Terrea.

Institución Ararteko. 1996. *Informe extraordinario sobre la asistencia no residencial a la tercera edad en la Comunidad Autónoma del País Vasco–Informe extraordinario al Parlamento Vasco (1994–1995).* Bilbao: Ararteko.

López Basaguren, Alberto. 2007. "La politica sociale nello Stato autonomista spagnolo: Welfare Mix o asistencialismo?" In *Federalismo fiscale, principipio de sussidiarietà e neutralità dei servizi sociali erogati. Esperienze a confronto.* Papers from the Ravenna Conference. Bologna: Bologna University Press.

Paugam, Serge. 2002. *La disqualification sociale. Essai sur la nouvelle pauvreté.* 2nd edition. Paris: Cuadrige/Puf.

Pérez Yruela, Manuel, Hilario Sáez Méndez, and Manuel Trujillo Carmona. 2002. *Pobreza y exclusión social en Andalucía.* Madrid: CSIC.

Simón Alfonso, Lola. 2000. "La protección a la familia en la Unión Europea." In *Familias y Bienestar Social*, edited by Lola Simón Alfonso and Ma. Montserrat Rejado Corcuera. Valencia: Tirant lo Blanch.

Susín Beltrán, Raúl. 2000. *La regulación de la pobreza: El tratamiento jurídico-político de la pobreza: Los ingresos mínimos de inserción.* Logroño: Universidad de La Rioja, Servicio de Publicaciones.

Index

List of Contributors

For full biographical information about the contributors, links to their projects, and more, visit www.basque.unr.edu/currentresearch/contributors

Eneka Albizu
Javier Bilbao-Ubillos
Vicente Camino-Beldarrain
Auxkin Galarraga Ezponda
Sandra González
Ander Gurrutxaga Abad
Álvaro Luna
Manuel González Portilla
Mikel Olazarán
Beatriz Otero
Antonio Rivera
Natxo Rodríguez Arkaute
Lola Simón Alfonso
José Urrutikoextea Lizarraga
Marce Masa